Letter from the Publishers

CITY OF ANGELS

Whether you look at the political landscape, the cultural scene or the entrepreneurial arena, there is no doubt that an amazing amount of female energy is in the air in 2019. Even without considering this, it was a no-brainer for us to choose Leticia "Tiza" Maldonado as the cover artist for *DTLA Book*'s 2019 edition. She is part of a small band of female neon-benders insisting on breaking down the walls of what has traditionally been a boys' club (page 48).

We also visit Meyghan Hill, who, just like Tiza, uses fire to create her magic. In Hill's case, that means welding geometric furniture in steel, brass and maple (page 88). Rounding up our exploration of Downtown's female creativity, we check in with four clothing labels who have set up shop in the Fashion District in recent years (page 18).

These trailblazers are all thoroughly modern women, but every day in our *DTLA Book* editorial office we are reminded that the (DT)LA Woman wasn't born yesterday. The 1926 Gothic Revival building in which we're located was developed by pioneer Florence C. Casler. She is responsible for 10 of Downtown's most distinctive towers (most of them with Douglas Lee of Chateau Marmont fame as an architect), and we show them all in our story about this surprising female force behind our skyline (page 78).

Just as women have, other groups have had to stand up for their right to flourish in DTLA. The story of Bronzeville tells us about two such groups. Large numbers of blacks from the South came to L.A. to join the war industry just as Little Tokyo's Japanese population was sent to internment camps in 1942. The city's segregation laws prohibited African Americans from living in 95 percent of its neighborhoods, so more than 50,000 black workers ended up in Little Tokyo, which became known as Bronzeville. Surprisingly, this double repression created an exciting (if short-lived) jazz scene. For a time, you could catch jazz great Miles Davis playing with Charlie Parker in The Finale Club on 1st Avenue (page 94).

Some 75 years later, the efforts to secure equal opportunities in our neighborhood continue. We visit the organizations Inner-City Arts, Skid Row Housing Trust and Chrysalis to learn about their work for the most vulnerable groups in DTLA (page 98). The angels that gave our city its name are alive and well, and we dedicate this book to them.

—*Kayoko & Shana*

BUSINESS BANKING IN LOS ANGELES FOR OVER 55 YEARS

Founded in 1962, Manufacturers Bank has been L.A.'s business bank for over 55 years, actively supporting the growth of small and mid-sized businesses locally.

A community bank, *Locally Committed - Internationally Connected*, offering large bank services and solutions along with the personal attention you would expect from a small bank. Keeping your money safe while making sure it stays in our community, supporting local nonprofits and helping local mid-sized businesses succeed in DTLA.

A SUBSIDIARY OF SUMITOMO MITSUI BANKING CORPORATION

515 S. Figueroa Street, Los Angeles, CA 90071
(877) 560-9812 www.manufacturersbank.com

CONTENTS
Vol. 03 // 2019

WATCH TIZA ON VIDEO
By Jiro Schneider

 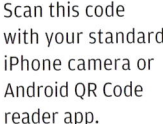 Scan this code with your standard iPhone camera or Android QR Code reader app.

Cover

Neon art by **Leticia Maldonado** (below at her studio near Downtown). Photographed and videographed by Jiro Schneider.

Features

1 LETTER FROM THE PUBLISHERS
The angels that gave our city its name are alive and well, and we dedicate this book to them.

4

4 5 ESSENTIAL RULES FOR TOTALLY ENJOYING DTLA
New shops, restaurants, bars and art galleries pop up every week. Here's how to take it all in.

12 DTLA'S 15 DISTRICTS
Get to know each vibrant area of the hottest neighborhood in L.A.

18 STYLE COUNCIL
Check out these four see-now-buy-now fashion labels that all have roots in Downtown L.A.'s creative scene.

26 FRESH FINDS
DTLA may not be known for green space, but tucked both between and near the bustling streets of this urban core are a handful of spots where you can temporarily retreat and connect with nature. From large parks to small gardens, here are eight places to explore.

32 IT TAKES TWO
A surprising number of Downtown's most tempting restaurants are helmed by husband-and-wife teams. What makes it work: "We get to see each other—otherwise we never would."

38 TWO ANGELS ON A STRING
For a trip back in time, take a ride on 118-year-old Angels Flight, the shortest

48

 26
 32
 78

railway in the world and a link back to old Bunker Hill.

48   NEON DREAMS
Inspired by the glowing signs of Los Angeles and Las Vegas, Leticia "Tiza" Maldonado is part of a new-wave group of artists taking the art of neon to the next level.

54   PEAK SNEAKER MOMENT
With the arrival of the Nike Air Jordan megastore on Broadway, Downtown's bubbling-up sneakerhead culture gets serious lift.

60   COLORS OF THE CITY
Learn where to find more than 35 street-art walls that together make DTLA one of the mural capitals of the world.

72   DTLA NOIR
Five writers and tour guides narrate the tales from Downtown's sordid history of murder and mayhem that obsess them.

78   TOWERING PIONEER
With a taste for Gothic Revival architecture, Florence Casler went from being the wife of a plumber to developing 10 DTLA buildings that all endure to this day.

84   THE DANCE TROUPES OF DOWNTOWN
Five companies, plus two performance venues, reside in DTLA, bringing grace and exuberance to the urban core.

88   FLAMES OF CREATIVITY
Since picking up a welding torch, former model Meyghan Hill has forged a second career as one of the city's most in-demand furniture and object makers, working out of a DTLA warehouse.

94   BECOMING BRONZEVILLE
For a period during World War II—when Japanese Americans were sent to internment camps—Little Tokyo became known by a new name, reflecting an influx of tens of thousands of African Americans who reshaped the community and made late nights swing with jazz.

98   DTLA'S ANGEL NONPROFITS
Seven of the city's most effective and big-hearted charitable groups are based Downtown, doing everything from giving kids art instruction that they can't find in school to building housing for the homeless and helping people learn job skills.

102   GO METRO!
Four L.A. transit lines—each of which you can catch right in DTLA—are ready to whisk you away to destinations as varied as Pasadena, Hollywood, Koreatown and Santa Monica.

108   RAISING CLEAN AND GREEN
The Los Angeles Cleantech Incubator gives a leg up to environmentally friendly startups.

112   GOOD TIMES
Inside an enormous DTLA warehouse, high-tech "micro-amusement park" Two Bit Circus is bringing folks together with its unique brand of interactive fun: "We're making entertainment more personal."

Our Faves

114	Eat	147	Observation Decks
130	Drink	148	Arts
138	Wellness	154	Play
141	Shop		

End Notes

156   Contributors, the Team and Thank-Yous

5 ESSENTIAL RULES FOR TOTALLY ENJOYING DTLA

RULE NO. 1

WALK IT!

Welcome to the most walkable neighborhood in all of Los Angeles.

By Degen Pener // Photography by Joshua Spencer

With a walk score of 95—the highest in the entire city of Los Angeles—Downtown L.A. is a paradise for people who love exploring and experiencing the urban landscape on foot. People who live in or visit DTLA can stroll to an average of 33 restaurants, bars and coffee shops in five minutes—a welcome thing in a metropolis that's so famous for its car culture. According to a 2015 survey, 22 percent of DTLA locals live and work here, and 62 percent of that group walk to work every day.

It's a trend that's sure to intensify. In 2018, an estimated 4,000 new residential units were expected to enter the market. Less than two decades ago—in 1999—the population of DTLA was just 18,700 people; it had almost quadrupled by 2017, hitting 70,000 people. New shops, restaurants, bars and art galleries pop up every week, inviting residents and visitors alike to hit the streets in search of the next great thing.

Throughout the following pages, Meng of Freedom Models wears clothing by DTLA-based fashion brand Skingraft. Walking on a bridge near City Hall, Meng sports Skingraft's Lily Dress in burnt orange ($160) and Long Meadow skirt in black ($110).

RULE NO. 2

SHOP TILL YOU DROP

Buy local. Get eclectic.

While many international brands have flooded into DTLA, you will discover scores of independent fashion, gift and home shops, plus wholesale stores and markets that are often open to the public. In the heart of the Fashion District, Santee Alley is a pedestrian mall and ultimate bargain shopping area, offering more than 150 stores selling apparel, footwear, accessories, cosmetics and more. Like Takeshita Street in Tokyo's Harajuku neighborhood, Santee Alley is a jumble of wacky, colorful and youth-driven fashion finds. Get lost in this two-block-long shopping haven—without breaking the bank.

SANTEE ALLEY
319 E. Olympic Blvd., Fashion District

GOOD DEALS
Meng explores the busy scene inside Santee Alley, between Santee Street and Maple Avenue, from Olympic Boulevard to 12th Street. Open 365 days a year.

Bowed Shirt in dusty rose ($38), Crossover Zip Cardigan in black ($270) and Cassidy Bumbag ($150)

AT THE EDGES
Meng stands on the North Broadway Bridge over the Los Angeles River, near Elysian Park.

RULE NO. 3

BE AN EXPLORER!

Revelations await around every corner.

As Downtown grows, more and more pockets of the district become hot. Go beyond traditional boundaries to discover up-and-coming areas like Far Chinatown, home to majordōmo restaurant, Apotheke bar and Highland Park Brewery, with more spots on the way (see page 14 & 126). Nearby is Elysian Park, one of a surprising number of green spaces within reach of the urban jungle (see page 28).

NORTH BROADWAY BRIDGE
1580 N. Broadway, Far Chinatown

RULE *NO. 4*

EAT, DRINK, ENJOY
So many flavors, so little time.

The DTLA dining scene is so fired up, it's lured such talents as Eleven Madison Park's Daniel Humm, David Chang of the Momofuku empire and James Beard Award-winning chef Jessica Largey, who all opened restaurants here in 2018. It's also a destination for delicious Instagram-worthy treats, from taiyaki ice cream (traditional Japanese fish-shaped cakes stuffed with soft serve) to oh-so-classic donuts.

SPRING STREET ARCADE
541 S. Spring St., Historic Core

SWEET CRAVING
Meng nibbles a classic cake donut with sprinkles at Downtown Donuts inside the Spring Street Arcade, a burgeoning food mall (see page 128) that's part of the 1924 Spring Arcade Building.

"THE GOLDEN HOUR"
OUE Skyspace LA's signature cocktail ($16) includes Elyx vodka, St. Germain, grapefruit bitters and prosecco, and is finished with gold leaf flakes on the rim.

GET ENGAGED 1,000 FEET UP
Popping the question nearly 1,000 feet above Downtown is now possible thanks to OUE Skyspace LA's marriage-proposal package, which includes champagne/wine/beer service, floral hat boxes from Aquafuzion and photography from CB Photo Studio to capture the magical and unforgettable moment.

RULE
NO. 5

GO UP HIGH
Elevate your spirits with the Golden Hour.

Downtown's ever-growing skyline isn't just something to be admired from below. Catch an elevator to one of the neighborhood's lofty bars. The new Skyspace Bar dramatically ups the city's mixology game, pairing signature cocktails and locally sourced beers and spirits with unparalleled 360-degree views.

SKYSPACE BAR AT OUE SKYSPACE LA
633 W. 5th St., Financial District // 213-894-9000
Open daily 10 a.m. - 10 p.m.
General admission: $25 for adults; $19 for youth
General admission + Skyslide ride: $33 for adults; $27 for youth
For more information: oue-skyspace.com/tickets

GET IT NOW!

You can shop the looks from Meng's day exploring Downtown—either online or by dropping by Skingraft's flagship store.

LEFT:
Meng wears Skingraft's Track Jacket in black ($337), Jersey Short Sleeve in black ($35), Jogger Sweat Pant in black ($190) and Cassidy Bumbag $150.

ABOVE:
Skingraft's Cropped Parachute Bomber ($220), Chapter Shirt RAE ($90), Leather Pocket Dress Pant (Sample).

SKINGRAFT
758 S. Spring St. // 213-626-2662 // skingraftdesigns.com

DTLA'S 15 DISTRICTS

Get to know each vibrant area of L.A.'s hot neighborhood

By Liz Ohanesian // Illustrations by Lulu

Public transportation in DTLA includes the Metro subway, above-ground light rail and buses. But you'll find that you can explore Downtown quite comfortably on foot. To navigate the area, check out one of the following walking tours, which group the neighborhood's many districts into a handful of easy-to-explore clusters. Go ahead, set forth!

The numbers on this map correspond to the tours on subsequent pages.

1. SOUTH PARK
2. JEWELRY DISTRICT
3. FINANCIAL DISTRICT
4. FLOWER DISTRICT
5. FASHION DISTRICT
6. CIVIC CENTER
7. BUNKER HILL
8. HISTORIC CORE
9. GALLERY ROW
10. TOY DISTRICT
11. LITTLE TOKYO
12. ARTS DISTRICT
13. EL PUEBLO
14. CHINATOWN
15. INDUSTRIAL DISTRICT

LOS ANGELES RIVER

12 DTLA BOOK 2019

1
SOUTH PARK
You will find the bulk of Downtown's crowds in South Park gathered along Figueroa Street, where the Los Angeles Convention Center, Staples Center and L.A. LIVE sit side by side.

2
JEWELRY DISTRICT
Los Angeles' Jewelry District sits next to Pershing Square and comprises close to 5,000 businesses, with vendors on Hill Street, Olive Street, and Broadway between 5th and 8th streets.

3
FINANCIAL DISTRICT
Downtown's skyscrapers will lead you to the Financial District. If you make it to the top of one of these buildings, you'll get a phenomenal view of the city.

DID YOU KNOW?
Two of the earliest jewelers to establish stores in DTLA were the Laykin Diamond Company (Laykin et Cie) and Harry Winston & Co. in 1932. Both stores were housed at the historic Alexandria Hotel on 5th Street, just behind the district on S. Broadway.

EXPLORE THE BLOCKS AROUND L.A. LIVE

South Park > Financial District > Jewelry District

L.A. LIVE often pulses with music at night. During the day, though, you can take a deep dive into pop music history at the **GRAMMY Museum (1)** on Figueroa. For a bite to eat, walk over to **The Original Pantry Cafe (2)**, on the same street. This L.A. institution has been open 24/7 since 1924 and some breakfast items are available at all hours. Bring cash. Stroll north into the Financial District and stop by the Los Angeles Public Library's flagship **Central Library (3)**. This massive, historic building is filled with art as well as books and there is a daily tour. If your sweet tooth needs a fix, make a stop at **Bottega Louie (4)** on 7th Street, known for its colorful selection of macarons in flavors like Earl Grey and Birthday Cake. Keep walking and you'll quickly enter the Jewelry District. Said to be the largest of its kind in the U.S., it encompasses blocks of Downtown with buildings like **St. Vincent Jewelry Center (5)** and **California Jewelry Mart (6)** filled with adornments. Return to the Financial District and head up to the highest observation deck in the state. **OUE Skyspace (7)** is situated near the top of the U.S. Bank building and offers a fantastic view of the city. Ride the Skyslide, a 45-foot enclosed glass slide, or grab a drink at the **Skyspace Bar.** Check their calendar for upcoming events, like their monthly yoga session.

WALKING TOUR TOTAL: 1.8 MILES

FROM FLOWERS AND STYLE FINDS TO GALLERY OPENINGS

Flower District > Fashion District

4 FLOWER DISTRICT
Located within the Fashion District, the Flower District is a six-block floral marketplace. Consisting of nearly 200 wholesale flower dealers, it's the largest flower market in the United States.

5 FASHION DISTRICT
As a top destination for wholesale buyers, retail shoppers, designers, fashion students and Hollywood stylists, this area attracts over 1.5 million people from all around the world annually.

Los Angeles' **Flower District** is tucked inside the Fashion District on Wall Street between 7th and 8th. Its **Original Los Angeles Flower Market** blooms early, opening to the public at 6 a.m. or 8 a.m. depending on the day (closed Sundays). For breakfast, swing by **Poppy & Rose** across the street. The bustling Fashion District greets you with bolts of colorful fabrics along the sidewalk. For inexpensive, on-trend clothing and accessories, head to **Santee Alley** (see page 6), between Santee Street and Maple Avenue. Unlike the Fashion District's showrooms—generally only accessible to folks in the fashion business—Santee Alley is always open to the public. (Many showrooms do hold public sample sales, though, typically the last Friday of the month.) Later, head to **City Market South**. This historic warehouse complex has been transformed into a work-and-play space with dining options. **Cognoscenti Coffee** can refresh you after a long day, while Italian restaurant **Rossoblu**, Latin-inspired **Dama** restaurant/lounge and **Superfine Pizza** are here too. To see a clutch of art galleries all in one place, check out the historic **Bendix Building** on Maple.

Areas of DTLA With New Names to Know
As Downtown continues to rapidly grow, these four sections of the district are gaining recognition

8TH STREET CORRIDOR
The 8th Street Corridor is a gateway into the Fashion District. The up-and-coming area is home to a few brand-centric boutiques, like COS and Skingraft, and many restaurants. Adventure-seekers may want to check out Escape Room L.A.

FAR CHINATOWN
As L.A.'s Chinatown extends far beyond the neighborhood's bustling Broadway core, a once warehouse-heavy corner is getting known as Far Chinatown now that majordōmo, David Chang's restaurant, and cocktail bar Apotheke have opened here.

THEATER DISTRICT
In the early days of film, grand movie palaces popped up across Los Angeles. You'll find restored theaters along Broadway in Downtown, such as The Orpheum and Theatre at the Ace Hotel, hosting evening events. The Los Angeles Conservancy offers walking tours of the district.

PIÑATA DISTRICT
Near the Fashion District, the Piñata District is known for the large, colorful piñatas sold here. But this small area has more than just party favors to offer. You'll find vendors grilling up lunch and serving agua frescas as well.

14 DTLA BOOK 2019

6 CIVIC CENTER

While home to Los Angeles' City Hall, the LAPD and other official structures, it's not all business here. Enjoy live performances at The Music Center or find a moment of peace at Grand Park.

7 BUNKER HILL

Once home to Victorian residences, Bunker Hill is now known for office buildings, MOCA, The Broad and Walt Disney Concert Hall. Use the 298-foot-long Angels Flight Railway for easy access to this district.

8. HISTORIC CORE

Many of Downtown's vintage buildings, bars and restaurants are clustered together within this district, including Grand Central Market, Broadway theaters, and the Bradbury Building, built in 1893.

9 GALLERY ROW

Centered around Spring and Main streets, Gallery Row overlaps the Historic Core and is known as the home of Downtown's Art Walk on the second Thursday of the month.

TAKING IN DTLA'S BIGGEST ATTRACTIONS

Bunker Hill > Civic Center > Historic Core > Gallery Row

Want a view of the city that comes without an entrance fee? Head to **City Hall**. A trip to the **observation deck** here is free. The building opens at 8 a.m. on weekdays and is a good place to start this tour of Downtown. Head into the Historic Core and take a peek inside the **Bradbury Building**, which you'll recognize from movies like *Blade Runner*. Then stop for a late breakfast or early lunch at **Grand Central Market**. This historic marketplace is now home to some of the city's hippest food joints. It gets crowded, so try to beat the lunch rush. **Angels Flight** (page 38) will take you on a quick ride up to Bunker Hill. It's $1 (or 50 cents with your Metro pass). Once at the top, tour Downtown's cultural institutions. Both **MOCA** and **The Broad** are right here. You can also head over to **Walt Disney Concert Hall** for a tour or to chill in the **Blue Ribbon Garden**. Continue your walk through **The Music Center** and **Grand Park**, then veer back toward the Historic Core. Stop by **Redbird** at Vibiana, a former cathedral, for happy hour. Move along to **The Last Bookstore** for shopping and a quick Instagram snap in the Labyrinth, a book-filled, maze-like space on the mezzanine level. Finish your day with cocktails and dinner at **Perch**.

What About Skid Row?

A few things to know about Downtown's area that's home to homelessness

Los Angeles' homeless population has surged in recent years, reaching crisis levels. The city's most populated area is Skid Row, historically the section of Downtown surrounding shelters like the Midnight Mission. If you venture through—for instance, if you try to walk directly from the Historic Core east to the Arts District—proceed with caution and compassion. You will find that people have set up tents throughout Skid Row's boundaries, usually considered the area south of 3rd Street, east of Main, west of Alameda and north of 7th.

HIP AND COOL HANGOUTS

Toy District > Little Tokyo > Arts District

Perk up in the Arts District, with coffee options from **Café Société** to **Urth** to **Eat Drink Americano**. For shopping, head to **One Santa Fe**, where you can stock up on comics at **A Shop Called Quest** or try out skincare products at **Malin + Goetz**. Art lovers should explore the many murals that cover the Arts District (page 60), and check out the exhibits inside **Hauser & Wirth**, **A+D Museum** and **ArtShare L.A.**. Beer lovers can stop by **Angel City Brewery**—tours of the brewery happen daily. For lunch, hit Little Tokyo, where you can find okonomiyaki at **Chinchikurin**. Visit the **Japanese American National Museum**, which features both history and art exhibitions. For shopping, **Make Asobi** is stocked with popular facial masks; **Fickle Wish** offers fun fashion from indie Japanese designers; and **Anime Jungle** is a popular stop for everything from manga to toys. Take a minute to relax at the **Japanese American Cultural and Community Center's James Irvine Japanese Garden** (page 26). Don't forget to pick up mochi before you leave: Little Tokyo's **Fugetsu-Do** has been serving sweets for more than a century and is known for its variety of mochi treats, including ones filled with peanut butter or chocolate.

10 TOY DISTRICT
You will find lifelong supplies of Baby Jesuses, party trappings, and $1 pom-pom key chains, but you may also stumble on Bong Alley, a spot for now-legal paraphernalia at wholesale prices.

11 LITTLE TOKYO
This historically Japanese neighborhood draws multigenerational crowds for its mix of shopping and dining, as well as the Japanese American National Museum and MOCA's Geffen Contemporary.

12 ARTS DISTRICT
You'll find murals throughout Downtown, but the collection inside the Arts District is bountiful. Restaurants, coffee spots and boutiques are found within the painted buildings.

Rocking Indie Scenes

On monthly first Saturdays, **The Great Rock and Roll Flea Market** goes down at The Regent theater. Vendors specialize in everything from vinyl to crafts, and the event features DJs and bingo. Around the corner on Winston Street is **These Days**, an edgy gallery and boutique with an eclectic collection of items, including zines and vintage concert flyers. Nearby is **Indian Alley**, a street art tribute to Native Americans (page 70). This isn't always accessible, but you can glimpse it through a gate on Winston Street.

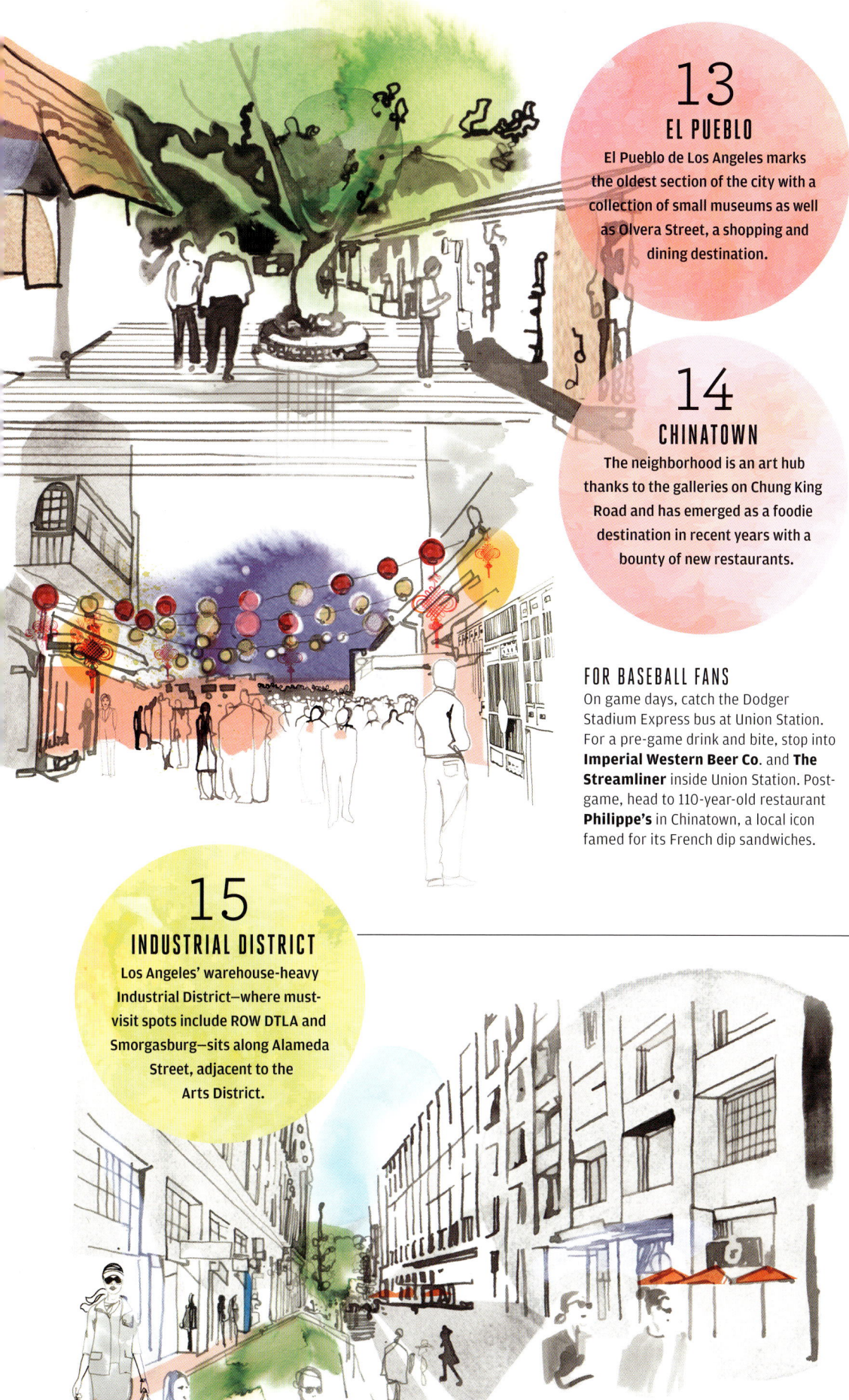

13 EL PUEBLO
El Pueblo de Los Angeles marks the oldest section of the city with a collection of small museums as well as Olvera Street, a shopping and dining destination.

14 CHINATOWN
The neighborhood is an art hub thanks to the galleries on Chung King Road and has emerged as a foodie destination in recent years with a bounty of new restaurants.

FOR BASEBALL FANS
On game days, catch the Dodger Stadium Express bus at Union Station. For a pre-game drink and bite, stop into **Imperial Western Beer Co.** and **The Streamliner** inside Union Station. Post-game, head to 110-year-old restaurant **Philippe's** in Chinatown, a local icon famed for its French dip sandwiches.

15 INDUSTRIAL DISTRICT
Los Angeles' warehouse-heavy Industrial District—where must-visit spots include ROW DTLA and Smorgasburg—sits along Alameda Street, adjacent to the Arts District.

L.A.'S BIRTHPLACE AND BEYOND
El Pueblo > Chinatown

You'll find Los Angeles' birthplace near **Union Station**. **El Pueblo de Los Angeles Historical Monument** is home to multiple museums that explore the city's history and its present. These include **La Plaza de Cultura y Artes**, **Chinese American Museum** and **Italian American Museum of Los Angeles**, all of which are free to enter. It's also home to cultural events like Día de los Muertos. **Olvera Street** is a shopping/dining center founded in 1930. You'll find David Alfaro Siqueiros' mural "La América Tropical" here. For lunch, order taquitos from **Cielito Lindo**, an L.A. classic, and then continue shopping for souvenirs among Olvera Street's shops and stalls. Take a short walk into Chinatown, known for both food and art. Many of the galleries are on **Chung King Road**, with some in Central Plaza and on Broadway as well. For dinner, you can pick from classic Chinatown spots like **Yang Chow** or new, popular joints like **Chego** or **Lao Tao**. After dinner, drinks can be found at local bars like **General Lee's** or **Melody Lounge**.

Fun Sunday
Smorgasburg and shopping at ROW DTLA

ROW DTLA is lit on Sundays, when it's home to **Smorgasburg**. This weekly food fest features an eclectic mix of vendors serving up everything from oysters to donuts and includes a healthy amount of businesses specializing in vegan eats. Open from 10 a.m. to 4 p.m., Smorgasburg is a destination for brunch or lunch. Shop at beyond-cool sneaker shop **Bodega** (page 58), or sit down for a more proper meal at **Rappahannock Oyster Bar** or **Paramount Coffee Project**.

STYLE COUNCIL

Check out these four see-now-buy-now fashion labels that all have roots in Downtown L.A.'s creative scene.

By Leslie McKenzie

ANINE BING
Rocker-chick vibe for every day

Anine Bing's upbringing in rural Denmark and Sweden is in stark contrast to the gritty urban surrounds of Downtown Los Angeles, where her globally recognized namesake fashion brand is based.

"The neighborhood has a roughness to it, and it really inspires me," says the former model. For proof, look no further than her of-the-moment womenswear line, from the bestselling studded Charlie boot ("Those put us on the map," she explains) to her figure-hugging jeans and rockstar-worthy leather jackets. She launched the label out of her garage in L.A.'s Silver Lake neighborhood in 2012 before moving the company to its current location.

"Ever since I was a kid, I dreamed about being a designer," explains Bing. "I was always finding vintage pieces and making them my own—but I never imagined that I would have stores around the world." She started off cultivating an online following for her model-off-duty

Anine Bing in the Fashion District wearing the Madeleine Blazer and Cigarette Pants in Leo

ANINE BING

Items from the Anine Bing x Janessa Leone capsule hat collection collaboration

The label's DTLA headquarters

ALL PHOTOS COURTESY ANINE BING

DTLA BOOK 2019   19

ANINE'S WORLD
Clockwise from right: Bing in the line's Bar Silk Skirt ($229) and silk camisole ($169) in Red Leo; a mood board in her office; Bing in the Madeleine Blazer in red and blue plaid ($349) and Larchmont Sunglasses in tortoise; the designer with model Maya Stepper.

sense of style through a now-defunct blog. That led to the creation of her direct-to-consumer line of edgy basics—"all pieces I think women should have in their wardrobes," she says. Today, the business has expanded to nine boutiques, including two in Los Angeles (in Pacific Palisades and in Beverly Grove on W. 3rd Street). In 2019, Bing expects to open five more doors—part of the brand's larger plan for growth after securing $15 million in a Series A financing round last September.

Even with the brand's dazzling rise, Bing remains hands on in day-to-day operations. "I want to know, and need to know, a little about everything," says the designer, whose 600,000-plus Instagram fans continue to watch her every stylish move. Creativity remains her strong suit, she says, including working on the brand's jewelry line, which is manufactured a stone's throw away from the brand's headquarters on Los Angeles Street (the rest of the products are made in Turkey).

But working Downtown has more advantages than just its proximity to L.A.'s nearby Jewelry District. "[The neighborhood] is evolving," says Bing, citing the rise of the local dining scene as an example, including personal favorites such as Bottega Louie on Grand Avenue. "I love coming down here from a more polished part of the city," says Bing, who commutes from her home in Hancock Park, where she resides with her husband and two children. "It's a really cool place."

ANINEBING.COM

Sarah Staudinger and George Augusto

STAUD

A vintage view on contemporary style

In 2015, Sarah Staudinger and George Augusto joined forces to create Staud, a womenswear brand with a vintage-driven approach. Beloved by the likes of Dakota Fanning, Emily Ratajkowski and Alexa Chung, the line was created with "a smart shopper" in mind, says Staudinger, "someone who understands versatility and is aware of price points."

Launched Downtown—the same neighborhood whose jewelry district Staudinger frequented with her mother while growing up—the expanding brand recently outgrew its original Arts District space and relocated to a larger studio in nearby Echo Park. "We wanted to stay as close to Downtown as possible," explains Augusto, also an L.A. native, noting that the ready-to-wear collection will continue to be made at local factories.

In between producing the line, which spans bubblegum-pink patent leather coats, lilac satin jumpsuits and rainbow-striped poplin dresses, the duo and their team find time to hit their favorite local hangs such as Maru Coffee in the Arts District ("They make one of the best matcha lattes I've ever had," says Staudinger), Filipino-inspired restaurant Lasa in Chinatown's Far East Plaza, and Santee Alley, where they occasionally spend lunch breaks scouting the outdoor market for styling props. Both co-founders admit to feeling like part of the neighborhood's creative class, thanks to an incoming wave of cutting-edge chefs, artists and fellow designers who have helped establish Downtown's reputation as a hub of innovation.

For spring 2019, Staud is planning its first shoe collection—a natural step for the label, which has already built a following with best-selling bags such as the structured PVC Shirley tote and the leather Moreau bucket bag encased in netting. So what's the secret formula? "We like to have fun," says Staudinger. "There are lots of trims and fun elements, but we don't want to make anything too trendy or overly sexy. It's pieces you can wear in a lot of different ways."

STAUD.CLOTHING

Pieces from Staud's fall 2018 collection, including the patent Dion Jacket in citrine with faux fur collar ($295) worn with the patent Murray Skirt ($205), full knit Shawn Sweater Dress in rose quartz ($175), and patent Liam Coat in rose quartz ($325)

Inside the designer's Fashion District studio

LYKKE WULFF
Inspired by Western-wear classics

Jemma Swatek didn't have a game plan when she launched her line, Lykke Wulff, in 2011 while she was wrapping up a degree in knitwear design at Academy of Art University in San Francisco. "I just starting making things because I found the perfect fabric and it evolved from there," says the English-born designer who now calls Echo Park home. "But who I am has always been someone who cares and has wanted to make a difference in this world." That meant making her line locally and involving her community.

Fast-forward to the present. Swatek's western-inspired collection of women's ready-to-wear and accessories includes gingham cowboy shirts and the best-selling Ranch jacket and pants in fabrics such as heavyweight denim, flannel plaid and twill. It's manufactured between a factory in Vernon and her studio on 8th Street (where clients can also shop by appointment only), so she frequents Sonoratown for a quick bite and Verve for her morning fix.

"I want the line to be for the conscious consumer who cares where their goods are coming from," says Swatek, whose pieces are also stocked by the likes of Free People and Urban Outfitters. "I am still packing up orders and am involved with every aspect of my business."

LYKKE WULFF
120 E. 8th St., Ste. 200, Fashion District // lykkewullf.com

Lykke Wullf's Lilith Lace-Up Bustier in cotton corduroy ($198)

Allegra wears the Puff Sleeve Shirt Dress in gold pebble satin ($435) and Shawl Blazer in peacock pebble satin ($495).

RAQUEL ALLEGRA
Topanga Canyon boho chic

Raquel Allegra describes her namesake womenswear line as "metropolitan bohemian"—a term that just as easily applies to the designer herself, who resides in laid-back Topanga Canyon and works out of a Downtown Los Angeles studio. Since landing on the fashion map with her shredded designs fashioned from vintage Los Angeles County Prison California tees, the Berkeley native—who formally launched a more expanded line in 2009—has become known for her flowy silhouettes in the form of tie-dye dresses and tops, silk kimonos, shawl blazers and cozy knits. "There's a quality in the clothing that's hard to describe, a humanity," says Allegra, who carefully selects her fabrics for their softness. From the brand's seventh-floor perch on Broadway (in 2016, the company opened a store in Beverly Grove on W. 3rd Street), Allegra is in close proximity to the Fashion District, as well as other Downtown haunts, such as the Freehand Hotel and its adjoining Flowerboy shop, and an outpost of Sweden's Il Caffe next to Acne Studios, which she loves for its coffee and its multicultural clientele. "You always hear different languages being spoken," she says. "It feels like a representation of a beautiful culture we have in Downtown Los Angeles that we don't have anywhere else in L.A."

RAQUELALLEGRA.COM

The designer in the Pop Over Top in mulberry silk tie dye ($495), Cropped Pant ($425) and Macintosh Coat ($875) in natural/brown plaid cotton stripe

FRESH FINDS

DTLA may not be known for green space, but tucked both between and near the bustling streets of this urban core are a handful of spots where you can temporarily retreat and connect with nature. From large parks to small gardens, here are eight places to explore.

By Liz Ohanesian // Photography by Mark Esguerra

1. Vista Hermosa Park

Located on the border of Downtown and Angeleno Heights (a bit west of Disney Concert Hall), 10-acre Vista Hermosa Park is nearly hidden from view. You could drive by not realizing that you're missing out on one of the city's hidden treasures. Situated on a hilltop, it provides gorgeous views of Downtown. Peek through the ample foliage and you can catch a glimpse of the top of a skyscraper. There's a small, soothing waterfall and picnic areas. It's designated wildlife habitat, so be on the lookout for critters. *100 N. Toluca St., laparks.org*

2. Los Angeles State Historic Park

Los Angeles State Historic Park is a fairly new spot to enjoy urban nature, but one with a long history. Look around and you'll see nods to Zanja Madre, the city's first aqueduct. This is also the site of a former rail yard and it was redeveloped as a park after lobbying by locals. Located just to the northeast of Chinatown, it officially opened on Earth Day 2017 and it's still a work in progress; the trees are young and small. You'll find less shade here and more open space on its 32 acres to play soccer or fly a kite. A bridge in the center of the park provides a fantastic view of Downtown and a small orchard (courtesy of the art collective Fallen Fruit) does bear oranges that, when ripe, can be picked and eaten by visitors. Events are frequent and include campfires, film screenings and more. *1245 N. Spring St., lashp.com*

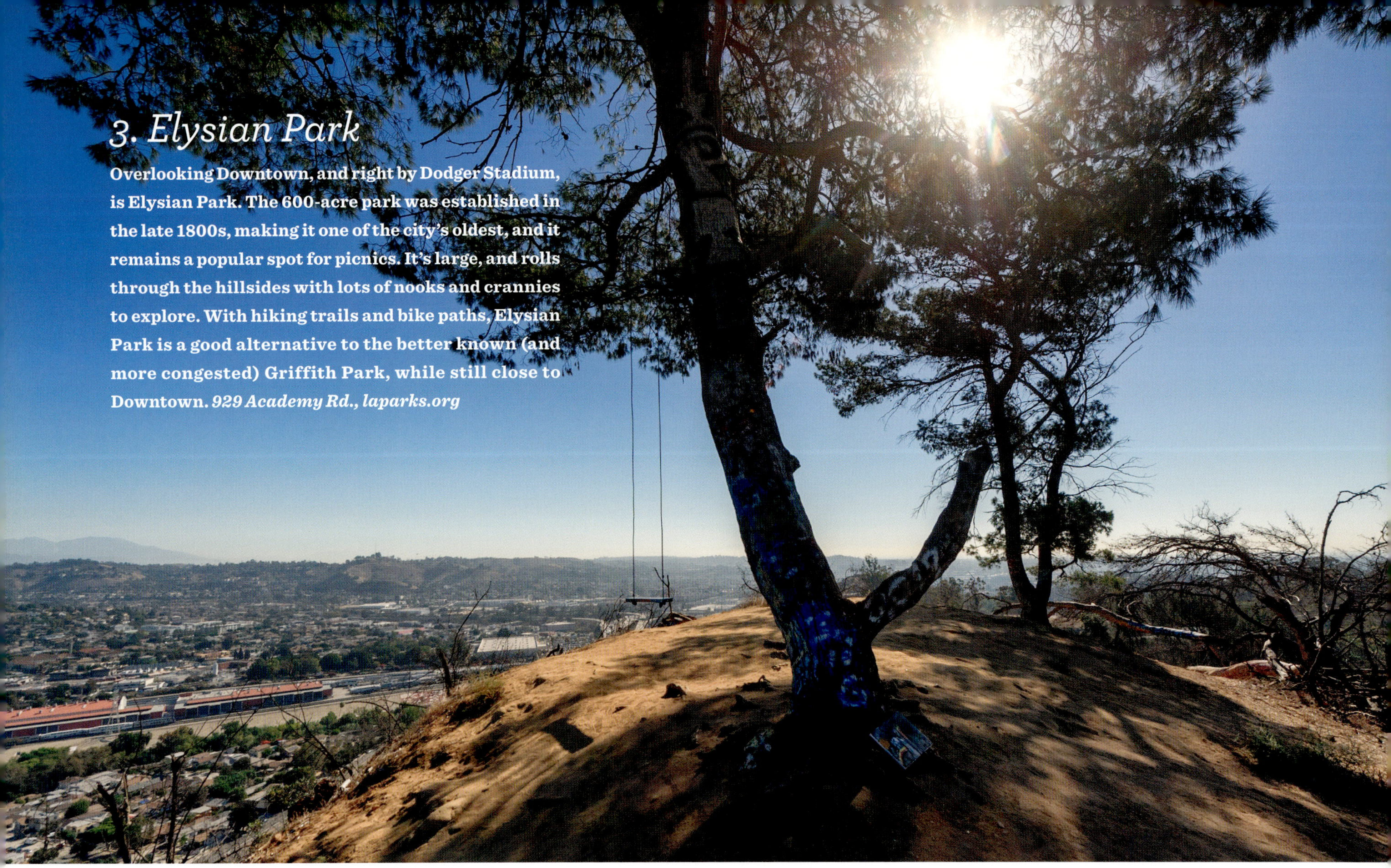

3. Elysian Park

Overlooking Downtown, and right by Dodger Stadium, is Elysian Park. The 600-acre park was established in the late 1800s, making it one of the city's oldest, and it remains a popular spot for picnics. It's large, and rolls through the hillsides with lots of nooks and crannies to explore. With hiking trails and bike paths, Elysian Park is a good alternative to the better known (and more congested) Griffith Park, while still close to Downtown. *929 Academy Rd., laparks.org*

4. Kyoto Gardens at the DoubleTree Hotel

Little Tokyo's DoubleTree by Hilton Hotel is home to a not-so-secret rooftop garden. The Kyoto Gardens are split into two compact levels. On the top is a tree-lined, grassy space that's ideal for wedding ceremonies. A small stream tumbles down rocks to the bottom level, where guests can lounge in a lush Japanese garden. Technically, the Kyoto Gardens are available only to hotel patrons, but it's not hard to walk in unnoticed. It is also available to rent for events. *120 S. Los Angeles St., doubletree3.hilton.com*

5. James Irvine Japanese Garden at Japanese American Cultural & Community Center

James Irvine Japanese Garden (also known as Seiryu-en or "Garden of the Clear Stream") is a small but breathtakingly beautiful space tucked outside of the bottom level of the Japanese American Cultural & Community Center. It's an award-winning garden with a 170-foot stream that symbolizes Japanese-American history. If you spot dragonflies darting between plants, you might start to think you're somewhere other than DTLA. This garden is open to the public (closed on Mondays) and is free to enter. *244 San Pedro St., jaccc.org*

6. Maguire Gardens

The Maguire Gardens surrounds the front entrance of the Central Library. It's an artful and serene space that merges the vintage appeal of the historic library with its modern Downtown surroundings. An adjacent restaurant, Cafe Pinot, offers outdoor seating where you can take in the sights of the garden while dining, and the garden itself is a well-known spot for eating lunch al fresco. *630 W. 5th St., lapl.org*

7. Blue Ribbon Garden at Walt Disney Concert Hall

The Blue Ribbon is a fundraising group for the Music Center and its donors are responsible for this rooftop garden at Walt Disney Concert Hall, home to the LA Phil. Pink ball and coral trees help provide a leafy canopy that makes this an ideal escape on days when Los Angeles sunshine beats hard against the streets. The Blue Ribbon Garden is easy to access via outdoor staircases on the sides of the concert hall and it's open to the public. *111 S. Grand Ave., musiccenter.org*

PERSHING SQUARE

A public gathering spot since the the mid-1800s, this was once a picture-postcard-worthy green space until a major redesign in the 1990s made concrete predominant. It's now better known for concerts and events than nature. However, L.A.'s oldest park is due for another face-lift and, this time, plans are to bring back a much-needed dose of flora.

8. Grand Park

Between City Hall and the Music Center, Grand Park is often called "the park for everyone." This 12-acre landscape is easily accessible—only steps away from a Metro Red/Purple subway station—and reflects Los Angeles' multicultural population. The Floristic Gardens of Grand Park features a global array of plant life organized by geographic regions, from South Africa to the Mediterranean. The park is a food truck destination several days a week. Enjoy lunch under the shade of an olive tree and take in the cool breeze near the Arthur J. Will Memorial Fountain as you stroll. *200 N. Grand Ave., grandparkla.org*

IT TAKES TWO

A surprising number of Downtown's most tempting restaurants are helmed by husband-and-wife teams. What makes it work: "We get to see each other—otherwise we never would."

By Lesley McKenzie

DINA & STEVE SAMSON
The owners of Rossoblu and Superfine

Whether you're craving handcrafted pastas or a quick slice of pizza, Dina and Steve Samson, the driving forces behind Italian stalwarts **Rossoblu** and **Superfine** in the Fashion District's City Market South complex (not to mention Sotto, just east of Century City) have you covered. "I often joke that Dina's the brains and I'm the talent. She does so much for each restaurant: operations, marketing, finances," says Steve, who met his wife while they were both undergrads at UC San Diego. "Her hard work allows me to focus on the kitchens." At Superfine, that means manning the electric pizza oven, turning out New York-meets-Neapolitan hits served whole or by the slice. A stone's throw away at Rossoblu, Steve's Bolognese heritage informs a family-style menu, ranging from handmade fennel tagliolini to whole-grilled orata.

OPENED Rossoblu in 2017; Superfine in 2018.
MUST-TRY DISHES "All of our pasta is great, but I especially love the tagliatelle al ragu. I've been eating this dish my whole life, so it has a special place in my heart," says Steve of Rossoblu. At Superfine, the spotlight is on produce-driven fare, including the Es-Ca-Role white pizza with escarole, salt-cured olives, chilies, mozzarella and smoked provolone.
WHY THEY LOVE WORKING TOGETHER "We complement each other very well. We want everyone at our restaurants to work to his or her strengths, so we try to lead by example," says Steve.

ROSSOBLU
1124 San Julian St., Fashion District // rossoblula.com

SUPERFINE
1101 S. San Pedro St., Fashion District // superfinepizza.com

32 DTLA BOOK 2019

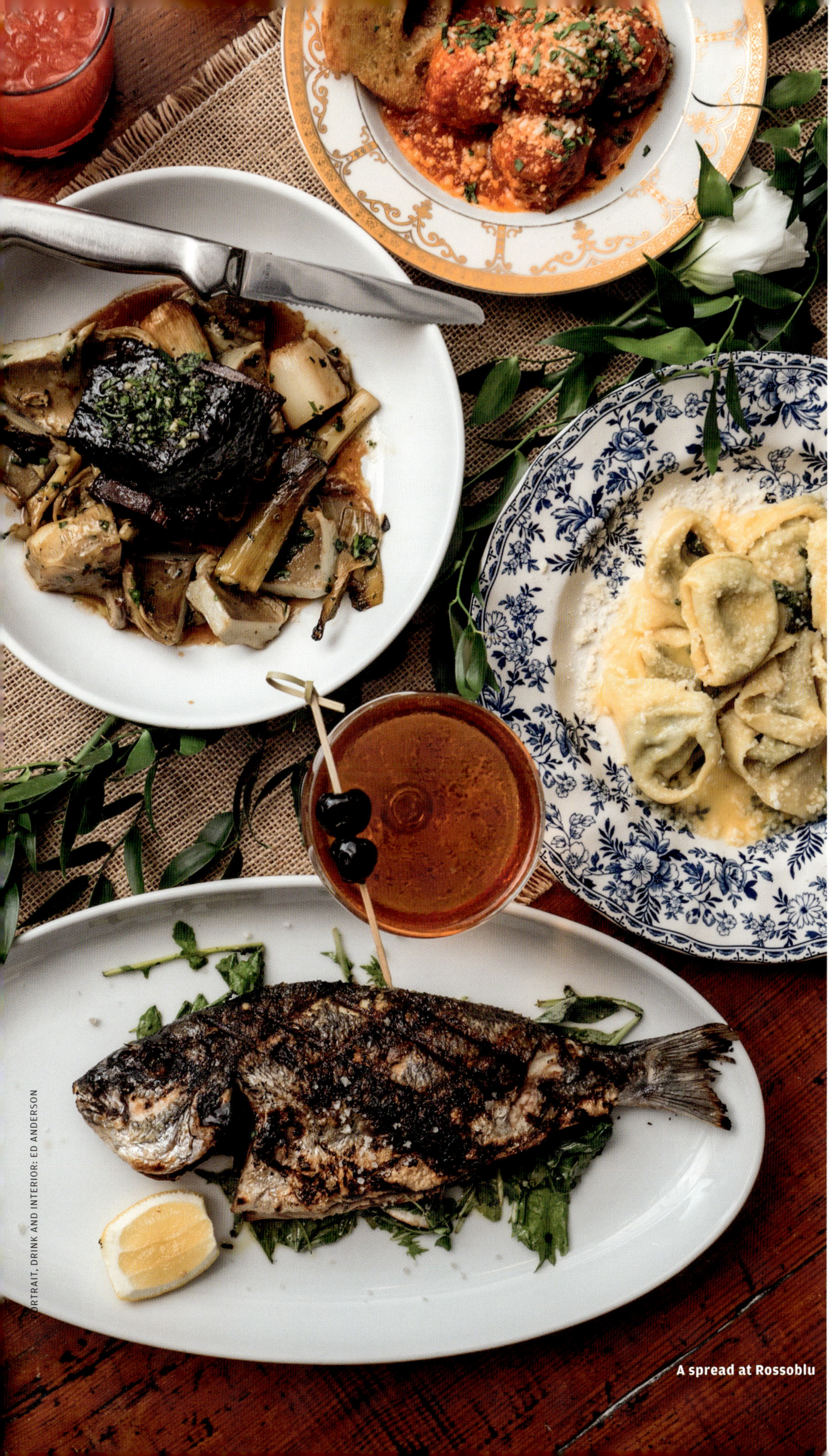

A spread at Rossoblu

PORTRAIT, DRINK AND INTERIOR: ED ANDERSON

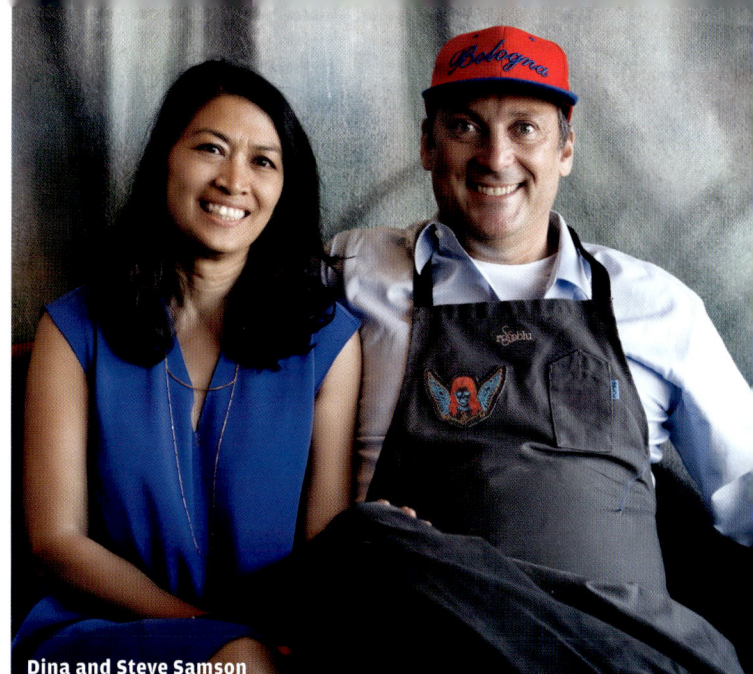

Dina and Steve Samson

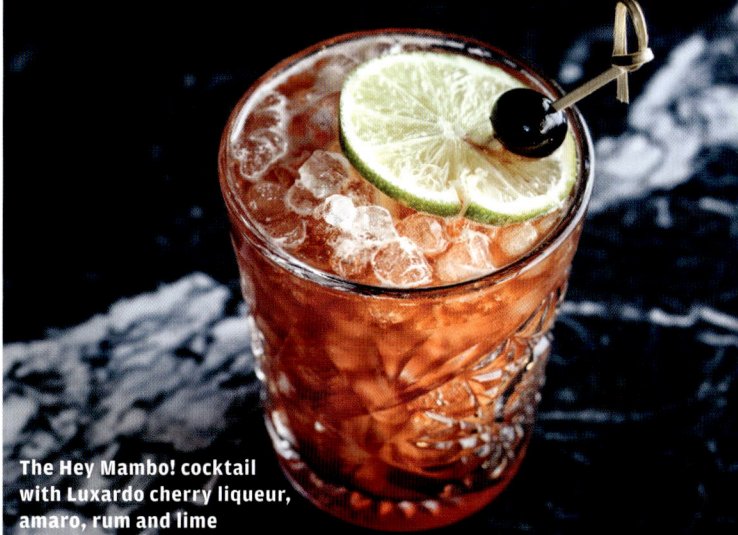

The Hey Mambo! cocktail with Luxardo cherry liqueur, amaro, rum and lime

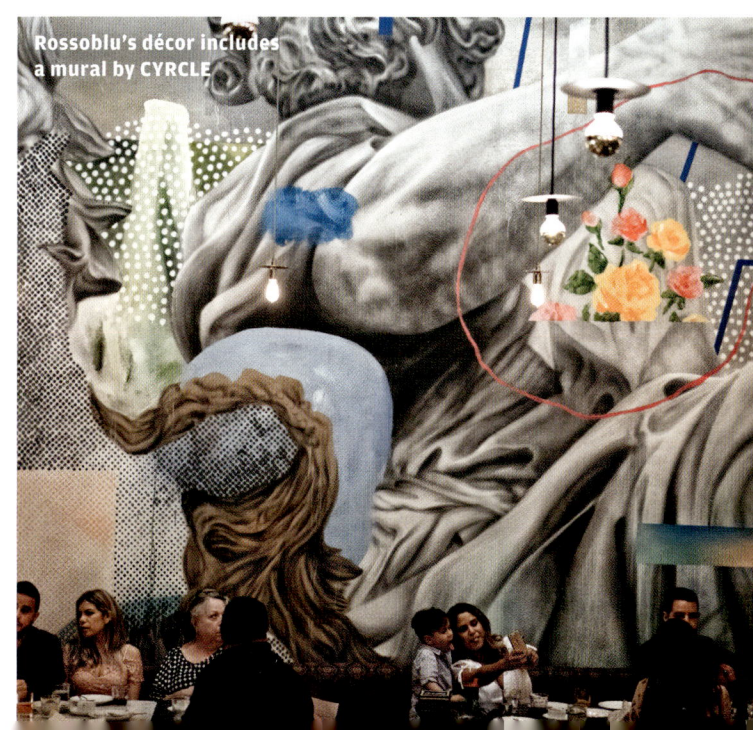

Rossoblu's décor includes a mural by CYRCLE

ORI MENASHE & GENEVIEVE GERGIS

The owners of Bestia and Bavel

After chef Ori Menashe and pastry chef Genevieve Gergis debuted their critically acclaimed multiregional Italian restaurant **Bestia** in 2012, the Arts District landed national attention as a dining destination. Six years later, the neighborhood's culinary cred was upped even further with the debut of **Bavel**, Menashe and Gergis' infinitely Instagram-able Middle Eastern spot. "What we pride ourselves on is having a diverse enough menu that we can accommodate anyone—even vegans," says Gergis, who met Menashe while they were both working at the now-shuttered La Terza. While Bestia has garnered a following with its house-cured meats and pastas, Bavel's shared-plates menu is a boundary-pushing ode to Menashe's cultural roots and formative years spent in Israel: Think spreads such as a silky foie gras halva, and mains like slow-roasted lamb-neck shawarma—all complemented by Gergis' memorable riffs on regional sweets. We'll have the roasted fig tart, please.

OPENED Bestia in 2012; Bavel in 2018.

MUST-TRY DISHES At Bestia, it's the cavatelli alla Norcina with housemade pork sausage "because it's synonymous with Bestia. It's been on the menu since day one," says Gergis. Bavel's licorice root ice cream bon bon is a can't-miss treat.

WHAT THEY LOVE ABOUT WORKING TOGETHER "Bouncing ideas off each other and being able to actually see each other despite our crazy long work hours," says Gergis.

BESTIA 2121 E. 7th Pl., Arts District // bestiala.com

BAVEL 500 Mateo St., Arts District // baveldtla.com

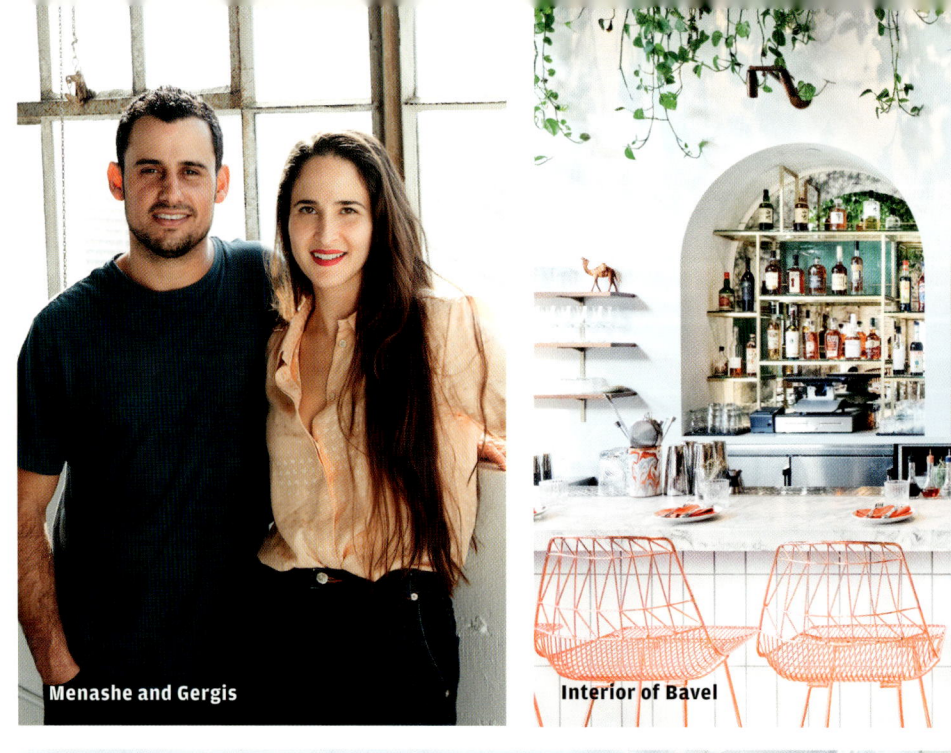

Menashe and Gergis

Interior of Bavel

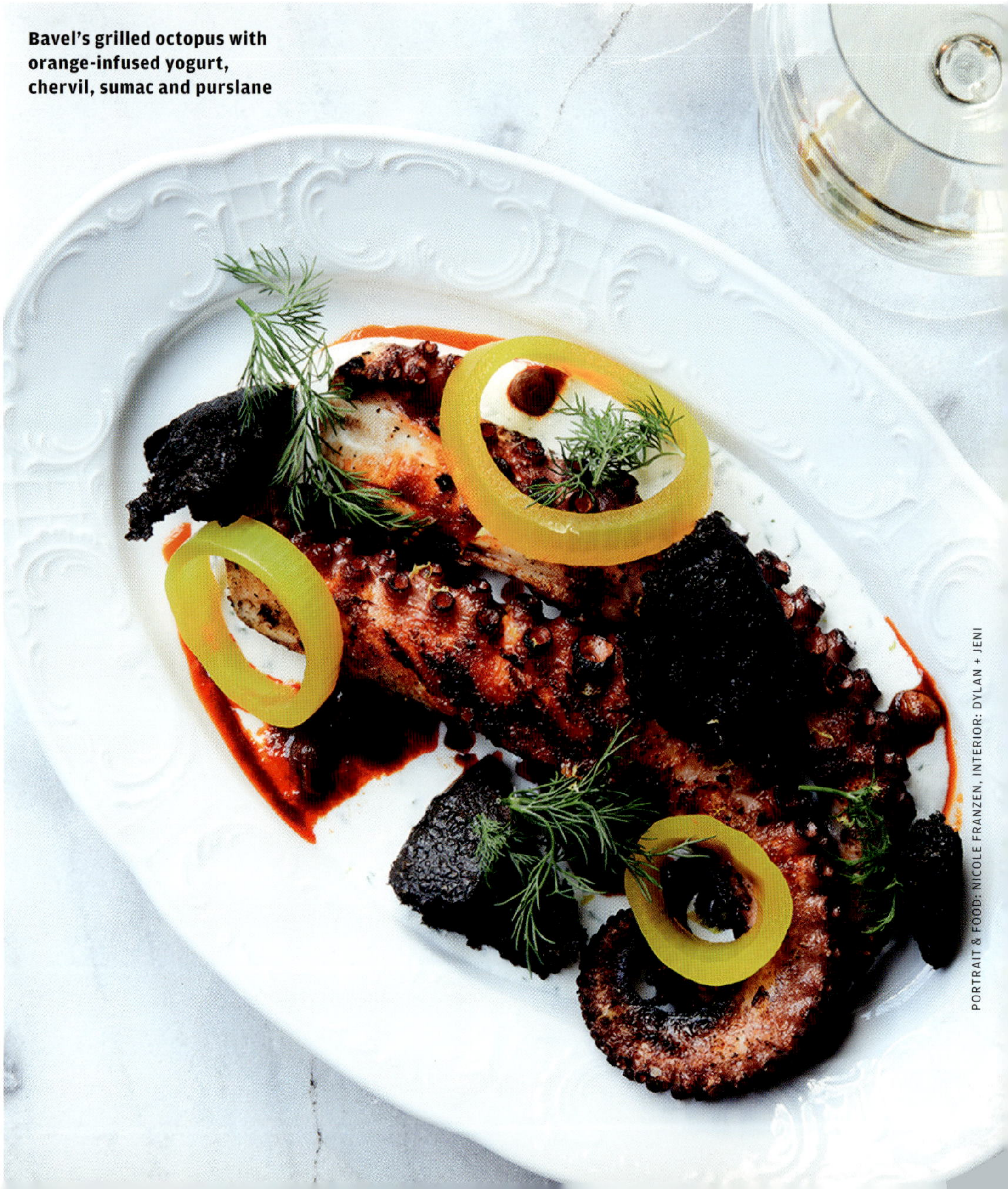

Bavel's grilled octopus with orange-infused yogurt, chervil, sumac and purslane

PORTRAIT & FOOD: NICOLE FRANZEN, INTERIOR: DYLAN + JENI

Fraser and Knoll Fraser

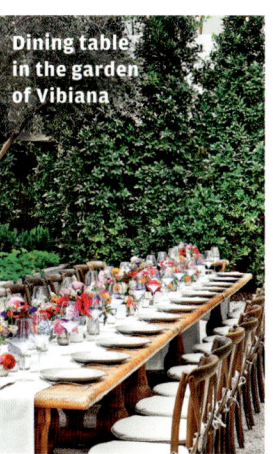

Dining table in the garden of Vibiana

Splendor in the Grass

Cured salmon on rye

NEAL FRASER & AMY KNOLL FRASER

Since taking over the deconsecrated Archdiocese cathedral **Vibiana** as owners-operators with their business partners in 2012, Neal Fraser and wife Amy Knoll Fraser reimagined the 19th-century landmark as a top events venue as well as home to their flagship restaurant, **Redbird**. As a lifelong Angeleno, Fraser's modern American fare pays homage to the city's multicultural flavors with spins on classic dishes (duck confit chilaquiles, barbecue smoked tofu). Knoll Fraser oversees the couple's catering business and operations for the 1,400-person venue.

REDBIRD 114 E. 2nd St., Historic Core // redbird-la
VIVIANA 214 S. Main St., Historic Core // vibiana.com

TIM & LOUISE LEE

Tim and Louise Lee, who met while both were working at restaurants in the neighborhood, weren't planning on opening their own spot. But all that changed when they stumbled upon a vacant space in the Fashion District, now home to Hawaiian-inspired **Broken Mouth**. "Our guests are welcomed with *aloha* spirit to dine with us with the feeling of being in our home," says Louise of the mom-and-pop-style concept, which puts a fresh take on homestyle plates, including the can't-miss Spam musubi (seaweed-wrapped spam on rice).

BROKEN MOUTH 213 E. 9th St., Fashion District // eatbrokenmouth.com

Spicy chicken sandwich

Tim and Louise Lee

Spam musubi

EUNAH KANG & MARCUS CHRISTIANA-BENIGER

Husband-and-wife co-owners Marcus Christiana-Beniger and Eunah Kang don't cut any corners at **The Little Jewel** of New Orleans, their Southern market and deli in Chinatown inspired by executive chef Christiana-Beniger's NOLA roots. Bread is flown in from New Orleans' Leidenheimer Bakery for a menu of more than 30 po'boys, accompanied by the likes of hush puppies and fried okra.

THE LITTLE JEWEL 207 Ord St., Chinatown // littlejewel.la

Christiana-Beniger and Kang

Crawfish Bisque special

DTLA BOOK 2019   35

YASSMIN SARMADI & TONY ESNAULT

The owners of Church & State

When Yassmin Sarmadi opened the doors to her debut restaurant, **Church & State**, in the once-desolate Arts District 11 years ago, there were crack dealers and prostitutes on the street corner, she says. "There wasn't a resurgence of Downtown yet, but there was an idea that there could be," says the Claremont native. A lot has changed since then. Not only did the French bistro quickly become a celebrated dining destination and a game changer for the neighborhood (when they first opened, "it was this hidden secret," she says), but Sarmadi met—and later married—her now business partner, Michelin-starred chef Tony Esnault (formerly of L.A.'s Patina and Essex House in New York City). Together the Downtown residents also opened the since-shuttered Spring in the historic Douglas building in 2016, and have set their sights on a forthcoming French restaurant in Orange County.

OPENED 2008.
MUST-TRY DISHES "The chicken liver mousse because it's made with 100 percent free-range organic chicken and it has a delicious, velvety texture that is complemented by the sweetness of the port wine gelée on top," says Esnault, who hails from the Loire Valley in France. For Sarmadi, it's all about the steak frites. "We use pasture-raised, grass-fed beef served with a delicious Bearnaise sauce and perfectly cooked fries," she says.
WHAT THEY LOVE ABOUT WORKING TOGETHER "We get to see each other—otherwise we never would," says Sarmadi. Adds Esnault: "I can't even imagine it otherwise."

CHURCH & STATE
1850 Industrial St., #100, Arts District // churchandstatebistro.com

Sarmadi and Esnault

Wild Burgundy snails in puff pastry

Daily oyster selection

French fries with aioli

The mesquite grill

Carne asada tacos

Diaz-Rodriguez and Feltham

JEN FELTHAM & TEODORO DIAZ-RODRIGUEZ

Housemade flour tortillas steal the show at **Sonoratown**, a modest, off-the-beaten-path taqueria opened in 2016 by Jen Feltham and Teodoro Diaz-Rodriguez, who were drawn to the neighborhood because it's "dynamic and diverse," says Feltham. Tacos, including a mesquite-grilled carne asada option, are served in the style of Diaz-Rodriguez's Northern Mexican hometown of San Luis Rio Colorado in Sonora. And don't miss the shredded chicken chimichangas, filled with grilled Anaheim chiles, blistered tomatoes, mild cheddar and Monterey Jack cheese.

SONORATOWN 208 E. 8th St., Fashion District // sonoratownla.com

NIGHTLIFE KING AND QUEEN: TIM KREHBIEL AND BRIDGET VAGEDES

Not many people choose to live above a bar. But Tim Krehbiel and Bridget Vagedes, who have owned a warehouse building in the Arts District since 2001, welcomed the idea. In 2015, Krehbiel—along with architect/designer Jacek Ostoya, music aficionado Larry Little and restaurateur Paul Oberman—opened **Resident**. It's an all-in-one bar, beer garden and live music venue with a regular food truck. As a managing partner, "I'm involved more than one would think," says Krehbiel. He started frequenting Downtown as a SCI-Arc student in the '80s and later as a classic-car restorer. Vagedes' work as a jeweler drew her to the neighborhood; today, her artistic touches can be seen in the plantings on the property as well as an on-site diorama. What do they love most about life Downtown? "Being part of a growing community that in many ways has taken on a life of its own," says Krehbiel. "We're proud of weathering all the change and being part of it. I think we continue to have something to offer newcomers."

RESIDENT 428 S. Hewitt St., Arts District // residentdtla.com

DTLA BOOK 2019   37

The Angels Flight, Los Angeles, Cal.

TWO ANGELS ON A STRING

For a trip back in time, take a ride on 118-year-old Angels Flight, the shortest railway in the world and a link back to old Bunker Hill.

By Jim Dawson // Archival photography courtesy of Marc Wanamaker/Bison Archives

When you look at the skyscrapers of Bunker Hill today, it's hard to imagine the stately Victorian mansions that once dominated its skyline. Built in the late 1800s as an exclusive residential enclave, Bunker Hill soon became a crowded working-class area of apartments and flophouses after the rich moved to wealthier precincts.

The demise of the old Bunker Hill came when L.A.'s Community Redevelopment Agency flattened the hilltop, carried off the last Victorian in 1969, and replaced everything with the office high-rises of today. Fortunately, the former Bunker Hill attracted scores of filmmakers, writers and painters, so plenty of evidence of the neighborhood is left for us.

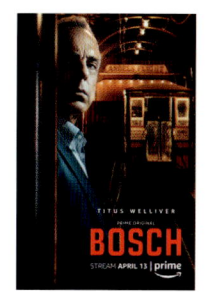

If the wooden mansions are long gone, there is one historical landmark still in existence to connect us with the lost neighborhood on the hill: Angels Flight. This funicular railway—which appeared in the 2016 movie *La La Land* and in season 4 of the popular *Bosch* detective show (based on Michael Connelly's 1999 novel, *Angels Flight*)—opened on the last day of 1901. Its two counterbalanced cars, Olivet and Sinai, controlled by a single cable, went up and down the hill at a grade of 33 degrees, connecting Hill and Olive Streets. Besides being considered the "world's shortest railroad," Angels Flight is probably also the only one to have been moved. Originally located next to the 3rd Street Tunnel, it was dismantled and put in storage in 1969, then rebuilt in 1996 half a block south, across from Grand Central Market. It now connects Hill Street with the California Plaza. In recent decades, Bunker Hill has enjoyed a renaissance as a cultural center around MOCA, Walt Disney Concert Hall, the Music Center and the Broad, where you can experience cutting-edge art framed by world-class architecture. But with all the shining objects on the hill, those little orange cars, Olivet and Sinai, will still give you the best 298 feet of time travel a dollar (50 cents with Metro Card) can buy.

ANGELS FLIGHT TODAY
FROM LEFT: The railway retains its distinctive 1910 Beaux-Arts gateway; Ryan Gosling and Emma Stone stole a kiss on it in *La La Land*; it appears in the Amazon Prime Original series *Bosch*.

> "I found Fante, I'd guess, when I was about 19. He didn't live in a house in this novel but described his window and his place and his hotel somewhere in his writings and it was along the cement stairway opposite Angel's Flight—downtown L.A. I used to pass the place he described and glance at it and quickly pass. I admired his writing so much that just looking at where he had once possibly lived was quite magic to me."
> —**CHARLES BUKOWSKI** from a 1978 letter to poet and playwright Ben Pleasants

A view from the top of the Casa Alta Apartments on Olive Street looked down on Angels Flight and its disappearing neighborhood in 1965.

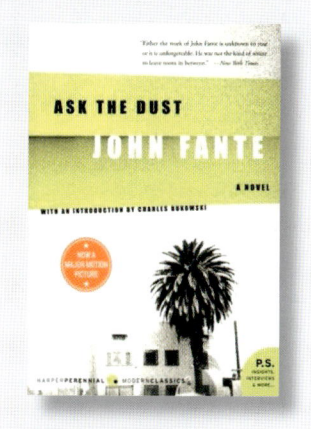

ASK THE DUST
BY JOHN FANTE
Harper Perennial Modern Classics

Charles Bukowski was a huge fan of the writer John Fante. He helped get some of Fante's work back into circulation when he successfully lobbied his publisher, Black Sparrow, to start publishing Fante's out-of-print books. Bukowski wrote the introduction for Fante's most famous novel, *Ask the Dust*.

PART 1: HARD-BOILED MEMORIES
Gritty Los Angeles writers fell in love with the train to nowhere on Bunker Hill.

Angels Flight has appeared in many books and short stories (see the list of notable books on page 42). Raymond Chandler lived on Bunker Hill, first with his mother and later his wife, and visited Angels Flight both in a novella called *The King in Yellow* and in the Philip Marlowe novel *The High Window*. But if Angels Flight had a poet, it was John Fante, a young Italian American from Colorado who lived at the Alta Vista apartments on Bunker Hill Avenue in the early 1930s with dreams of becoming a writer. In his second novel, *Ask the Dust* (1939), Fante so vividly evoked Angels Flight and the topography of Bunker Hill that today's Angelenos consider it a local literary classic. Later in his life, after diabetes ended his screenwriting career, Fante dictated to his wife his last novel, *Dreams from Bunker Hill*, published in 1982, a year before his death. When struggling writer Charles Bukowski found a copy of *Ask the Dust* in the L.A. Public Library in Downtown, he declared it "the finest novel ever written." Just as Bukowski often wandered around Bunker Hill looking for some traces of Fante's life, we may find ourselves daydreaming about those writers' lives—on a very sweet and short ride on the same railway they once rode.

DTLA BOOK 2019 41

CLASSIC BOOKS
Six authors inspired by Bunker Hill

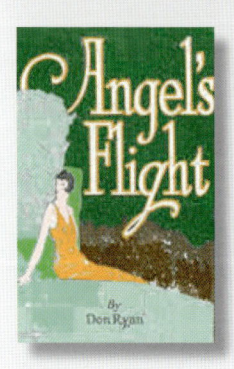

ANGEL'S FLIGHT
By Don Ryan
Boni & Liveright, 1927

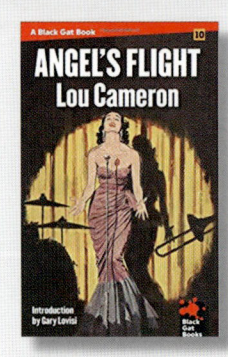

ANGEL'S FLIGHT
By Lou Cameron
Black Gat Books, 1946

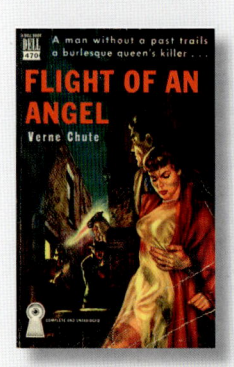

FLIGHT OF AN ANGEL
By Verne Chute
Dell, 1947

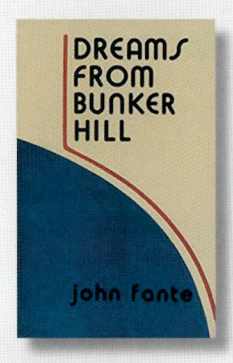

DREAMS FROM BUNKER HILL
By John Fante
Black Sparrow Press, 1982

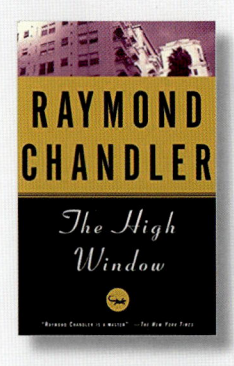

THE HIGH WINDOW
By Raymond Chandler
Vintage Crime/Black Lizard, 1988; originally published 1942

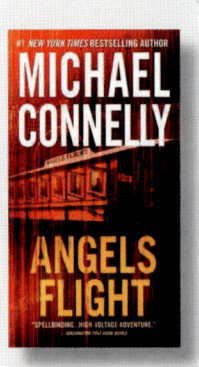

ANGELS FLIGHT
By Michael Connelly
Grand Central Publishing, 2014; originally published 1999

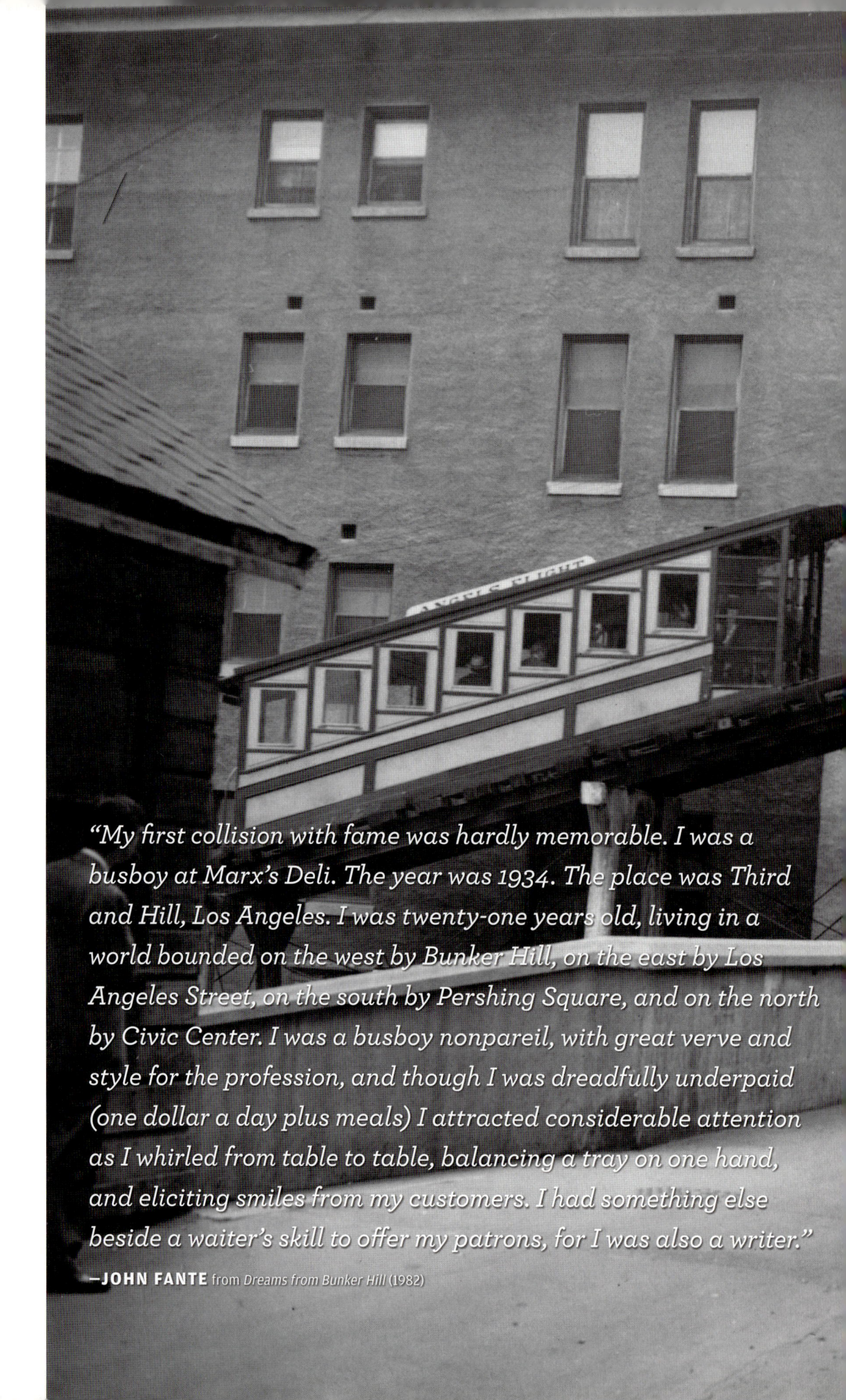

"My first collision with fame was hardly memorable. I was a busboy at Marx's Deli. The year was 1934. The place was Third and Hill, Los Angeles. I was twenty-one years old, living in a world bounded on the west by Bunker Hill, on the east by Los Angeles Street, on the south by Pershing Square, and on the north by Civic Center. I was a busboy nonpareil, with great verve and style for the profession, and though I was dreadfully underpaid (one dollar a day plus meals) I attracted considerable attention as I whirled from table to table, balancing a tray on one hand, and eliciting smiles from my customers. I had something else beside a waiter's skill to offer my patrons, for I was also a writer."

—JOHN FANTE from *Dreams from Bunker Hill* (1982)

"Walking across Third and Hill to Angel's Flight, I climbed aboard the trolley and sat down. The only other passenger was a girl across the aisle reading a book. She was in a plain dress and without stockings. She was rather attractive but not my style. As the trolley lurched into motion she moved to another seat."

—JOHN FANTE
from *Dreams from Bunker Hill* (1982)

ANGELS
FLIGHT
DRUGS
BREAKFAST
Served
BROMO SELTZER
HEADACHES
Coca-Cola
LIGHT
LUNCHES

"Bunker Hill was [Fante's] neighborhood ... I lived there too before they leveled off the poor and put up high-rises. It was the best place for the poor, the best place for cabbage and fish heads, boiled carrots, the old, the insane, the young who couldn't fit into the offices down there."

—**CHARLES BUKOWSKI** from his 1978 letter to Ben Pleasants

Van Heflin ran from a dark past beneath Angels Flight in MGM's *Act of Violence* (1949).

PART 2: FILM NOIR'S GROUND ZERO
When Angels Flight appeared on screen, it signified you'd entered a strange neighborhood.

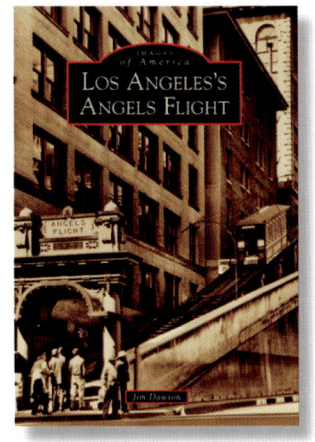

ABOUT THE WRITER
Jim Dawson is the author of *Los Angeles's Angels Flight* (Arcadia Publishing, 2008).

Angels Flight found a true home in the movies. Beginning in 1914, directors came from nearby Hollywood to build silent comedy adventures around the moving cars, including *Their Ups and Downs* (1914) and *All Jazzed Up* (1920). After World War II, business really picked up when film noir auteurs needed mean streets and picturesque neighborhoods. Bunker Hill, with its aging Queen Annes and twisting stairways, was the perfect location for mayhem, and Angels Flight instantly identified the neighborhood as an unusual place where anything could happen: A newspaper-reading passenger could learn that her husband had been murdered (*The Unfaithful*, 1947) or a serial killer could ride up to his seedy Victorian aerie (*M*, 1950). The two cars crisscrossing above Clay Street also became a motif in such films as *Act of Violence*, *The Turning Point* and *Kiss Me Deadly*. In one memorable moment, Yvonne DeCarlo smoked a cigarette in a boardinghouse in 1949's *Criss Cross* as the cars passed outside the window.

ANGELS FLIGHT
Upper Station: 350 S. Grand Ave., Financial District
Lower Station: 351 S. Hill St., Historic Core

46 DTLA BOOK 2019

M *Columbia, 1951*
David Wayne, playing a child murderer, ran through the 3rd Street Tunnel with Janine Perreau and rounded the corner at the foot of Angels Flight.

ALL JAZZED UP *Christie Film Company, 1920*
Giddy tourist bride Helen Darling rode up and down Angels Flight as if it were an amusement park ride in the Al Christie comedy.

THE TURNING POINT *Paramount, 1952*
Angels Flight took William Holden and Alexis Smith to a Bunker Hill flophouse where a mob witness was hiding.

THE MONEY TRAP *MGM, 1966*
Los Angeles police detective Glenn Ford tailed the wife of a fugitive murderer on Angels Flight.

CRISS CROSS *Universal Pictures, 1949*
Angels Flight's cars passed in the night outside gun moll Yvonne DeCarlo's window.

COURTESY COLUMBIA, PARAMOUNT, MGM, UNIVERSAL PICTURES

GONE AND FORGOTTEN

Court Flight: The Unglamorous Sister

Built just three blocks away from Angels Flight in 1904, Court Flight never had the cachet of its older, shorter sister. Samuel G. Vandergrift built the 335-feet funicular from Hill Street on Bunker Hill to the 200 block of North Broadway, across the street from the Los Angeles Courthouse. Its two very utilitarian-looking cars ran on separate tracks. Comedians from Hal Roach's nearby studio, including young Harold Lloyd, used it for several movies, but none of the films appear to have survived. It ceased operations during World War II and was dismantled.

DTLA BOOK 2019 47

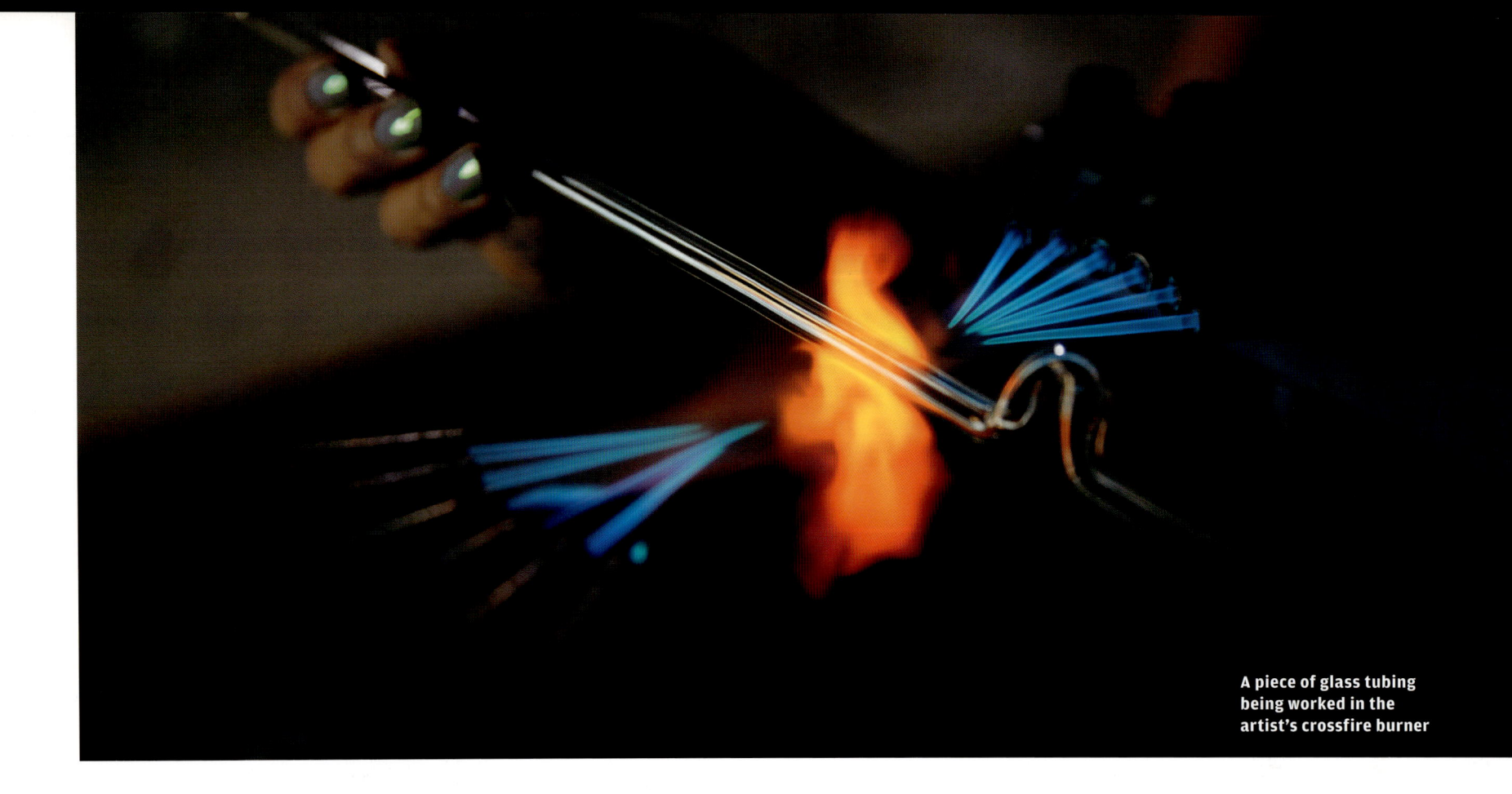

A piece of glass tubing being worked in the artist's crossfire burner

NEON DREAMS

Inspired by the glowing signs of Los Angeles and Las Vegas, Leticia "Tiza" Maldonado is part of a new-wave group of artists taking the art of neon to the next level.

By Molly Creeden
Photography and videography by Jiro Schneider

The blinking, hypnotic history of neon in Los Angeles begins with the convergence of consumerism and art in the 1920s, booms through the golden age of new advertising in the 1930s, falls out of favor as an emblem of urban decay in the 1960s and '70s, and resurfaces, thanks to the Museum of Neon Art, in the 1980s. In the future, however, it might look something like the organic forms of Leticia Maldonado. The 38-year-old artist grew up in Las Vegas, where many evenings, she sat in the car with her stepfather, waiting for her mother, a showgirl known as Gypsy Louise, to come off her shift at the Flamingo Hotel.

"It represented adult autonomy to me," she recalls of those late nights sitting in the backseat and gazing up at the lights. "This beautiful electric wonderland that I couldn't get close to." Once, when her mother didn't have a babysitter, she brought "Tiza" (Maldonado's nickname since she was little) to the club, and when the boss arrived backstage, she hastily placed the young girl under a chair draped with costumes. "I remember looking out through sparkly, colorful fabric at high heels going back and forth," Maldonado recalls. "That buildup of energy when people are getting ready to perform; it made a huge impression."

Decades later, Maldonado had already been working as a neon artist in L.A. for five years when she was invited to create a piece outside of DTLA's Palace Theatre for 2018's Night on Broadway. "Electric Hustlers" featured two glowing, feather-flanked showgirls in a backstage vignette. At her daughter's invitation, Gypsy Louise came from Vegas to see the installation. When she saw the buzzing tribute, she wept.

Like the anticipation of a performer before the curtain goes up, the moment that Maldonado plugs her work into a power source feels exhilarating every time. It comes after

Maldonado in front of her work "The Crimson Ghost." Says the artist, "It's the logo of one of my favorite bands, The Misfits."

WATCH TIZA IN ACTION
Video by Jiro Schneider

Scan this code with your standard iPhone camera or Android QR Code reader app.

she has drawn and amplified a sketch, traced around a glass tube to create a pattern, then placed the tubes atop heat-resistant fabric to torch and bend them swiftly according to the blueprint. She fuses electrodes to the tubes before hooking the work up to a source of neon, krypton or argon (the latter with mercury). The instant she flips the switch that sends gas and electricity through her sculpture, the sight of it snapping alive feels like "a kick in my chest, heart, eyeballs, all at the same time," she says.

Maldonado's foray into the form began in an Arts District class with Lili Lakich, a longtime fabricator of neon public works. Eager to apprentice with a bender, she cold-called artists until Michael Flechtner, a 20-year industry veteran and creator of the U.S. Postal Service's "Celebrate!" stamp, took her on for a two-month course. Maldonado credits Flechtner and Lakich for introducing her to neon's possibilities. "I love the tactile experience of working with neon and feeling connected to my hands," she notes of the highly technical medium. "And that it's not a static drawing; it's an active, physical reaction happening in front of you."

Notes Meryl Pataky, a young bender herself, who curated the 2017 show "She Bends: Women in Neon" at the Museum of Neon Art (MONA) in Glendale: "Tiza is part of a new generation of neon benders who are female in a predominantly older white male community."

At MONA, Maldonado's self-taught illustration background and fascination with symbols of personal power came together in her interpretation of tarot cards. "The Lovers" and "Death" were conceived as flowers leaning in graceful, painterly gestures. "No one else is doing what she is—bending neon in illustrative, intricate ways—and the best part is that she's making it herself," says Pataky.

"No one else is doing what she is—bending neon in illustrative, intricate ways—and the best part is that she's making it herself."
—MERYL PATAKY, CURATOR AND FELLOW NEON ARTIST

A piece of glass in Maldonado's ribbon burner

The artist using a blowhose, a glass-blowing tool, while working material in her crossfire burner

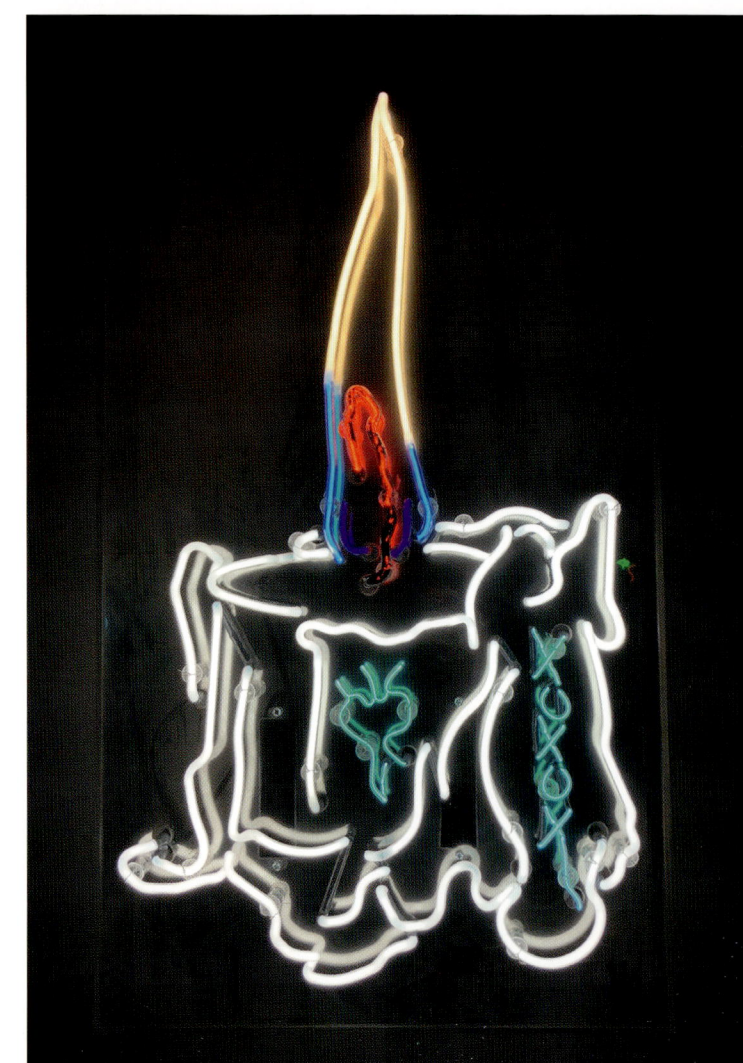

A TRIO OF TIZAS

ABOVE: The artist made "Inner Sight," from her Moon series, to help "keep a bigger perspective when faced with an acute sadness," she says.
RIGHT, TOP: Her 2018 work "Soledad" is named after her grandmother. "We are very close and this piece is in tribute to her vitality and light."
RIGHT, BOTTOM: A 2018 piece titled "I left the light on for you, but I guess you ain't coming home." Says Maldonado, "I made this as I was processing the end of a long-term romantic relationship."

52 DTLA BOOK 2019

TIZA'S FAVES

BOTTEGA LOUIE
"I dream about their huge selection of delicious macarons."

CLIFTON'S REPUBLIC
"I love the variety of its California-themed bars on different levels."

MARIE'S SANDWICH SHOP
"My go-to for a quick lunch, including baguette sandwiches."

SEVEN GRAND
"I love the old-timey decor. They have delicious whiskey-based cocktails, pool tables and, on some nights, a rad jazz band."

BRIGHT LIGHTS
The luminaries of L.A.'s neon artist community

MICHAEL FLECHTNER
Bending since the mid-'80s, Flechtner is known for both his private and public commissions, including 2011's "Celebrate!" stamp. The artist creates his sculptural neon at a studio in Van Nuys and is a member of the MONA advisory board.

LILI LAKICH
Lakich's studio in the Arts District welcomes students and drop-ins alike. There, they observe and learn from one of the industry's most experienced craftswomen, bending in the field for 45 years.

LINDA SUE PRICE
After 30 years spent creating motion graphics in the video production world, Price took a neon workshop from Flechtner at MONA that changed her creative course. The MONA advisory board member's optimistic abstract works are regularly on view throughout galleries in L.A.

ROXY ROSE
Rose started working in neon in 1978 and took over her grandfather's manufacturing company in 2000. In addition to commissions and commercial projects, her latest works explore politics, sexuality and gender.

LISA SCHULTE
Owner of Nights of Neon, a Van Nuys fabrication studio, Schulte sits on the board of MONA. In addition to sculpture, she is known for her neon film and music video credits.

Maldonado has also taken botanical forms, an influence from her grandmother, an avid gardener, and given them sculptural dimension, hanging her incandescent florals in the window of Hang Arts in San Francisco and traveling with the same installation to Mexico City, where she was part of "Bridges in a Time of Walls: Mexican/Chicano Art from Los Angeles to Mexico City," curated by Julian Bermudez of Chinatown's Bermudez Projects. Her works were part of a section about the Mexican-American experience; it was her first time in Mexico. After those shows and "All Lit Up," a 2018 group exhibit at DTLA's Eastern Projects, Maldonado's work is next on view in Milwaukee, when "She Bends" arrives at the Var Gallery in January 2019.

Los Angeles, however, is where Maldonado continues to challenge herself—influenced by her forebears; a burgeoning group of fellow benders; and the signs dotting the city and its freeways.

After a new owner of Downtown L.A.'s Santa Fe Art Colony raised rents by as much as 82 percent, she relocated her studio to a corner of painter Frank Romero's working space on the crease of the Arts District and Boyle Heights. Though the climate toward artists in the neighborhood is changing, Maldonado loves DTLA, where she has waitressed and tended bar, taken visitors to Clifton's Republic, and found herself in the frequent pull of Chinatown, drawn by its neon glow. "It's where my favorite public artwork in the city lives. It's known as the Dragon Gate, by artist Rupert Mok, depicting two Chinese dragons fighting over a glowing pearl that spans Broadway. It's beautiful relief for my imagination. I hope L.A. maintains it forever."

Her ultimate goal, however, is to return to the hallowed fluorescent thoroughfare of her youth, whose neon flamingos, palm trees and vintage signs continue flickering in her mind: "The Strip is like the neon hall of fame to me."

PEAK SNEAKER MOMENT

With the arrival of the Nike Air Jordan megastore on Broadway, Downtown's bubbling-up sneakerhead culture gets serious lift.

By Maxwell Williams

Terry Bailey looks tired, but proud. It's the grand opening of Downtown's new three-story Nike Air Jordan store called **Jumpman LA** on Broadway, and Bailey is exiting with a bag full of new kicks sporting the logo (a silhouette of Michael Jordan flying through the air) so famous among sneakerheads. He'd been in line outside for three days, sleeping in a camping chair. "I didn't cheat either," he says, referring to people who pay line-standers to wait for them. "I was there the whole time." And unlike others who waited for their chance to buy the glossy Air Jordan 1 "Gold Toe" sneaker or the limited re-release of the Air Jordan 3 with cracked "black cement" design, Bailey isn't going to sell them right away. "I'm going to take some pictures," he says with a smile, "and get my clout up."

It's generally thought that L.A.'s sneaker scene— where people clamor for slightly different shades of kick

54 DTLA BOOK 2019

JUMPMAN LA
DTLA's sneaker scene has arrived in a big way with this 19,000-square-foot, three-story behemoth dedicated to the Air Jordan Brand, the most iconic name in kick collecting. Started by Hall of Fame basketball player Michael Jordan with Nike in 1984, the brand that features the Jumpman logo was the original coveted shoe. Their new shop on Broadway offers new kicks and reproductions of classics, as well as refreshments, brand history displays and a rooftop hoops court.

Jumpman LA's rooftop hoops court

Jumpman LA exterior

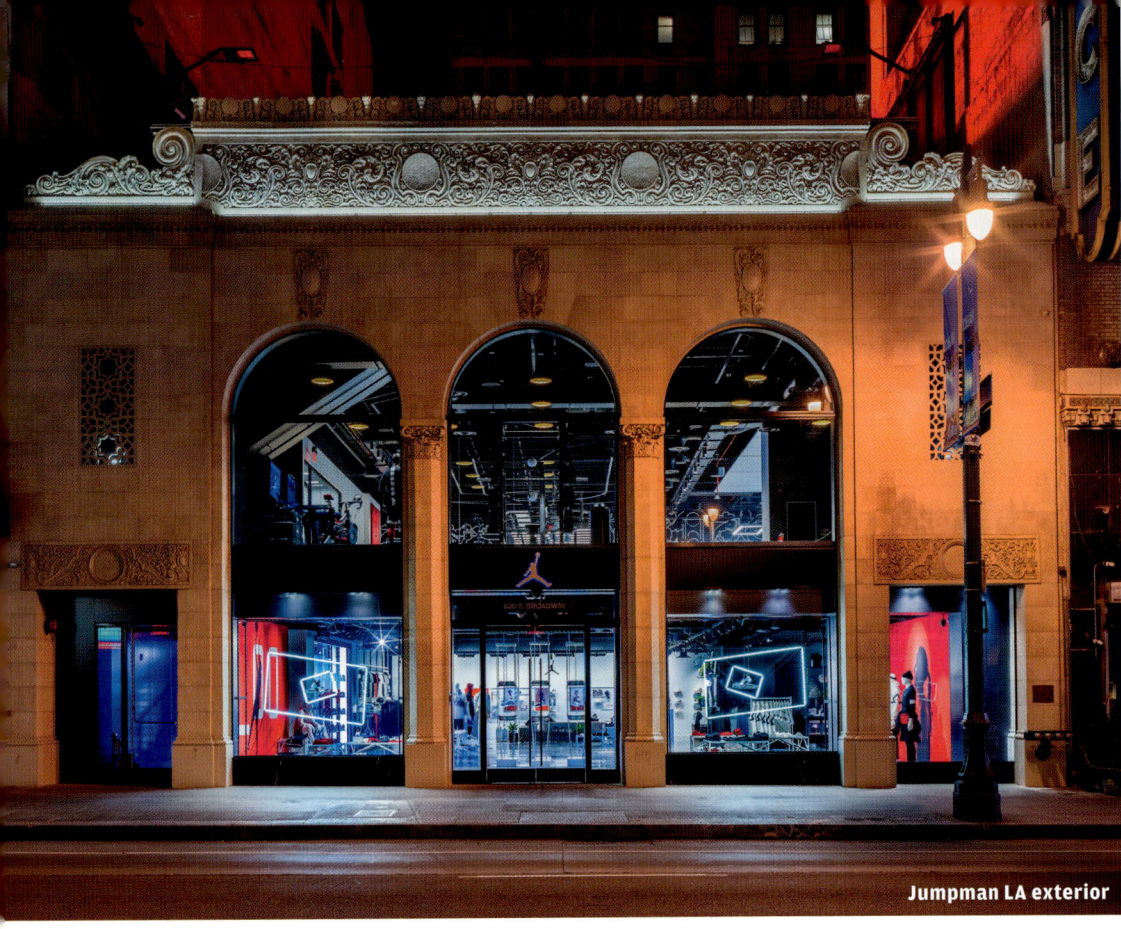

Blends

PEEK INSIDE THE AIR JORDAN ARCHIVAL COLLECTION
History of the legendary kicks

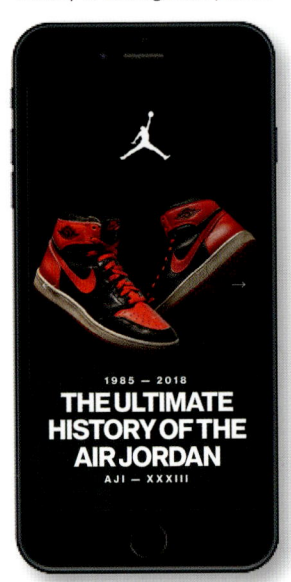

(like the Yeezy Boost 700 in a mauve colorway) or limited-edition collabs (like the Dragon Ball Z x adidas Deerupt "Son Gohan" inspired by the classic anime)—revolves around Fairfax Avenue. And while Fairfax has its staples like Supreme, Flight Club, Diamond Supply Co. and the Hundreds, Downtown is becoming a serious rival.

Downtown "was empty," says Mikey Dosen, a manager of **Nice Kicks**, a sneaker shop on South Main Street that carries a variety of new kicks, including fashion-forward options like adidas designed by designers Raf Simons and Alexander Wang. "Now we've had a ton of neighborhood stores popping up. It's totally revamped."

Downtown's sneaker culture revolves around two distinct locales: the Fashion District and ROW DTLA. The latter has the three-story multibrand store **Bodega** (which has an entrance that resembles the loading dock of a bodega), while the Fashion District is home to Nice Kicks and its punkier neighbor **Blends** (owned by Japanese-born sneakerhead duo Tak Kato and Mike Toe); streetwear gods Virgil Abloh and Don C.'s luxury boutique **RSVP Gallery** (which carries sneakers by the likes of Fear of God and Converse x JW Anderson); and consignment stores **The Holy Grail** and **RIF**, where finds can include vintage Air Jordans and the Nike Air Mags released to honor the shoes Marty McFly wore in *Back to the Future II*.

Rich Torres opened The Holy Grail near Staples Center in 2007, before realizing that the Fashion District was the place to be. Today, his shop carries sneakers from nearly every brand, and some are *very* valuable. For example, adidas Yeezy Boosts in the right colorway and size can cost nearly $2,000 on the resale market—you can see why kids stand in line all day to buy them at the retail price of $200.

"When we first opened, we had a really specific customer—big Jordan fans who would wear Jordan jerseys," says Torres, who also owns the nearby plant-based restaurant Wild Living Foods. "Now, it's gone mainstream. It's expanded—partly because of the financial motivation to buy and sell and make a profit—sometime around 2012, people from all over the city started buying shoes." The culture is even about to get its own documentary series, being developed by actress Lena Waithe, who has admitted she owns more than 100 pairs of sneakers.

56 DTLA BOOK 2019

Sneaker Lab

Sneaker Lab Sneaker Cleaner

SNEAKER LAB

721 S. Los Angeles St., Historic Core // us.sneakerlab.com
Opened in 2018, this U.S. shop uses probiotic technology for both its on-the-spot sneaker touch-ups and drop-off shoe service ($9 to $45 per pair). Additional treatments include lace detailing and odor protection.

JASON MARKK

329 E. 2nd St., Little Tokyo // jasonmarkk.com
Using biodegradable, water-based products, Jason Markk's flagship Little Tokyo store offers drop-off shoe service ($14 to $75 per pair) and sells its cleaning products, which are available in 2,000 stores worldwide. L.A.-based founder Jason Mark Angsuvarn's personal sneaker collection numbers more than 400 pairs.

The Jason Markk store

And with all that growth, there needs to be upkeep. The latest addition to the scene is **Sneaker Lab**, a South African company that trades on an environmentally friendly, bacteria-based cleaning solution so sneakerheads can keep their new kicks looking crispy. "You have people who are obsessed, and they own nothing else but expensive sneakers," says Sneaker Lab's general manager Joe Villarreal. "They want to protect them as much as they can."

SHOPS IN DTLA

BLENDS 725 S. Los Angeles St., Fashion District // blendsus.com

BODEGA ROW DTLA, 1320 E. 7th St., Ste. 150, Industrial District // shop.bdgastore.com

COMUNITY 584 Mateo St., Arts District // comunitymade.com

THE HOLY GRAIL 836 S. Los Angeles St., Fashion District // holygrailgallery.com

JUMPMAN LA 620 S. Broadway, Historic Core // nike.com

NICE KICKS 862 S. Main St., Fashion District // nicekicks.com

RIF 334 E. 2nd St., Little Tokyo // rif.la

RSVP GALLERY 905 S. Hill St., South Park // rsvpgallery.com

CORTEZ: THE ICONIC SNEAK'S LAID-BACK LOOK

Bodega interprets the new Nike x Kendrick Lamar collaboration with an only-in-L.A. fashion shoot

Introduced in 1972, Nike's Cortez was the brand's first track shoe, eventually becoming a mainstay of L.A. street culture. Its latest iteration: the Nike Cortez Kenny IV. The fourth collaboration between the brand and the Pulitzer Prize-winning singer, this sleek slip-on kick has the ease of a house shoe. "There are fewer shoes with a connection to a specific geographic location stronger than the one between Nike's iconic Cortez and Los Angeles," explains an ode to the Cortez on the website of Bodega, the streetwear boutique at ROW DTLA. "Simplicity of design, widespread availability and, perhaps most importantly, an inexpensive price tag made the Cortez an instant hit."

A model sports the latest Cortez in a new Bodega fashion shoot

"House shoes have always been part of L.A. culture. The shoe is all about being able to get up and just go out in style."

—KENDRICK LAMAR

COLORS OF THE CITY

Learn where to find more than 35 street-art walls that together make DTLA one of the mural capitals of the world.

By Degen Pener // Photography by Poul Lange

THE CONTAINER YARD

Located in a former mochi factory, The Container Yard is an event space that invites artists from all over the globe to paint its surfaces. The many murals on its outer walls, seen below, include Bisco Smith's flag, Tom Bob's smiley heart and It's a Living's "Ain't Easy." The compound recently debuted a retail store (Wednesday–Sunday, 11 a.m. to 7 p.m.). 800 E. 4th St. // thecontaineryard.com // No. 6 on map, page 71

TRISTAN EATON

A self-described "skateboarding punk" in his youth, Eaton grew up in Los Angeles, London and Detroit before becoming a toy designer early in his career. The New York-based artist's 2015 mural "Peace by Piece" on an exterior wall at The Container Yard addresses the epidemic of gun violence in America.

800 E. 4th St. // No. 6 on map

WATCH HOW EATON DID IT
TIME-LAPSE VIDEO
By Jordan Ahern

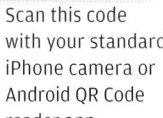

Scan this code with your standard iPhone camera or Android QR Code reader app.

ARTS DISTRICT: 3RD & 4TH STREET VICINITY

One of the biggest concentrations of murals in DTLA is on and around 3rd and 4th Streets. Explore the area that also is home to Hauser & Wirth art gallery, Art Share L.A., A+D: Architecture and Design Museum, and the enormous One Santa Fe residential and retail development.

KIM WEST

The artist painted her climate-change-inspired image of a dangling polar bear in 2011. After Hauser & Wirth opened in the building, the gallery commissioned West to expand the work, titled "Only One Way Through." A great place from which to view it is at Eat Drink Americano, opposite.
901 E. 3rd St. // No. 2 on map

OFA, ICR, ELSE ONER, SPIRO, JEANETTE PARADES

This gritty multi-artist mural, titled "Los Angeles," overlooks a garden at Hauser & Wirth, which has worked to preserve the work.
901 E. 3rd St. // No. 3 on map

PETER GRECO

Among the spots Greco's intricate calligraffiti (calligraphy meets graffiti) works can be seen are One Santa Fe and The American Hotel.

Left: One Santa Fe, No. 1 on map; Above: American Hotel, 303 S. Hewitt St. // No. 4 on map

KIM WEST: JOSHUA TARGOWNIK, COURTESY HAUSER & WIRTH

JR

The French artist wheat-pasted this piece—a reaction to Hollywood's youth obsession—on the Angel City Brewery in 2011. It's one of a number of still-extant pieces in L.A. from his "Wrinkles of the City" project. The face is that of late actor Louis Waldon, who was part of Warhol's Factory circle.
216 S. Alameda St. // No. 7 on map

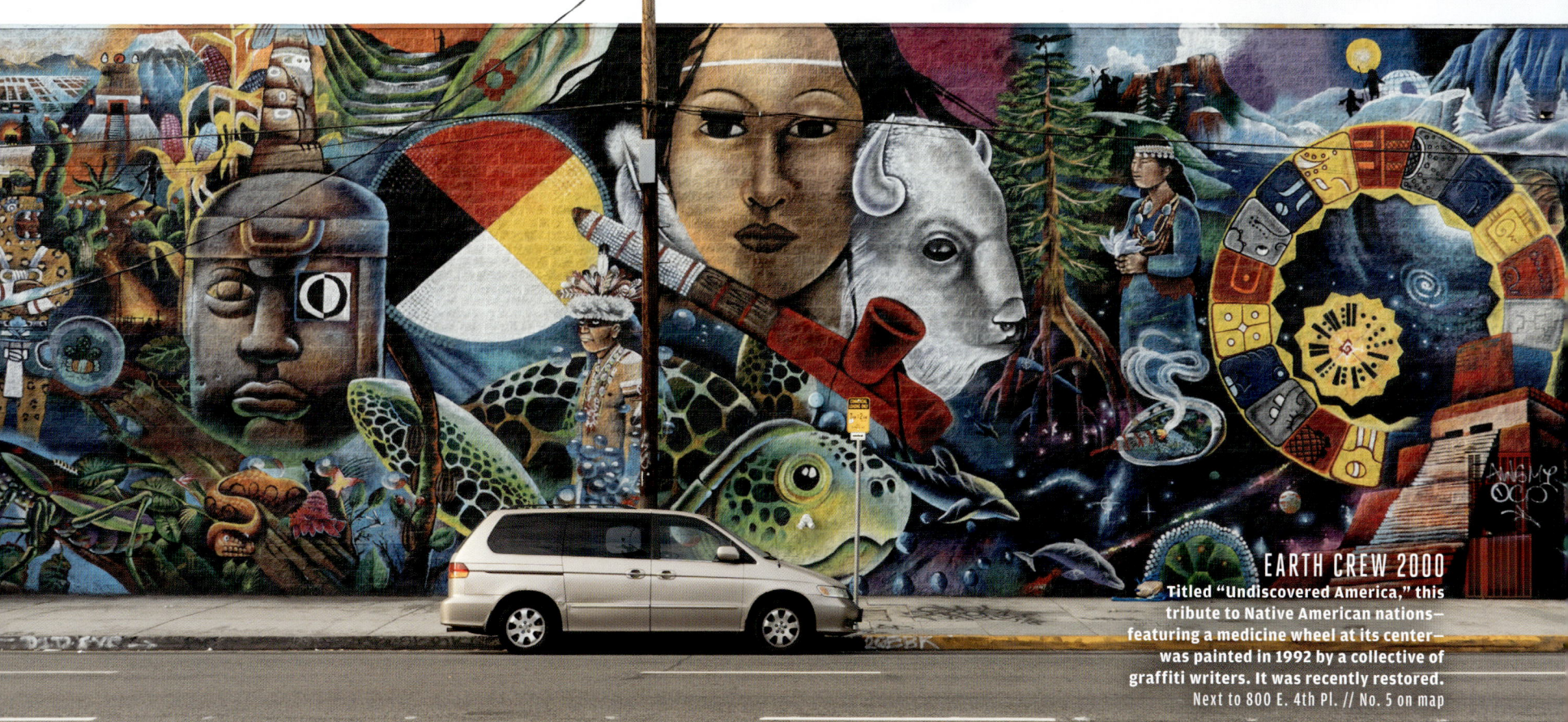

EARTH CREW 2000

Titled "Undiscovered America," this tribute to Native American nations—featuring a medicine wheel at its center—was painted in 1992 by a collective of graffiti writers. It was recently restored.
Next to 800 E. 4th Pl. // No. 5 on map

LOWER ARTS DISTRICT: ALONG E. 7TH STREET

Many more murals can be found in the more southern part of the Arts District along E. 7th Street, Mateo Street, Violet Street and Santa Fe Avenue, where influential graffiti artist Retna has a studio. You can also check out a number of works painted inside the new brick-and-mortar Guerrilla Tacos while grabbing a bite.

DAME, RETNA, RISK, REVOK, ABEL (ABOVE)

On the side of the Rendon Hotel is this piece by some of the most influential graffiti artists in L.A. street-art history. To "read" a piece like this, advises Steve Grody, author of *Graffiti L.A.*, "Search for the letter forms and don't be distracted by the color or design within the letters. Letter 'breaks' and smooth connections can be confusing, but often the letters can be discerned." Grody walks by this piece on a new Cartwheel Art mural tour of the area.
2055 E. 7th St., wall facing Santa Fe Ave. // No. 10 on map

AUGUSTINE KOFIE & AISEBORNE (LEFT)

Also on the Rendon is this work by two L.A.-based artists. It was commissioned for a recent art project there, curated by Cartwheel Art founder Cindy Schwarzstein.
2055 E. 7th St. // No. 10 on map

DAVID CHOE & ARYZ (ABOVE)

Located on the Mateo Street side of Silver Lake Wine, this work is by David Choe, known for painting murals at Facebook for stock options, and Spanish artist Aryz.
1948 E. 7th St. // No. 11 on map

DTLA BOOK 2019

FROM ROW DTLA TO THE FLOWER DISTRICT

Make sure to take in the massive Retna and Ricardo Estrada murals at ROW DTLA. From there, walk down San Pedro Street and west on 8th Street to the Flower District (a route that avoids Skid Row's tent cities) to see "Mr. Rooster."

ETAM CRU
This six-story work, "Mr. Rooster," was painted entirely freehand in less than a week by Polish artists Sainer and Bezt, who together make up Etam Cru. The wall was produced by Thinkspace Gallery and Branded Arts.
514 E. 8th St., overlooking a parking lot // No. 14 on map

RETNA AND RICARDO ESTRADA
Retna—along with Ricardo Estrada (who painted the human figure below)—was commissioned by ROW DTLA to cover the facades of three of its buildings facing E. 7th Street. Retna has said that his influences include Old English, gang writing, Thai wood carvings and hieroglyphics.
ROW DTLA's address is 777 S. Alameda St.; murals viewable from 7th St. // No. 13 on map

LOWER WERDIN PLACE: BELOW 8TH STREET

An inconspicuous alley, Werdin Place is broken into two noncontiguous stretches running north-south. The more southerly part—bounded by Main, Los Angeles, 7th and 8th Streets—has been adopted by the nearby Avenue des Arts gallery. Owner Dimitri Lorin has worked with a dozen artists—including Matt Gondek and Hopare—to transform the alleyway into a colorful procession of expression.

Start on the north end of the alley, adjacent to 120 E. 8th St. (near Escape Room L.A.) // No. 15 on map

Hopare's work depicting a woman holding a baby

A calligraffiti mural by Peter Greco (at left) on Werdin Place

Victor Castillo

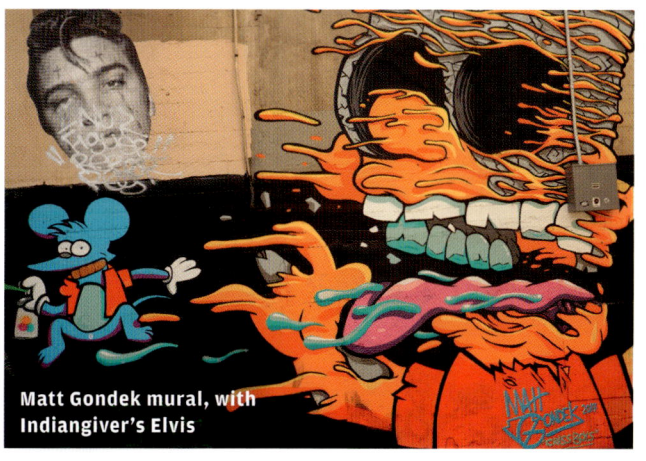

Matt Gondek mural, with Indiangiver's Elvis

DTLA BOOK 2019 67

HISTORIC CORE & GALLERY ROW

Some of DTLA's more massive works are displayed on the grand buildings of the Historic Core and Gallery Row.

JR AND VHILS (RIGHT)

Titled "Dona Benedita," this portrait of a Brazilian woman is a meeting of JR's wheat-paste approach and Portuguese artist Vhils' precise chiseling. A second work is opposite, across a parking lot.

621 S. Spring St. // No. 18 on map

ROBERT VARGAS (LEFT AND OPPOSIT PAGE BOTTOM)

Vargas' in-progress "Angelus," located by Metro's Pershing Square station, is vying to be the world's largest single-artist mural. Vargas often does live paintings of passersby during the monthly Art Walk in front of his earlier "Our Lady of DTLA."

"Angelus": 312 W. 5th St. // No. 21 on map
"Our Lady of DTLA": 600 S. Spring St. // No. 17 on map

CHRISTINA ANGELINA AND FIN DAC (BELOW)

Irish artist Fin DAC, known for his masked geishas, and L.A.-based Christina Angelina collaborated on "Upon Reflection" in 2014.

401-415 S. Los Angeles St. // No. 23 on map

TIME-LAPSE VIDEO
By Landon Taylor

WRDSMITH & COLETTE MILLER (ABOVE)

The Bloc gave shared space to two of Instagram's most snapped artists. The wings are part of Miller's Global Angel Wings Project reminding "humanity we are the angels of this earth," she says.

Northwest corner of W. 8th St. and S. Hope St. // No. 20 on map

DTLA BOOK 2019 69

INDIAN ALLEY

The north part of Werdin Place is also known as Indian Alley. Beginning in the 1970s through the '90s, the alleyway was adjacent to United American Indian Involvement, a service organization that helped Native Americans in need. Around 2010, Stephen Zeigler, co-owner of the nearby store/gallery These Days, began recruiting artists to honor that history. Works, including a depiction of medicine woman Toypurina, can be viewed through a gate on Winston Street. Adjacent to 118 Winston Pl., the address of These Days // No. 22 on map

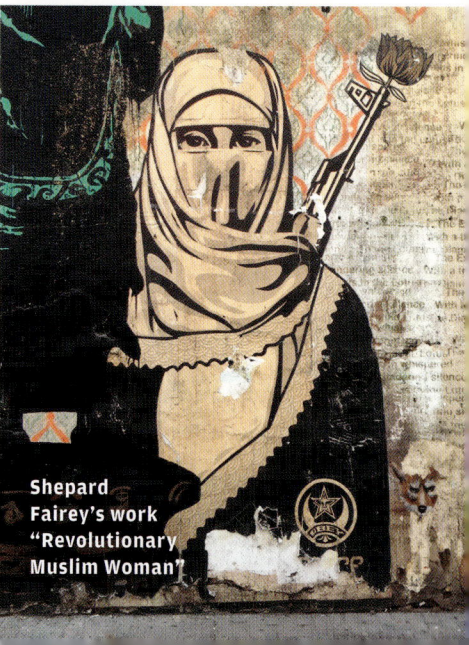

Dylan Egon's work portrays Comanche leader Quanah Parker

Shepard Fairey's "Pine Ridge (We Are Still Here)"

"Shamanic Energy Cache," a collaboration between Zeigler and artist Wild Life

Shepard Fairey's work "Revolutionary Muslim Woman"

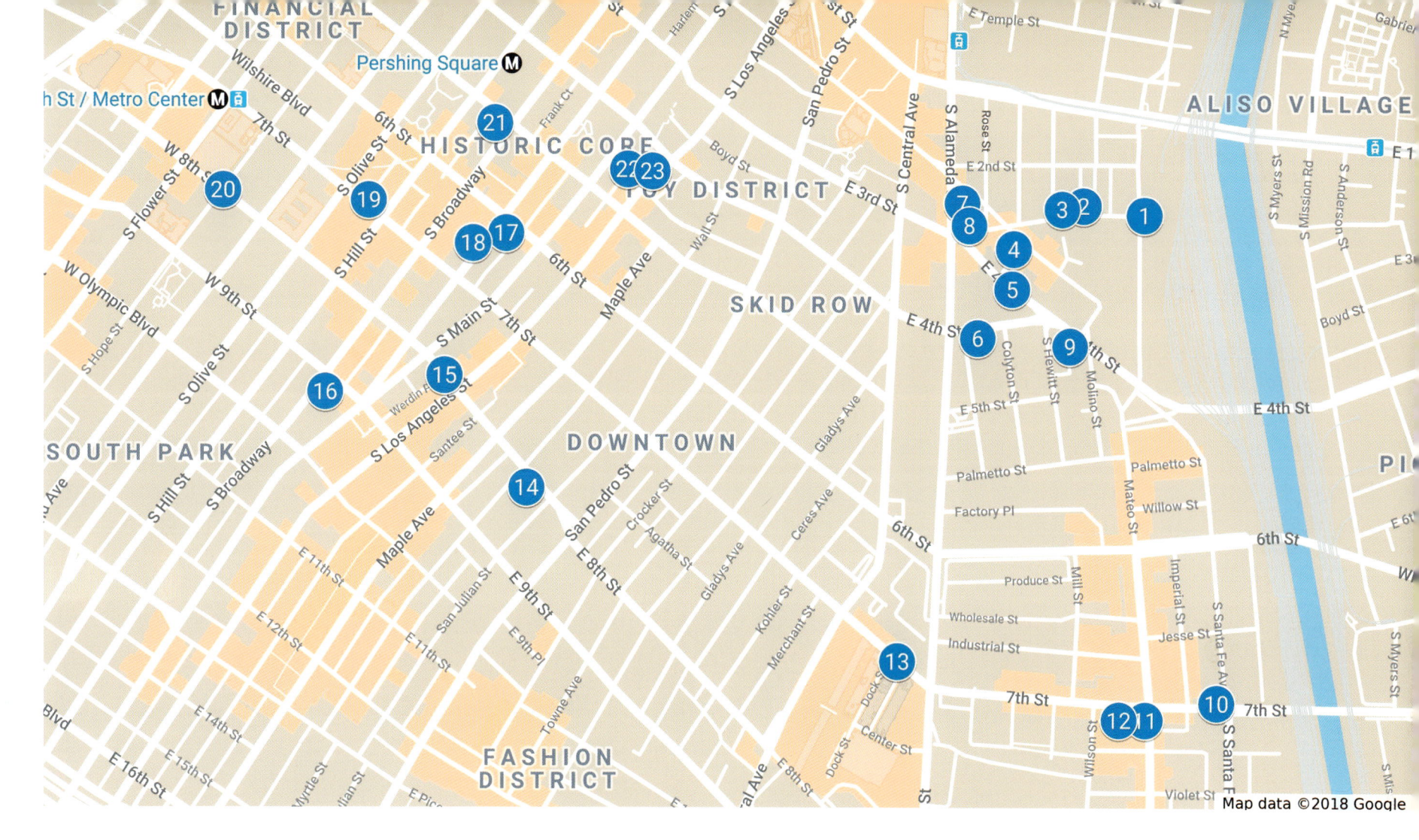

FAMOUS, BUT HIDDEN

RETNA ON MERCURY COURT
On little-known Mercury Court is this work by Retna, inspired by a poem in the archives of the nearby Los Angeles Athletic Club.

Mercury Court near 421 W. 7th St.
No. 19 on map

BANSKY ON BROADWAY
The British artist painted the side of the Sparkle Factory building in 2010, but it's now mostly blocked by the new Broadway Palace.

910 S. Broadway, south side of building // No. 16 on map

INSTAGRAM DARLINGS
Followings of some of DTLA's street-art roster

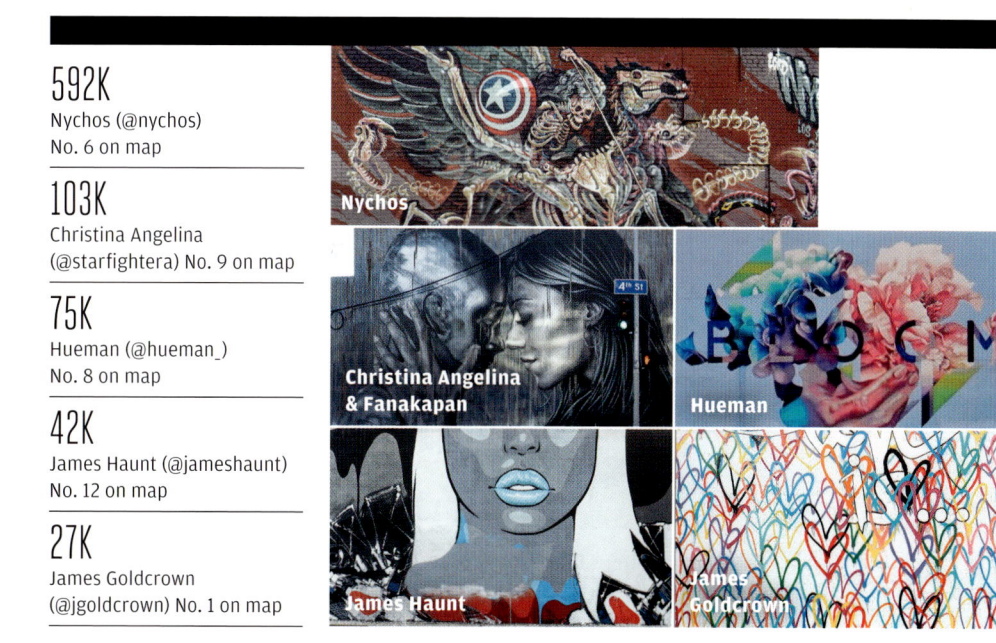

592K
Nychos (@nychos)
No. 6 on map

103K
Christina Angelina
(@starfightera) No. 9 on map

75K
Hueman (@hueman_)
No. 8 on map

42K
James Haunt (@jameshaunt)
No. 12 on map

27K
James Goldcrown
(@jgoldcrown) No. 1 on map

DTLA BOOK 2019 71

DTLA NOIR

Five writers and tour guides narrate the tales from Downtown's sordid history of murder and mayhem that obsess them.

Edited by Degen Pener // Illustrations by Brian Busch

RAYMOND CHANDLER'S "CROOK TOWN"

*As recounted by **Jim Dawson**, author of* Los Angeles' Bunker Hill: Pulp Fiction's Mean Streets and Film Noir's Ground Zero

In *The Long Goodbye*, Raymond Chandler called Downtown "the big sordid dirty city." During the booming 1920s, when the city was awash in petroleum dollars, he was a Dabney Oil Syndicate executive whose Olive Street office had a view of enough tabloid-worthy mayhem to fuel a life of crime writing. Along with the crooked water schemes and oil graft, Prohibition had turned every thirsty good-time Charlie into a lawbreaker, and underworld scuzzbags morphed into slick, bigger-than-life racketeers. Instead of fighting all this criminality, the LAPD decided to "manage" it, and thus became corrupt. There were plenty of exotic characters to inspire Chandler. For instance, Guy McAfee—an LAPD vice cop who became an icy gentleman kingpin running an offshore gambling ship and a Hollywood casino club—turned up as Eddie Mars in *The Big Sleep* and Laird Brunette in *Farewell, My Lovely*.

But where was the main locus of all this malfeasance? Chandler's main gumshoe, Philip Marlowe, who gallantly stood like a "slumming angel" above the urban blight, learned his trade and earned his cynicism working for the district attorney at the Hall of Justice on Temple and Broadway. Beyond that, Chandler repeatedly hinted in his writing that L.A.'s most crime-infested spot was City Hall.

The clues came gradually in the form of an address to a rundown building on Court Street on the top of Bunker Hill, which was then a casbah of stairways, aging Victorians, cliffside clapboard rooming houses and dusty storefronts. This particular building showed up in several of Chandler's stories and novels, always given a street number (such as 28 Court or 118 Court) that never existed Downtown. In his 1936 story "Guns at Cyrano's," the place was a gangster den where several people died in a blaze of gunfire. In "The King in Yellow," it was a flophouse in which hotel detective Steve Grayce discovered a female blackmailer's body under a bed and witnessed a gun battle in the hallway. When Chandler recycled part of this episode in *The High Window*, the house was where Marlowe stumbled upon a down-on-his-luck shamus with a bloody hole in his head. In *The Big Sleep*, the address was a brothel fronting as an apartment house, to which a two-bit chiseler named Harry Jones misdirected a mob trigger man looking to kill his girlfriend. What was it about this place on Court Street that intrigued Chandler so much that, in *The High Window*, he even gave it the name of his mother: the Florence Apartments?

In real life, Court Street ended on the eastern crest of Bunker Hill, where Court Flight (see page 47), a 335-foot-long funicular, once carried passengers from Hill Street down to North Broadway. If Court Street, though, had continued east off Bunker Hill, it would have run smack dab into City Hall. The faux addresses in Chandler's stories would have been located inside the seat of the city government's bone-white walls.

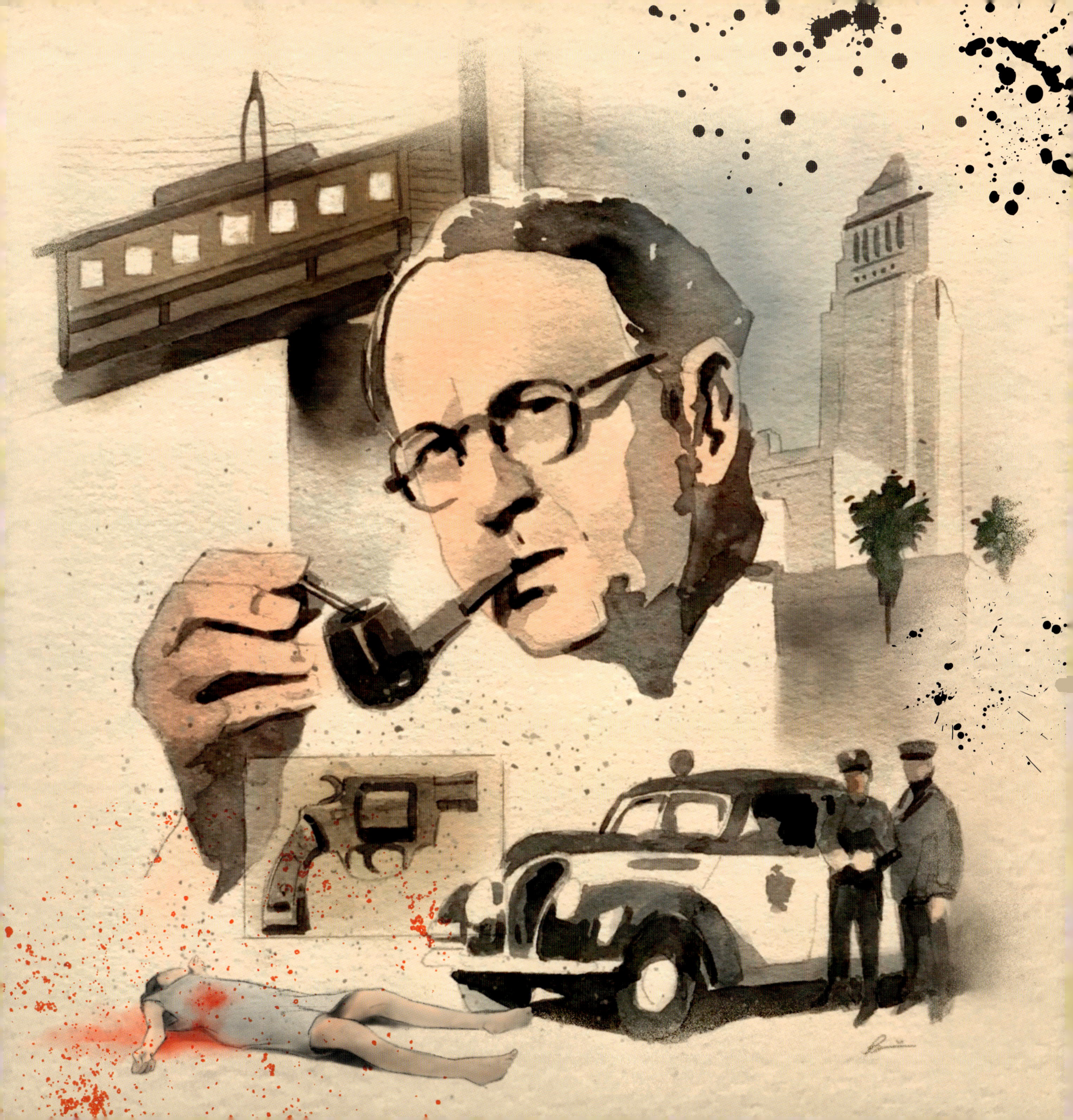

THE GHOSTS OF PICO HOUSE

As recounted by **Jordan Riefe,** *arts writer*

At the 149-year-old Pico House on 430 N. Main Street, supernatural tales have ranged from rattling toolboxes to a guard who claimed he was kicked in the leg, as recounted on TV's *Ghost Adventures*. All told, fairly mild paranormal activity—considering that the spirits believed to haunt this National Historic Landmark have every reason to be vengeful.

Opened in 1870, this 80-room hotel was the height of opulence, with indoor plumbing, an aviary, and a French restaurant with gaslit chandeliers. Built by Don Pío Pico, a wealthy businessman and the last Mexican to serve as governor of Alta California (1845-1846), Pico House bore witness to one of the country's most violent race riots, the Chinese Massacre of 1871. That year, tensions between two Chinatown gangs broke out into a shoot-out in a nearby alley. After a policeman was shot and a white rancher was killed amid the crossfire, a mob of 500 whites and Mexican Americans damaged buildings and storefronts, and lynched 17 to 20 Chinese, including children.

A Pico House employee at the time later recalled, "From the entrance of the Pico House I ... heard a steady roar of guns. I remember one fellow—big, hatless and coatless, with bulging maniacal eyes as he ran past us, brandishing huge butcher's axes." Amid rising discrimination in the U.S. against Chinese residents, the federal government passed the Chinese Exclusion Act in 1882, which barred any immigration by Chinese to the country. (It was repealed in 1943.) Some people believe that the ghosts of those lynched during the massacre took up residence in Pico House.

The hotel remained a leading accommodation for a time. But as Pico's fortunes waned and as the city's business district moved south, the former governor lost the hotel to foreclosure. It later became a flophouse. After Pico's death in 1894 at age 93, his ghost was said to have joined the spirits of the Chinese Massacre, often seen on the rooftop or upper-story windows, surveying what used to be his prized asset. In 1953, the state acquired it and today Pico House is part of the El Pueblo de Los Ángeles State Historic Monument.

THE NIGHT STALKER AT THE CECIL HOTEL

As recounted by **Damien Blackshaw**, founder of The Real Los Angeles Tours

One of the toughest parts of researching our DTLA Murder Mystery Ghost Tour was reading about all the horrible murders that have taken place in and around Downtown. Of all the killers that I researched, though, arguably the worst was Richard Ramirez, aka the Night Stalker.

Ramirez's reign of horror began in June 1984, and for more than a year he terrorized L.A. as he drove around looking for houses and apartments he could break into. Once inside, he would attempt to kill any men and rape and kill any women. He would also take all their money, jewelry or other valuables—often making his victims swear on Satan to not hide anything. In the end he killed 13 people.

The then-night clerk at Downtown's Cecil Hotel on Main Street swore that Ramirez spent a few weeks in a 14th-floor room during this period. It somehow seems preordained that he would stay at this hotel, as the Cecil has its own hellish history, including multiple suicides, murders, deaths and rapes almost going back to its 1927 opening. In 1991, Austrian serial killer Johan Unterweger also stayed at the Cecil, largely because of the Ramirez connection.

There's always been a debate as to whether killers like Ramirez are created by circumstance or if they are born that way. In Ramirez's case, it seems likely that his own childhood experiences of abuse had a big impact. He saw his cousin, Miguel, kill his wife by shooting her in the face. Later, Ramirez did that to several of his own victims. He almost seemed programmed to kill, rape and rob. Friends of mine who lived in L.A. at the time still remember the period with a shudder.

Thankfully he was stopped in August 1985. If it happened today, it's very likely nowadays that right-wing politicians would use the fact that Ramirez was Latino to encourage anti-immigrant sentiment, but it was a group of Hispanic women who pointed him out to police after recognizing him from a mug shot that had been released to the media. He was chased by a group of Latino men across a freeway and beaten up. It's said he was quite glad when the police showed up! An unremorseful Ramirez was convicted on all charges in 1989. He died due to complications from lymphoma in 2013 on Death Row.

THE L.A. VAMPIRE

As recounted by **Hadley Hall Meares**, *historical journalist and tour guide for Cartwheel Art*

LAPD policeman Harry Donlan knew the face of a wanted man when he saw one. It was November 16, 1944. Only 20 minutes earlier, at Central Station, he had read the description of the handsome young man who now sat before him, calmly drinking wine in the crowded Red Front Bar, a long-gone watering hole on Hill Street. According to reports, Donlan began to question the man, who replied, "I don't know what this is all about," before backing out of the bar. It was then that Donlan noticed the blood stains on the man's clothes and the bruises on his knuckles. Donlan apprehended the suspect with a quick judo hold, and thus ended the brief reign of Downtown L.A.'s very own vampire—Otto Stephen Wilson.

Wilson, who was described as looking like boyish movie star Robert Taylor, had been a fry cook in the naval shipyards. Recently divorced, his ex-wife had accused him of being a sadist with an odd thirst for blood. This culminated in horror when he "slashed her buttocks with a razor and licked the blood as he apologized to her for his actions."

One night, Wilson picked up a troubled waitress named Virgie Lee Griffin at a Downtown bar. He took her to the Barclay Hotel, which had once been the grandest hotel in town, before falling on hard times that have continued to the present day. According to court records: "He choked the woman and then indulged in an orgy of stabbing, cutting, and severing parts of the woman's body, using the knife he had just purchased ... He ... claimed that the choking took place during an argument following a demand by the woman for $20 after reaching the room."

Wilson then attempted to dismember Griffin's body but was only successful in severing one leg. He then stuffed her in the hotel room closet. As he walked through the quiet hallways of the Barclay, he passed a maid. "Please don't disturb my wife," he said, smiling politely.

Wilson then went to the Million Dollar Theater. The film that was playing? Boris Karloff's *The Walking Dead*. Afterward he picked up Lillian Johnson and took her to the Joyce Hotel, which was once next to Grand Central Market. Wilson checked in as O.S. Watson and took Johnson upstairs. He brutally killed and mutilated her, and again calmly exited, back into the mean streets of Downtown, which were a whole lot meaner with him around.

Wilson was apprehended a short time later. He was convicted of his monstrous crimes and executed in the gas chamber of San Quentin Prison on September 20, 1946.

A GRAND HOTEL'S "PHANTOM WING"

As recounted by **Neel Sodha**, *founder of Downtown LA Walking Tours*

In 1906, a hotel opened at 501 S. Spring Street that was so majestic that Presidents Taft, Wilson and Roosevelt would frequent it when in town. News articles cooed over the new Hotel Alexandria's "costly magnificence," thanks to abundant use of Italian and Egyptian marble and its Palm Court ballroom with a Tiffany stained-glass skylight. To increase the size of the hotel, its owners entered into an agreement with the owner of a livery stable next door, William Chick. Mr. Chick co-invested in the Alexandria, constructing an entire separate wing, with hallways connecting it to the main property.

However, the allure of the Alexandria started to vanish in the 1920s after the grand Biltmore Hotel opened two blocks west. The Great Depression was taking a toll as well. By 1934, the entire Alexandria Hotel shut down. However, four years later, in 1938, two new owners came along: Phil Gladstone, a movie producer, and Lee Roddie, the daughter of William Chick. The reopened hotel continued to function as one unit. However, soon after the reopening, fights ensued between Mr. Gladstone and Ms. Roddie, revolving around competition over retail tenants. But Mr. Gladstone remembered something: Mr. William Chick, Lee Roddie's father, was somewhat cheap. When he constructed his wing in 1906, he only built rooms and hallways, meaning there were no staircases or an elevator shaft. As the fight escalated between Ms. Roddie and Mr. Gladstone in 1938, the latter decided to brick up the hallways connecting his wing to the auxiliary wing. Ms. Roddie would call this "a grave mistake by my father."

And so it happened that no guests have slept in any of the auxiliary wing's hotel rooms for 80 years. While the retail stores have remained open since 1938, there is no access to floors 2–7 of what has since become known as the Alexandria's Phantom Wing. Ladders have been climbed to visit the top floors, only to see old rocking chairs, typewriters and hats from 1938. In 2012, a developer purchased the wing with the intention of converting it into a high-end apartment complex named The Chelsea; he recently filed plans to move the project forward. The Phantom Wing is located on the 5th Street side of the Alexandria in the Historic Core.

TOWERING PIONEER

With a taste for Gothic Revival architecture, Florence Casler went from being the wife of a plumber to developing 10 DTLA buildings that all endure to this day: "She was way ahead of her time."

By Marissa Gluck // Archival photography courtesy of Marcia Faris

The history of great buildings in Los Angeles is usually also the history of Great Men. Men such as architects Frank Lloyd Wright and Richard Neutra; or John Parkinson, who built City Hall; or Joseph Eichler, the developer who brought midcentury design to the masses in tract homes across Southern California. The contributions of women are often overlooked, forgotten or diminished—women such as trailblazer Florence Casler.

She may not be a household name, but in the 1920s, this former plumber developed bungalows, apartment buildings and commercial skyscrapers worth more than $74 million in today's money. Born in 1869 in Welland, Canada, Casler married an American plumber named John H. Casler and settled in Buffalo, New York, where she had two daughters. When her husband left to pursue the California Gold Rush, Casler stayed behind and took over her husband's plumbing business, despite the fact that as a woman she was not allowed to have a license in her name. By the time he returned eight years later (never having found his fortune in gold), his wife had built a small but thriving plumbing empire. She was proud of her origins running it. According to her great-granddaughter, Marcia Faris, "she put the plumbing license in a frame. It was hanging in a bathroom in the last house she [lived] in."

Plumbing led to an interest in construction, and when her husband died in 1921, Casler packed up her daughters and did what so many hopeful emigres to the city have done: came to Los Angeles to seek her fortune. She soon joined development firm J.K. Lloyd and Company. By 1923, Casler formed a new development company with her business partner, Jesse K. Lloyd, dubbed Lloyd & Casler. She had a loyal crew of builders who worked on each project with her, and despite her gentle demeanor, she managed every part of the construction. "She was so instrumental in building Downtown Los Angeles," recalls Faris, who remembers her as "very, very sweet and soft-spoken."

Casler also formed an intimate partnership with architect William Douglas Lee. Lee, who was already known for his work on the El Royale Apartments and the Chateau Marmont, found a kindred spirit in Casler, who shared his

In the large photo at left, Casler stands with workers inside the doorway of one of her projects. Her great-granddaughter Marcia Faris provided these archival images of Casler and her buildings. "She was way ahead of her time," says Faris.

TEXTILE CENTER BUILDING
Opened in 1926 as a center for manufacturing garments, this Gothic Revival- and Italian Renaissance-style 12-story structure was converted to condominiums in 2005. It's now known as the Textile Building.

affection for stone Gothic Revival accents combined with modern design.

Lee became her chosen architect for the development of an astounding seven buildings in the relatively short period between 1924 and 1928. They were each centered in the city's burgeoning Fashion District.

Lee was the architect for all seven, including the Allied Crafts Building, the Graphic Arts Building, the Garment Capitol Building, the Printing Center, the Furniture Exchange Building, the Merchant's Exchange Building and, perhaps most notably, the Bendix Building, which today is experiencing a rebirth as a home for artist studios and galleries. The buildings typically feature retail spaces on the ground floor, while large windows on the upper floors provide expansive views of the city.

By 1925, Casler could also add the title of banker to her expanding resume. She was elected director of the People's Bank, marking another milestone as the first female officer of a national bank in L.A. Casler went solo in 1928, establishing the Casler Construction Company. The local

IN THE TRENCHES
BELOW: Casler at a work site with her daughter Grace (in white) and granddaughter Jean (Faris' mother), standing on the arm of an excavator. A newspaper article from the time extolled, "This enterprising woman has accomplished in less than a decade what many men have taken a lifetime to achieve." RIGHT: Castler at another dig in an undated photo.

business community was fascinated by her meteoric rise from obscurity to magnate. The *Los Angeles Times* noted in 1931 that Casler, whom they dismissively called a "nice maternal little woman" had "eight Class A limit-height buildings to her credit, sixty flat buildings and a vast vision of the future of Los Angeles."

The triumph of the Bendix was short-lived, as the Great Depression hit and it was the last recorded project by Casler Construction. All of the buildings developed by Lloyd & Casler were sold after the stock market crash in 1929. Casler faded from public view and died in 1954. "I have a feeling she lost everything during the Depression," says Faris.

Assessing her legacy today, Casler indelibly changed Downtown's cityscape and her buildings endure as some of L.A.'s most prized real estate. Some have been converted into high-end lofts like the Textile Building, while others serve the Skid Row community, such as the Renaissance Building, now the nonprofit Downtown's Women's Center.

And Casler herself remains a proto-feminist model of "having it all." As the *Los Angeles Times* also noted in 1931, "she marvels that there could ever be any discussion as to whether women should try to combine both careers and matrimony. 'I had to,' she laughs, 'so I never thought about it.'"

Casler's Towers As Seen Today

Photography by Dean Paul De Leon

1. **RENAISSANCE BUILDING**
(Downtown Women's Center)
442 San Pedro St.

2. **MERCHANT'S EXCHANGE**
717 S. Los Angeles St.

3. **GARMENT CAPITOL**
217 E. 8th St.

4. **TEXTILE CENTER**
315 E. 8th St.

5. **FURNITURE EXCHANGE**
1200 Santee St.

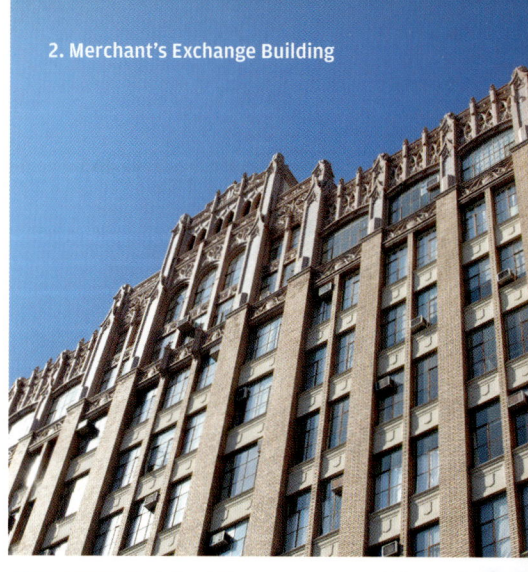

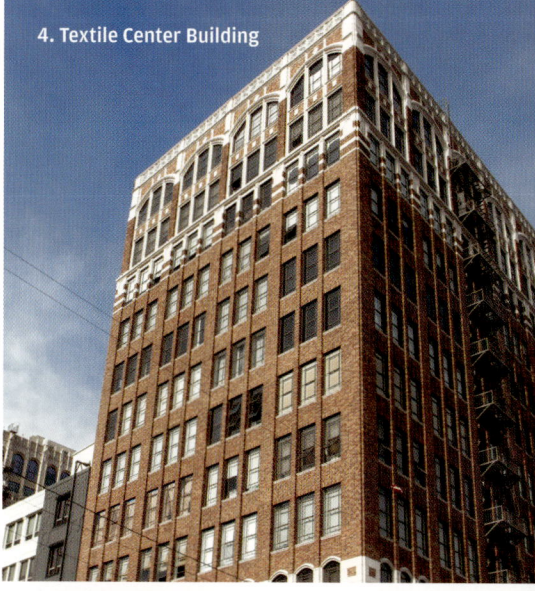

6. **BENDIX**
1206 Maple Ave.

7. **PRINTING CENTER**
1220 Maple Ave.

8. **ALLIED CRAFTS**
407 E. Pico Blvd.

9. **GRAPHIC ARTS**
417 E. Pico Blvd.

10. **LLOYD & CASLER**
1231 Wall St.

82 DTLA BOOK 2019

1. Renaissance Building, now home to Downtown Women's Center

2. Merchant's Exchange Building

3. Garment Capitol Building

4. Textile Center Building

3. Garment Capitol Building's Gothic Revival details

5. Furniture Exchange Building

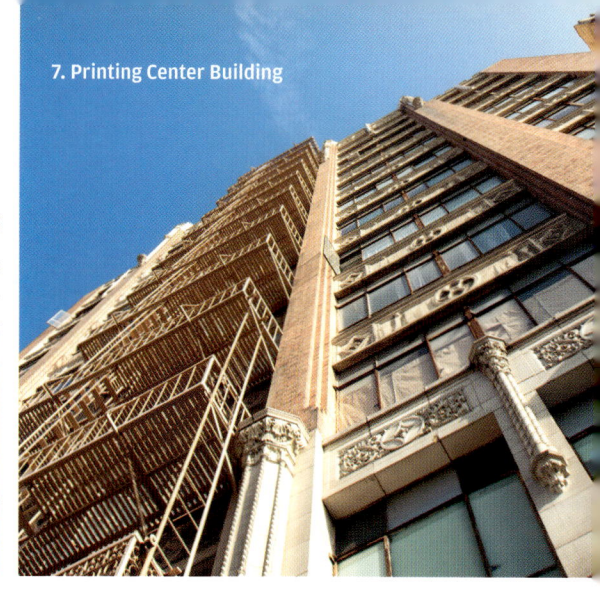

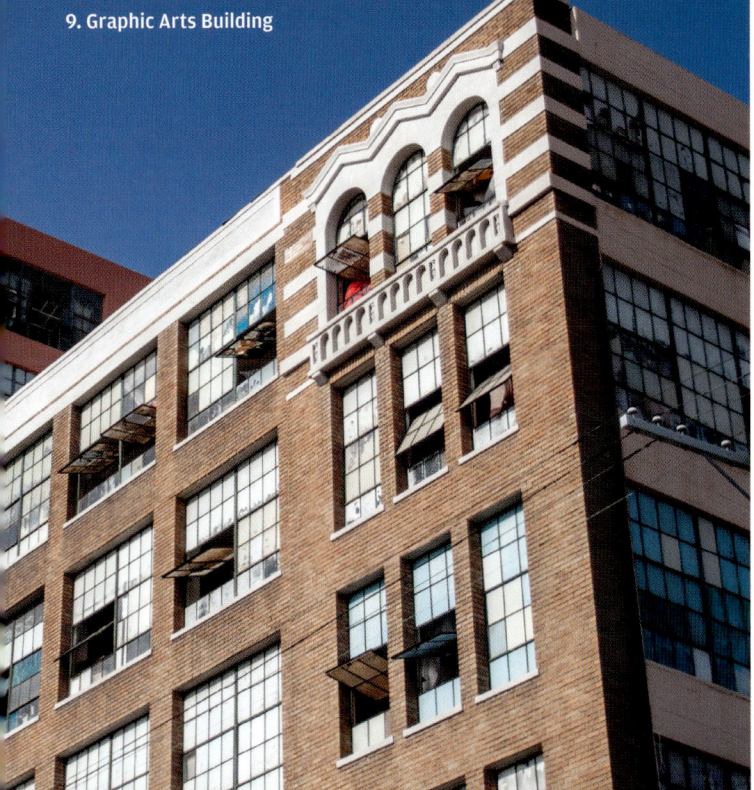

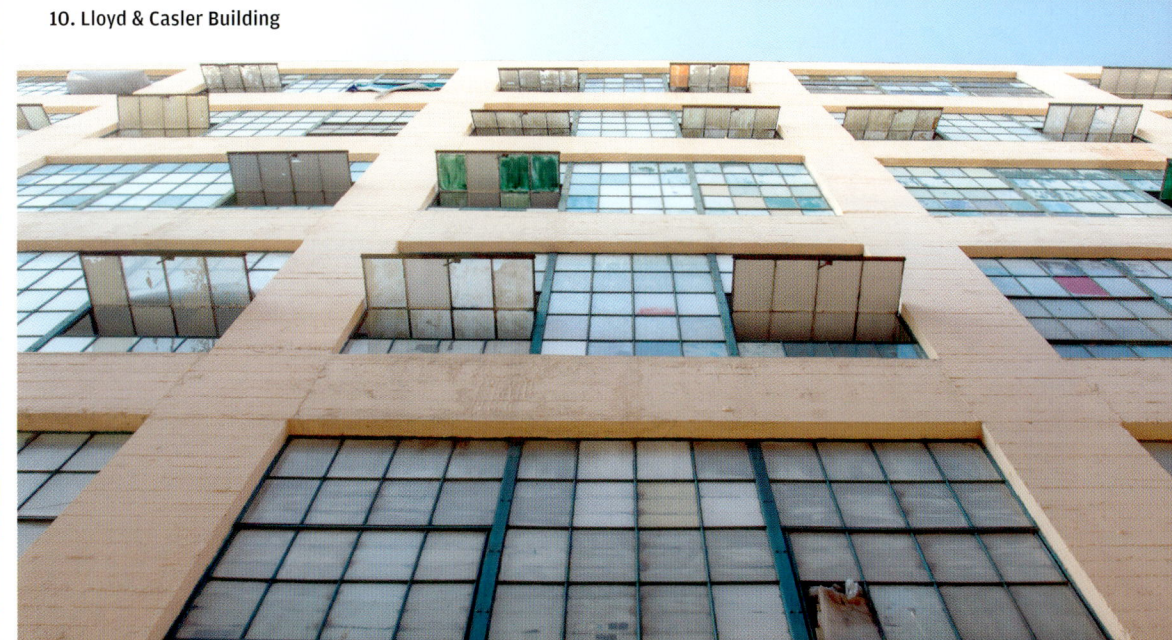

6. Bendix Building and its 150-foot-tall neon sign

7. Printing Center Building

8. Allied Crafts Building

6. Bendix Building details

9. Graphic Arts Building

10. Lloyd & Casler Building

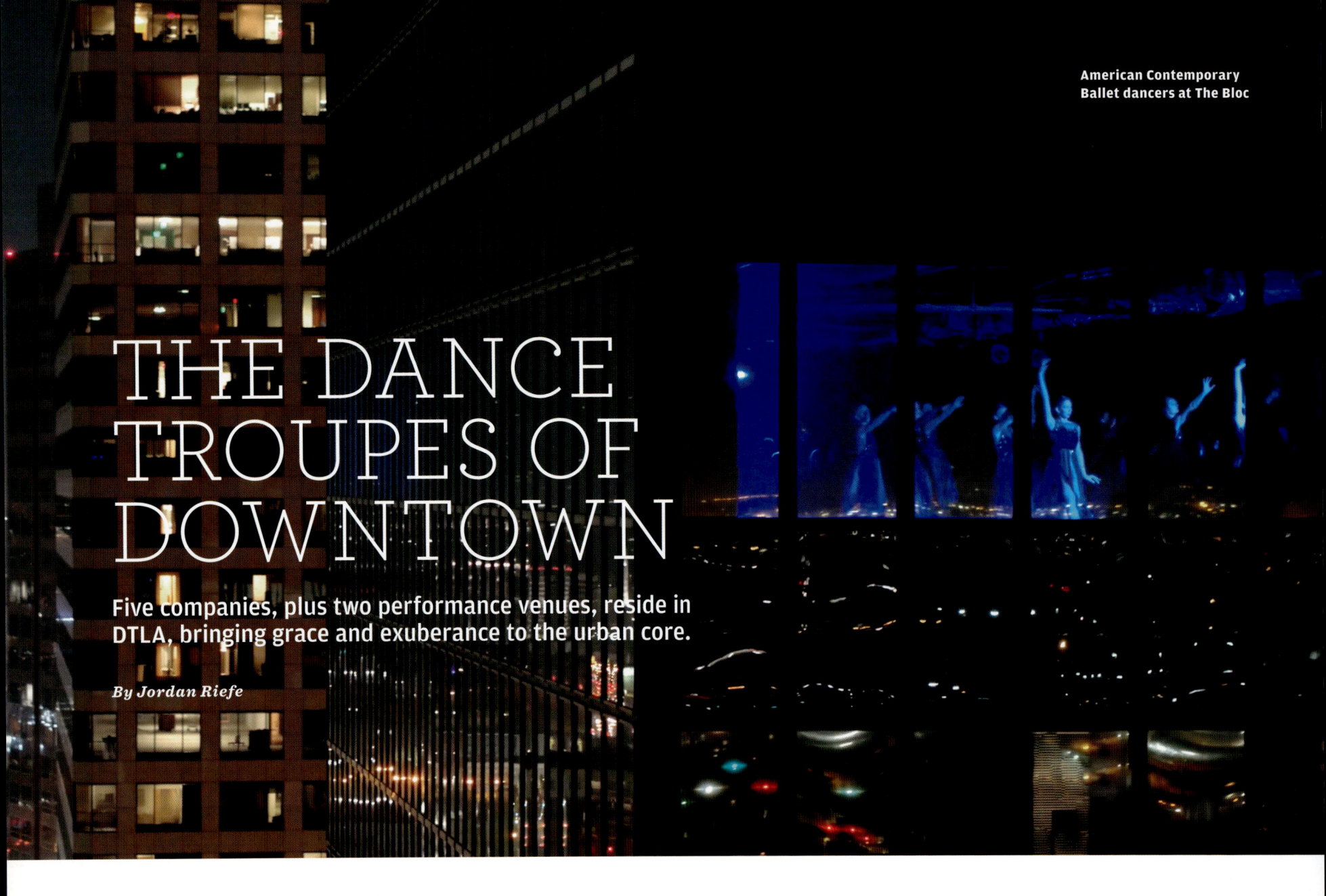

American Contemporary Ballet dancers at The Bloc

THE DANCE TROUPES OF DOWNTOWN

Five companies, plus two performance venues, reside in DTLA, bringing grace and exuberance to the urban core.

By Jordan Riefe

"L.A. Takes Lead as Dance Center," read a 1929 headline in the *Los Angeles Times*. That was a long time ago, when local names Ruth St. Denis and Ted Shawn of the famed Denishawn School resonated throughout the dance world. Today, the rapid expansion of the Downtown Arts District has seen a parallel resurgence in dance with a variety of contemporary, ballet and experimental companies calling the neighborhood their home.

Two venues present dance performances as well. Since 2003, Glorya Kaufman Presents Dance at The Music Center has been hosting venerable companies like American Ballet Theater, The Joffrey, The Royal Ballet, Paul Taylor and Alvin Ailey, while a few steps away, downstairs at Walt Disney Concert Hall, REDCAT features performances through its Sharon Disney Lund School of Dance at CalArts series. Seasons at REDCAT spotlight dancemakers from around the world, representing a panorama of cultures, styles and influences.

The distance between these organizations is just a short walk, but aesthetically it's as good as a mile. Luckily, there are numerous companies representing various styles to satisfy tastes both conventional and curious.

WATCH DRONE VIDEO AND GET YOUR TICKET

American Contemporary Ballet dancers captured by Matt Dutcher

Scan with your standard iPhone camera or Android QR Code Reader.

84 DTLA BOOK 2019

AMERICAN CONTEMPORARY BALLET

Performing classics and more, high in the sky

Choreographer Lincoln Jones and dancer Theresa Farrell established American Contemporary Ballet (ACB) in 2004, after relocating from New York City. Today, they occupy the 32nd floor of The Bloc, using the epic cityscape outside their window as a dramatic backdrop for performances. Their mission is to produce original works to add to a repertory that includes George Balanchine, Fred Astaire, Lincoln Jones and seminal works from ballet's history. "We take a very musical approach to ballet that draws the choreography out of the score," Jones says about engaging audiences in a new way. "We're innovative and, on the other hand, rooted in the history of ballet." ACB's performances are always accompanied by live music, which is frequently played by the Da Camera Society, as well as some of L.A.'s finest classical musicians including Martin Chalfour of the L.A. Phil and soloist Hilary Hahn. Each program is followed by a reception with the artists and live music.

The Bloc, 700 S. Flower St., Ste. 3200, Financial District // 213-878-9020
acbdances.com

DTLA BOOK 2019 85

A Heidi Duckler Dance Theater performance atop the Bendix Building

HEIDI DUCKLER DANCE THEATRE
The queen of site-specific dance shows

Heidi Duckler's dancers have made the city's diverse locations their stage, such as swimming pools and laundromats, as well as the terrace of its headquarters inside the Fashion District's historic Bendix Building. "We don't ever rehearse in a studio. We only rehearse on site," Duckler says about their process. "All the content of the rehearsal, everything comes from the environment." Collaborators include a cross section of visual and performing artists like muralist Kim West (see page 62). "We're nimble and try to be responsive to changes that are always happening in our city. Los Angeles is still a city of becoming. I think, as an artist, it's wonderful to be able to take advantage of that."

1206 Maple Ave., Ste. 1100B, Fashion District // 213-536-5820 // heididuckler.org

L.A. CONTEMPORARY DANCE COMPANY
At the cutting edge of modern movement

Since its founding in 2005 by a pair of dance students from USC, this resident company has served as a spotlight for L.A. talent, representing a wide diversity of dancers, composers and fine artists in an ever-evolving repertory of new danceworks and commissions. "We're dedicated to supporting L.A.-based dancers and choreographers and collaborators," says artistic director Genevieve Carson, a member since 2009. "It's become a booming community that is full of people who are starting their own companies and rethinking how dance is presented."

Brewery Arts Complex, the Brockus Project Studios, 618B Moulton Ave. // lacontemporarydance.org

Diavolo

L.A. Contemporary Dance Company

L.A. Dance Project

DIAVOLO: ARCHITECTURE IN MOTION

Exploring the meeting of the body and geometry

This acrobatic dance company combines the human body and sculptural structures to conjure visceral feats of movement exploring themes as varied as the Holocaust, corporate America and military veterans. Artistic director Jacques Heim has helmed Diavolo since 1992, employing rigorous choreography that has become the company's hallmark in a quest to understand how we are shaped by our physical environments.

Brewery Arts Complex, 616 Moulton Ave. // 323-225-4290 // diavolo.org

L.A. DANCE PROJECT

Star choreographer Benjamin Millepied's creation

Beginning in 2012, under artistic director Benjamin Millepied, this contemporary company has become a must-see for dance lovers. The choreographer on the movies *Black Swan* and *Vox Lux* (both starring his wife, Natalie Portman), Millepied served briefly as artistic director of the Paris Opera before returning his full attention to LADP. Known for works by Justin Peck, Kyle Abraham, Noe Soulier and, of course, Millepied, LADP famously collaborated with site-specific opera company The Industry on the 2013 Pulitzer finalist "Invisible Cities."

2245 E. Washington Blvd. // 213-622-5995 // ladanceproject.org

Natalie Portman & Benjamin Millepied

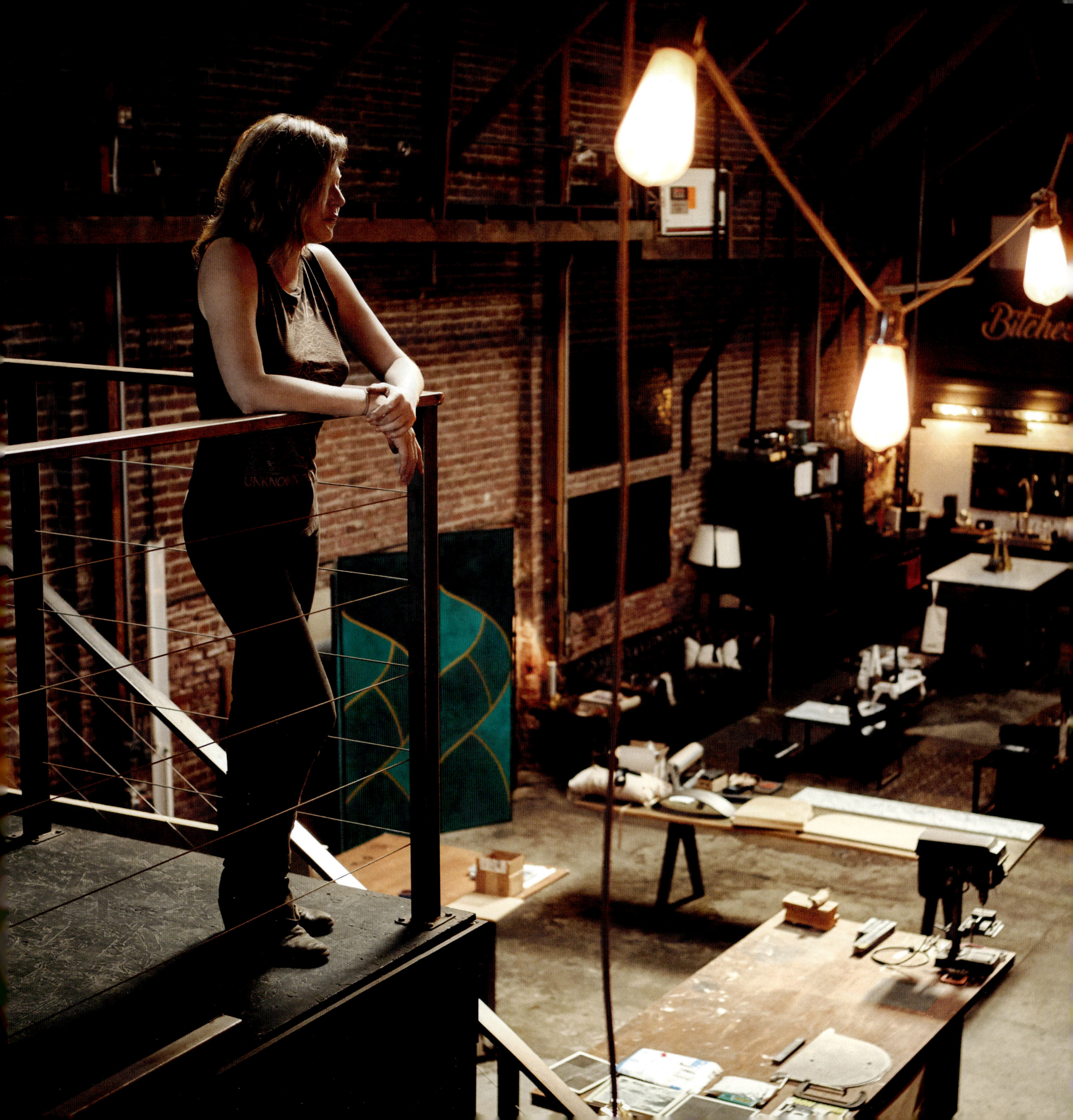

FLAMES OF CREATIVITY

Since picking up a welding torch, former model Meyghan Hill has forged a second career as one of the city's most in-demand furniture and object makers, working out of a DTLA warehouse.

By Abigail Stone

Meyghan Hill—who runs her provocative furniture fabrication and design business out of a large vine-covered DTLA loft—first picked up a welding torch after a bad breakup. She was living in Hollywood and faced with an empty apartment. So Hill, a former Ford model, decided to make things to fill it. She talked herself into an apprenticeship at a machine shop in the Valley. Her first efforts were pieces made from metal and stone scraps retrieved from the dumpster. Wielding fire to create felt empowering.

Her line of furniture and small goods retains that sense of raw energy and feeling while made in luxuriously elegant materials. There are jagged marble headboards and blackened

Daniel Dining Table

"My work is influenced by the geometry of Downtown— the design of the 4th Street Bridge, the outline of the U.S. Bank Tower."

steel consoles; tables clothed in leather and cinched with brass buckled belts. The work has gotten the attention of everyone from The Clippers, who have 10 of her marble and brass Daniel tables in their lounge, to Swiss luxury timepiece maker Audemars Piguet, for whom she's designed a custom couch and club chairs. "My work is influenced by the geometry of Downtown: the design of the 4th Street Bridge, the outline of the U.S. Bank Tower," she says.

Welding can at times be a lonely endeavor. So when she started out, she felt lucky to connect with two other makers, glassblower Uri Davillier of Neptune Glassworks and woodworker Westin Mitchell. Together, they formed The Kohler Street Collective in 2013, a group of Downtown craftspeople who worked out of a sprawling studio on said street, located in the Skid Row area. "I needed people around me who were doing the same thing. I thrive on Downtown's energy and talented people," says Hill.

HILL ON DINING DOWNTOWN:
"My neighbors, Comfort LA, make amazing soul food, including great vegan options. I love the truffle fries on The NoMad rooftop, and Rappahannock Oyster Bar at ROW DTLA."

Restraint Nightstand in blackened steel, marble and leather with brass detailing

90 DTLA BOOK 2019

COURTESY HANDCRAFTED PR

ON SHOPPING THE DISTRICT:
"My favorites are Hammer and Spear, Please Do Not Enter (I can't walk out of there without buying something), A+R, Hennessey + Ingalls (I'm a book nut) and Scent Bar DTLA (I can spend hours there)."

Chair in brass finished steel with travertine and leather

Couch in brass finished steel with travertine and leather

Brass Pinch Dish from the Small Goods Collection

ON SEEING ART:
"The Broad is hugely inspiring as are Hauser & Wirth, ICA LA and Wilding Cran. And I love studio visits with artist friends such as Mesplé, C.C. Boyce and Jason Koharik."

A year ago, as Kohler Street Collective expanded, she moved her shop across the street into a similarly raw warehouse. She continues to share her workspace with fellow creators who inspire her—her studio mates are now art and surface designers Brynn Gelbard and Lisa Donohoe of Londubh Studio and photographer Sarina Saletta.

Hill admits not everyone loves the name of her business, (wh)ORE HAüS Studios. She originally wanted to call it Orehaus, but the url was taken. So she decided to reclaim a word with negative connotations much in the same way she had reclaimed discarded materials and given them value at the start of her career. She says she wouldn't change a thing about her life right now. "Some people have a little notebook

ON DTLA'S BEST COCKTAILS:
"I go for anything spicy like the Rabbit Hole at Apotheke or the Old Hickory at Manuela. For old-fashioneds, I head to Tony's Saloon."

by the side of their bed where they jot down their ideas. I can just get up and build it right there. I really want to keep that."

For her, a perfect day in Downtown would be a Sunday spent with her community of friends. "I'd pick up ingredients at Urban Radish and the farmers' market on Spring, and booze at Flask & Field; then cook, welcoming fellow artists to a table set with their own creations: Uri Davillier's glasses; my brass salt cellars, candlesticks and place card holders; a tablecloth painted by artist Nicholas Knudson; coasters by Lindsey Kearns. We've created this beautiful community and so I love an opportunity to come together and celebrate our intense investment in our craft and the lives we've created here."

HILL: J SQUARED PHOTOGRAPHY

DTLA BOOK 2019   93

DREAM DUO: AHEAD OF THEIR TIME
Charlie Parker (left) and 19-year-old Miles Davis (right)—seen here at New York's Three Deuces club in 1947—played together at The Finale Club in Bronzeville in February–March 1946. A very rare recording of their L.A. gig was discovered and was included on the RLR Records album *Charlie Parker: At the Finale Club & More*. The Finale Club's location at 230½ E. 1st St. was later occupied by the store S.K. Uyeda, which recently closed.

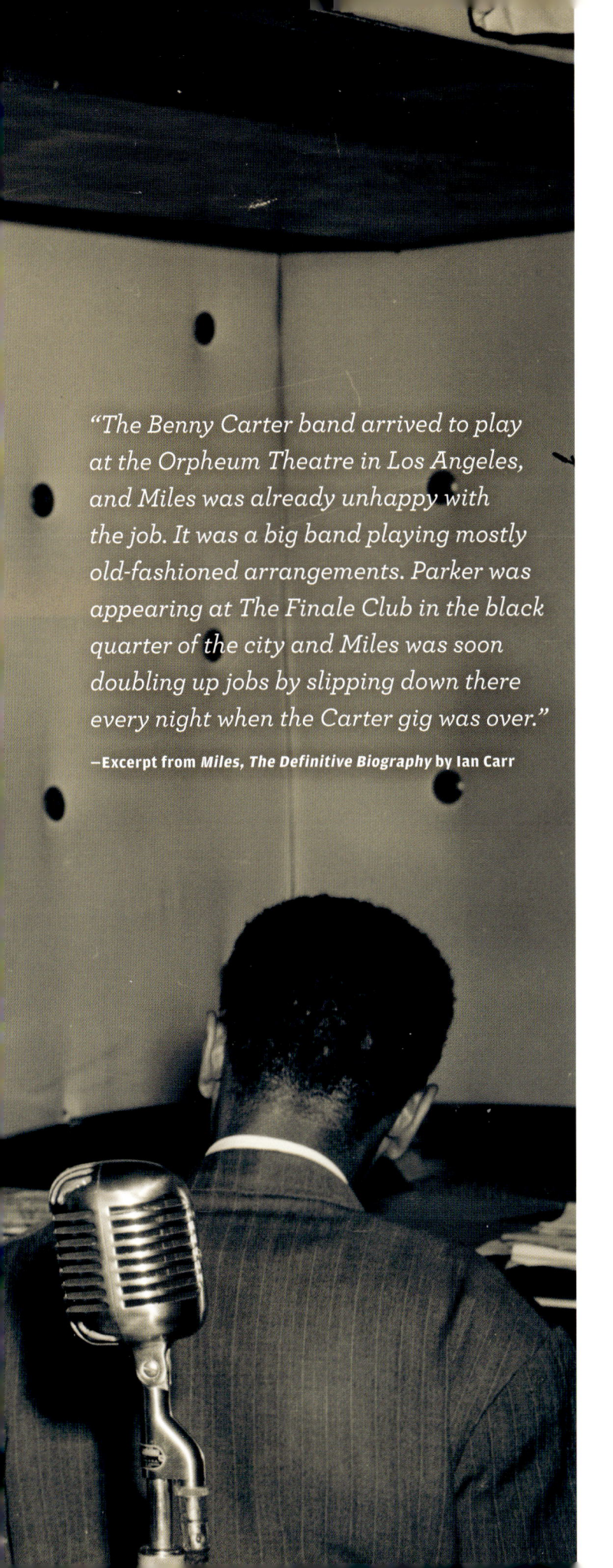

> "The Benny Carter band arrived to play at the Orpheum Theatre in Los Angeles, and Miles was already unhappy with the job. It was a big band playing mostly old-fashioned arrangements. Parker was appearing at The Finale Club in the black quarter of the city and Miles was soon doubling up jobs by slipping down there every night when the Carter gig was over."
>
> —Excerpt from *Miles, The Definitive Biography* by Ian Carr

BECOMING BRONZEVILLE

For a period during World War II—when Japanese Americans were sent to internment camps—Little Tokyo became known by a new name, reflecting an influx of tens of thousands of African Americans who reshaped the community and made late nights swing with jazz.

By Stacie Stukin

Los Angeles' Little Tokyo was founded in the 1880s when a Japanese sailor named Hamanosuke "Charles Hama" Shigeta opened an American-style café on E. 1st Street. The neighborhood continued to grow, and before World War II, it boasted a population of more than 35,000, making it the biggest Japanese commercial district in California. But in 1942, after Pearl Harbor attack, President Roosevelt issued Executive Order 9066, which forced roundups of Japanese residents, most of whom were U.S. citizens. Japanese-American families all over the country had mere days to decide what to do with their possessions, their farms and their businesses before, under the watch of soldiers with rifles, they boarded trains destined for internment camps like Manzanar, located in a remote desert near Owens Valley, California.

Almost overnight, Little Tokyo and its restaurants, hotels, newspapers, furniture stores, dry goods shops, churches and Buddhist temples went dark. It became an eerie ghost town just blocks away from City Hall. This bleak chapter in Japanese-American history and the involuntary evacuation of Little Tokyo dovetailed with the migration of African Americans from the South who came to Los Angeles seeking war industry jobs. Since the city's segregation laws prohibited blacks from living in 95 percent of Los Angeles neighborhoods, Little Tokyo became a destination for around 50,000 to as many as 80,000 African Americans who moved west to earn good wages.

The demographic change ushered in a new era and a new name. Little Tokyo became known as Bronzeville, a term that referred to the skin color of its residents and was at that time a name for many black metropolitan neighborhoods around the country. While the quarters were tight—many lived in squalor—a vibrant culture emerged that spawned newspapers, a chamber of commerce and new businesses including a spate of clubs where jazz and variety shows entertained patrons. Some were known as breakfast clubs, music spots that ran into the wee hours of the morning.

Martha Nakagawa, a journalist and historian, had heard about a time when African Americans lived in the neighborhood, but she didn't know much about the history until she

James Hodge, in hat, seen smiling at the camera, was the African-American owner of a newsstand at the corner of 1st and San Pedro Streets. Opened in 1942, it remained in business until the mid-1980s.

began studying the era more than a decade ago. In fact, as a kid growing up in L.A., she and her family shopped in Little Tokyo. There she saw James Hodge, the African-American proprietor of a newsstand on the corner of 1st and San Pedro Streets, which he opened during the Bronzeville era in 1942 and operated into the 1980s. In Ichiro Mike Murase's book *Little Tokyo: One Hundred Years in Pictures,* Hodge was quoted as saying: "This neighborhood here was nightclubs and gambling and prostitutes and pimps. But they weren't like today. They were civilized. The sun never went down in this neighborhood. Guys were spending money with both hands. It was real exciting...but it only lasted about three years."

During those three years, nightclubs showcased some of the era's most progressive jazz. "The jewel of Bronzeville was Shepp's Playhouse," says jazz journalist Kirk Silsbee. Located on 1st Street, Shepp's was a three-story entertainment mecca where, Silsbee explains, "there were comics, eccentric acts, ballad singers, contortionists, shake dancers and, of course jazz." At Shepp's, legendary bandleader Gerald Wilson, who had played with Duke Ellington and Count Basie, performed regularly, and other jazz greats like Coleman Hawkins, T-Bone Walker and Joe Liggins graced the stage, too, making Shepp's a destination for white Angelenos like Judy Garland and Gene Kelly.

But it was The Finale Club on E. 1st Street—with a bare-bones, low-ceilinged room located on the second floor and accessed by an alley—that, according to Silsbee, became the locus of modern jazz. "For a brief time, in the summer of 1946, The Finale Club became the destination for every modern jazz-minded musician and fan west of the Rockies," he says. The reason: Charlie "Bird" Parker, one of the most influential musicians of the 20th century, who defined the improvisational, bold jazz known as bebop.

Parker had left Dizzy Gillespie's band and found himself in Los Angeles looking for gigs and drugs. He assembled a small band and got booked at The Finale Club (which is the subject of a new documentary of the same name directed by Robert Shoji). Parker invited a 19-year-old trumpeter named Miles Davis to join him. In Davis, Parker found an equal with lots of talent. For Davis, Parker offered a creative challenge and someone to learn from. Davis said of his time at The Finale Club: "It was a nice place and I thought it was funky because the music was funky and the musicians were getting down."

Much like the limited run of The Finale Club, Bronzeville was a short-lived period in the history of Little Tokyo. The Supreme Court's Korematsu decision at the end of 1944 lifted the evacuation orders, and at the beginning of 1945, Japanese Americans were free to return home. Hillary Jenks, PhD, a historian who wrote a dissertation on the history of Little Tokyo, says the transition wasn't perfect—there was racism and tense moments as Japanese families returned to reclaim their homes and businesses. "It wasn't smooth, it wasn't roses, but there was a conscious effort to make it work," she says.

In fact, kinships between African Americans and Japanese developed—in some cases they hired one another to work in their businesses and assisted each other to find new housing. And in 1945 an editorial published in the black newspaper, *The California Eagle,* came out in defense of their Japanese brethren when it stated: "It is the question today of whether or not California shall live up to its tradition of democracy, or shall it become a breeding place for Fascism. Shall citizens of the United States of America be allowed to live in this state unmolested, free to enjoy all the privileges of the greatest democracy in the world, free to exercise the rights and responsibilities of that democracy?... It is not only we Negroes who are asking that question." The editorial ended with this appeal: "California's job in 1945 is to take the lead in the establishment of a democratic state of affairs in which the people of whatever race, color or creed may live together in peace and harmony."

Today, Little Tokyo is still a destination for Japanese Americans and tourists alike who come for confections like mochi from Fugetsu-Do, where the Kito family has been making their delicacies since 1903 and re-established the business upon their return from internment, or who shop at Anzen Hardware, which has been selling items like specialty knives and Japanese carpentry tools since it opened after the war. Among a newer wave of stores and restaurants, Popkiller carries vintage and contemporary gifts and clothing, while ramen enthusiasts patiently wait in line at Daikokuya.

Activists like Bill Watanabe, who was born while his parents were incarcerated in Manzanar internment camp and who founded The Little Tokyo Historical Society, want to ensure that DTLA's gentrification doesn't erase the legacy of the Japanese-American community. To that end, Watanabe helped organize a community-based investment program to purchase heritage-based businesses called the Little Tokyo Community Impact fund. "We need to keep a connection to our historic places, people, customs and culture," Watanabe says. "Our history and heritage live in these buildings and once they're torn down, the memories and connections go away as if they never existed."

For Watanabe, preservation isn't just about buildings; it's also about preserving history. When it comes to the legacy of Bronzeville, he observes, "racism, of course, was a huge underlying factor in why the Japanese were rounded up and incarcerated, and racism is why this area became Bronzeville because of the restrictive covenants. The fact that it happened to the Japanese-American community gives us a stronger sense that our civil rights can be taken away when people are afraid and suffering. That's when they look for a scapegoat. Unfortunately, today that message has not gone away."

TRANSITIONS AFTER WORLD WAR II

These photographs show the street scene outside Kiichi Uyeda's Bronzeville 5-10-25-Cent Store and the sales floor inside, soon after Uyeda (seen at right) opened it in 1945. The Japanese-American shopkeeper was one of the first to return to the neighborhood after being held in the Manzanar internment camp. Many African and Japanese Americans made efforts to bring a harmonious community into existence, with varying success. Uyeda hired African Americans as clerks, and Samuel Evans hired Japanese American waitresses to work in his restaurant, the Bamboo Room. Uyeda's store, which changed its name to S.K. Uyeda and became a department and specialty store run by his son, closed in 2016.

DTLA'S ANGEL NONPROFITS

Seven of the city's most effective and big-hearted charitable groups are based Downtown, doing everything from giving kids art instruction that they can't find in school to building housing for the homeless and helping people learn job skills.

By Shelly Levitt

Former Chrysalis client Omara

CHRYSALIS

Its cleaning crews, seen all around DTLA, can get something "much deeper than a paycheck"

Spend any time Downtown and you'll likely spot men and women in brightly colored safety vests and shirts sweeping streets or pressure-washing sidewalks. They're members of Chrysalis' transitional jobs program (which employs more than 1,100 people annually), and while they're helping to keep DTLA spick and span, they're also gaining job skills. Chrysalis contracts with five business improvement districts in Downtown who hire these street teams. This street maintenance program is a fully functioning business—a dynamic example of what's known as social enterprise—that provides temporary work for the nonprofit's clients.

It's just one element of the ambitious agenda of the nonprofit that was started in 1984 as a food and clothing distribution center and has grown into one of the country's leading service organizations. Since 1984, Chrysalis has served more than 60,000 clients. They assist people with challenges that might include history with the criminal justice system, a lack of work history or hardships due to unstable housing.

"How we measure success is through job outcomes," says Mark Loranger, the organization's president and CEO. The numbers are impressive: In 2017, for the third year in a row, more than 70 percent of clients reached were still employed six months after landing a job. Behind that statistic are moving stories of lives transformed. Loranger points to Omara, a woman who came to Chrysalis after being released from prison and who'd had her kids taken away from her.

"Getting out of prison, her number-one goal was to be reunited with her daughters," Loranger says, "but first she had to find a way to support them." Omara was placed in a job with a local jewelry manufacturer, The Giving Keys. She was eventually promoted to supervisor, and launched a cleaning service on the side. A year ago, she went out on her own and is working to gain custody of her children. "She didn't want to be a millionaire," Loranger says. "We see that over and over with our clients. They just want the dignity and respect that comes with having a job, so that they can be a part of their family and community, and buy a birthday gift for their kid. It's much deeper than a paycheck."

HOW YOU CAN HELP Volunteer time to help clients write their résumé or practice interview skills; make a financial contribution; or donate work-appropriate clothing.

CHANGELIVES.ORG

COURTESY CHRYSALIS

INNER-CITY ARTS

For kids who can't get arts classes at school, this nonprofit fills the gap at its Skid Row campus

Since 1989, Inner-City Arts has had a single mission: to provide a safe space where children and teens can express their creativity. The classes offered in the studios of its Skid Row campus embrace all the arts, including painting, dance, film and animation. More than 200,000 students have received hands-on instruction from their teaching artists. Some 10,000 educators have taken part in professional-development programs, extending the nonprofit's reach to 2.5 million kids. The group fills a critical gap in the city, where many schools don't have funds for art classes. "Inner-City Arts is not just a learning oasis in the heart of Skid Row—it's a creative movement," says Bob Smiland, the group's president and CEO. "We advocate for the arts and the power it has to transform communities."

HOW YOU CAN HELP Become a Inner-City Arts member for as little as $10 a month.

INNER-CITYARTS.ORG

100 DTLA BOOK 2019

MORE DTLA ANGELS

DOWNTOWN WOMEN'S CENTER
With the mission of empowering women experiencing homelessness, the 50-year old Downtown Women's Center is taking a lead role in the new Domestic Violence and Homeless Services Coalition. The nonprofit, founded in 1978, also runs a health clinic in Skid Row exclusively for women.
downtownwomenscenter.org

HOMEBOY INDUSTRIES
Serving men and women who are former gang members, Homeboy Industries has launched several social enterprises. The most well known is Homeboy Bakery; the made-from-scratch Banana Praline Cake is worth writing home about.
homeboyindustries.org

MIDNIGHT MISSION
For more than 100 years, The Midnight has been providing necessary services to Skid Row's homeless men and women: food, shelter, clothing, hygiene items and medical care.
midnightmission.org

THE PEOPLE CONCERN
Addressing the needs of the chronically homeless, The People Concern has been put in charge of running the first of the 15 emergency homeless shelters in L.A. Mayor Eric Garcetti's L.A. Bridge Home Program. Five trailers arranged around the common area of a wooden deck will provide housing for 45 residents.
thepeopleconcern.org

SKID ROW HOUSING TRUST

The group is a leader in providing attractively designed permanent housing for the homeless

For the first decade or so of its 30-year existence, the Skid Row Housing Trust was focused on the preservation of buildings where low-income people were living. But by the mid-'90s, with homelessness soaring, there was a recognition "that people needed more," says Dana Trujillo, the organization's chief investment and finance officer. Providing support services—including access to medical and mental health care and substance-abuse treatment—became seen as essential.

Today, the Skid Row Housing Trust provides homes and services to nearly 2,000 people in Los Angeles, in a variety of different housing models, including the New Genesis Apartments, a 106-unit mixed-income apartment building with an on-site health clinic. "The biggest impact we've had is that we've provided evidence that permanent supportive housing is the solution to homelessness," Trujillo says.

HOW YOU CAN HELP Speak up and insist that housing be built to address the homeless problem.

SKIDROW.ORG

STAR DESIGN
Skid Row Housing Trust's Star Apartments on 6th Street, designed by Michael Maltzan Architecture, provide housing to 100 formerly homeless individuals using innovative prefab units.

GO METRO!

Four L.A. transit lines—each of which you can catch right in DTLA—are ready to whisk you away to destinations as varied as Pasadena, Hollywood, Koreatown and Santa Monica.

By Liz Ohanesian // Illustrations by Lili Todd

GOLD LINE A DAY IN PASADENA

South Pasadena 11 a.m.
Mission Street is the heart of South Pasadena with a quirky, small-town vibe that makes it a perfect spot to start your day. Swing by **The Moo on Mission** for a caffeine fix first. The shopping scene here is eclectic and worth at least an hour of browsing. Head to **Vidéothèque** for indie and foreign film finds, **Old Focals** for vintage glasses, **Dinosaur Farm** for toys

and **Fair Oaks Pharmacy** for unusual candies. Make a stop at **Hotbox**—tucked into an alley off Mission Street—for an impeccable selection of vintage clothing.

Fillmore 12:30 p.m.
If you have a passion for vintage odds and ends, **Pasadena Antique Center** is a must-stop on your Gold Line adventure. The two-story, labyrinthian complex overflows with everything from furniture to dolls. Look for the closets and corners stocked with vintage clothing. The selection is high-end—we spotted everything from Hermès to Prada on a recent trip—and in tip-top shape. Check out the display cases with antique jewelry and don't forget to flip through the boxes of postcards and photos for an inexpensive retro souvenir.

Memorial Park 2 p.m.
The Gold Line's Memorial Park station lets off riders in Pasadena's Old Town district, where you can grab a late lunch. Dining options are plentiful, ranging from local chains like **Umami Burger** and **Taco King** to mom-and-pop spots. For a taste of Himalayan cuisine, head to **Tibet Nepal House**, where steamed mo-mo dumplings are made with either vegetables or meat. After lunch, visit **Armory Center for the Arts** and spend some time with the contemporary art on view. Admission is free.

7 DOWNTOWN AREA METRO STATIONS

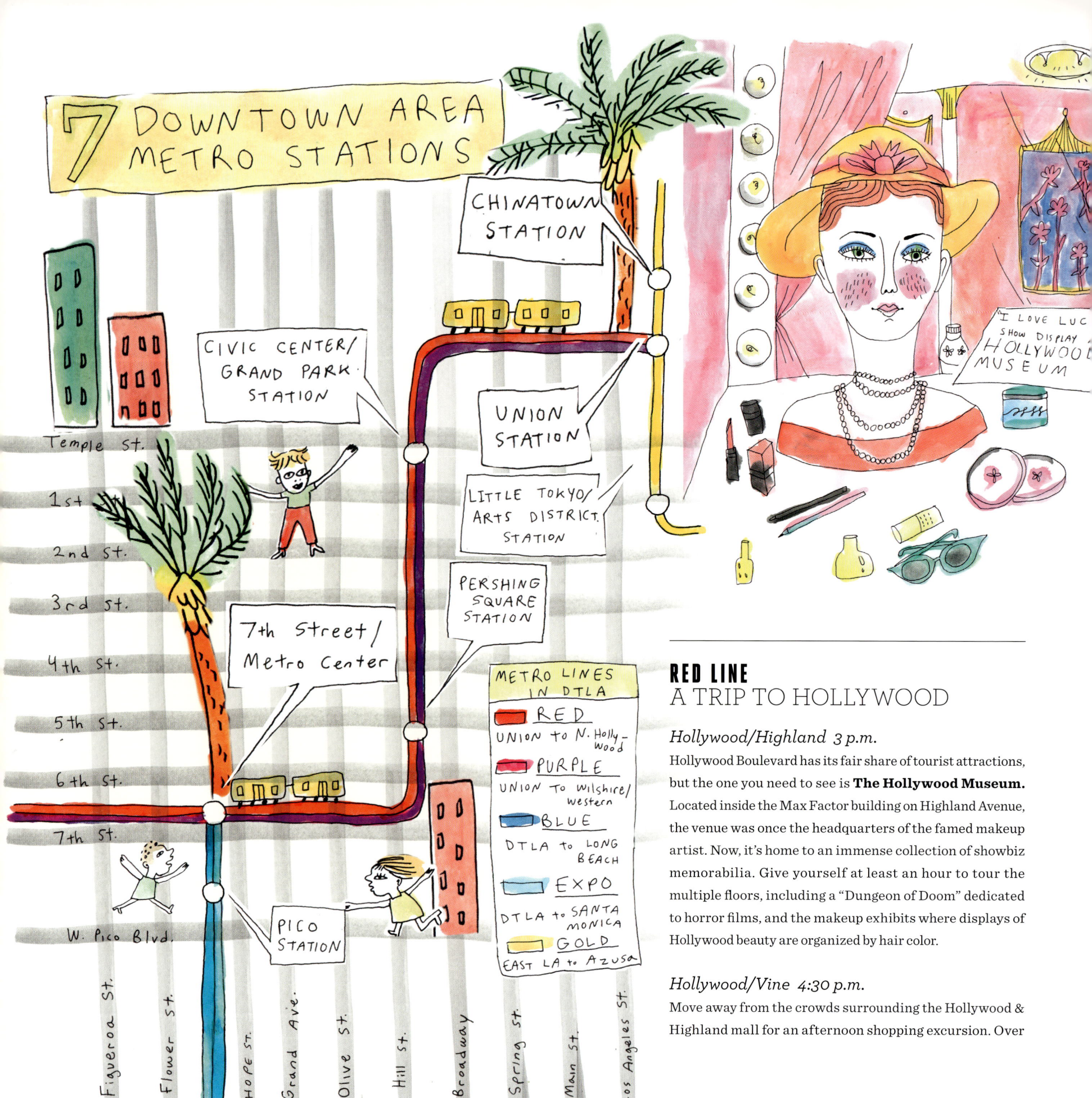

CHINATOWN STATION

CIVIC CENTER/ GRAND PARK STATION

UNION STATION

LITTLE TOKYO/ ARTS DISTRICT STATION

7th Street/ Metro Center

PERSHING SQUARE STATION

PICO STATION

Temple St.
1st
2nd St.
3rd St.
4th St.
5th St.
6th St.
7th St.
W. Pico Blvd.

Figueroa St. · Flower St. · Hope St. · Grand Ave. · Olive St. · Hill St. · Broadway · Spring St. · Main St. · Los Angeles St.

METRO LINES IN DTLA

- **RED** — Union to N. Hollywood
- **PURPLE** — Union to Wilshire/Western
- **BLUE** — DTLA to Long Beach
- **EXPO** — DTLA to Santa Monica
- **GOLD** — East LA to Azusa

I LOVE LUCY SHOW DISPLAY — HOLLYWOOD MUSEUM

RED LINE
A TRIP TO HOLLYWOOD

Hollywood/Highland 3 p.m.

Hollywood Boulevard has its fair share of tourist attractions, but the one you need to see is **The Hollywood Museum.** Located inside the Max Factor building on Highland Avenue, the venue was once the headquarters of the famed makeup artist. Now, it's home to an immense collection of showbiz memorabilia. Give yourself at least an hour to tour the multiple floors, including a "Dungeon of Doom" dedicated to horror films, and the makeup exhibits where displays of Hollywood beauty are organized by hair color.

Hollywood/Vine 4:30 p.m.

Move away from the crowds surrounding the Hollywood & Highland mall for an afternoon shopping excursion. Over on Cahuenga Boulevard, you'll find **Space 15 Twenty**, the Urban Outfitters hub that's also home to pop-ups and special events. **The Record Parlour**, on nearby Selma Avenue, is a record store that's jam-packed with used vinyl. On Hollywood Boulevard, comb through racks of secondhand threads at **Iguana Vintage Clothing** for everything from on-trend pieces to odds and ends for last-minute costumes.

Hollywood/Western 6:30 p.m.
Home to the enclaves of Little Armenia and Thai Town, East Hollywood has a bounty of dining options from large, sit-down restaurants to tiny bakeries. Inside a very '80s mini-mall is **Carousel**, a local favorite for Middle Eastern food with an expansive menu that includes meatless options. (Kim Kardashian is said to be a fan). For sweets, you can't go wrong with **Bhan Kanom Thai**. Pick up a bag of Pui Fai, fluffy cupcake-like pastries in pastel colors, and the coconut and cocoa candy Ar-Lua to take back home.

Sunset/Vermont 8:30 p.m.
After dinner, hop back on the Metro for one more stop to grab drinks at **Tiki-Ti**. This tiny Sunset Boulevard bar was launched in the early 1960s by Ray Buhen, whose own career as a bartender went back to the 1930s at the legendary Don the Beachcomber bar. This local mainstay is family-run and its ample menu includes tiki classics along with house specialities, like Ray's Mistake with passionfruit and rum. If you can't decide on a cocktail, take a chance and spin The Wheel for your selection.

DTLA BOOK 2019

PURPLE LINE
A JAUNT TO KOREATOWN

Wilshire/Vermont 10 a.m.
Start your day with an Instagram-able breakfast at **California Donuts**. The 24-hour donut shop has been around for several decades, but, in recent years, has gained a reputation for their extremely photogenic treats. From a window fronting a small parking lot, you can order donuts covered in cereal or candy, or ones made to resemble panda bears and unicorns. There's also a Pink D'oh-nut that channels *The Simpsons*, plus croissant donuts and donuts in flavors like chocolate bacon or matcha green tea.

Wilshire/Normandie 10:30 a.m.
Walk off that donut while checking out the art and architecture of Koreatown. At Wilshire/Normandie, the Purple Line lets off travelers in the midst of one of Los Angeles' most historically significant neighborhoods. Along Wilshire Boulevard, you'll find grand houses of worship, like **Wilshire Boulevard Temple**, and stately buildings

that were once home to local department stores. The city's old gems neighbor new spaces, like **The Line Hotel**, where you'll spot a mural from famed street artist D*Face.

Wilshire/Western 11:30 a.m.
The end of the Purple Line is also the best exit for shopping and dining in Koreatown. K-pop fans will want to walk to **Music Plaza**, at Koreatown Plaza, for the latest albums from hit-makers like BTS. **Louis Castel** offers stylish golf attire and you'll find facial masks galore at **Cosmetic World**. For grub, take your pick of everything from Korean barbecue to gastropub fare. Want dessert? **Milk Tavern** serves up ice cream sundaes with kids' cereal toppings. They also have beer, wine and bubbly, plus video game stations and ping-pong. If you're in the mood for a movie, too, **CGV Cinemas** screens both U.S. and Korean flicks.

EXPO LINE
SOJOURN IN SANTA MONICA

26th Street/Bergamot Station 1 p.m.
Start your Santa Monica adventure at the city's art hub. **Bergamot Station** is a collection of galleries situated right behind the Expo Line stop. **Copro Gallery**, launched by the late *Juxtapoz* magazine co-founder Greg Escalante, is renowned for its focus on new contemporary art. **Lois Lambert Gallery** includes a gift shop filled with unusual finds from jewelry to toys.

Downtown Santa Monica 2 p.m.
The Expo Line ends just blocks from the Pacific Ocean and, from here, you have a few options for your day trip. Right below the train platform is a Metro Bike Share rack. You can rent a bike and hit the coastal path toward Venice Beach to the south or Pacific Palisades to the north. Head less than two miles north and you'll find **Annenberg Community Beach House**. This public beach house is open year-round, although the pool is summer-only. The Beach House also hosts art exhibitions and cultural events. If you prefer to stroll, browse the **Third Street Promenade** pedestrian mall, walk through the gardens of **Tongva Park**, hit the sand or head to the amusement park at **Santa Monica Pier**. With so many activities and options for food, you can easily stay here until later in the evening.

DTLA Book asked Lili Todd to follow these itineraries and illustrate this story in the form of a diary. She and her friend Eliza Henderson use Metro to go everywhere in the city, including their school, Los Angeles County High School for the Arts (LACHSA).

METRO BIKE: HOW IT WORKS

1. GET A BIKE from any Metro Bike Share station, go for a ride and then return it at any station.

2. FIND A DOCKING STATION with Metro's online bike map (bikeshare.metro.net/stations) or app (bikeshare.metro.net/app).

3. PAY AT THE STATION KIOSK with a debit or credit card. The rate is $3.50 for the first half hour and $3.50 for each half hour after that.

4. RIDE ANY TIME OF THE DAY. Bikes are available 24/7/365. Call or text 844-857-BIKE for customer service.

A Department of Water and Power customer engagement lab, located inside LACI, where consumers can learn more about conservation and clean energy

LACI's large amphitheater, which hosts 30,000 visitors annually

The breakroom at LACI's La Kretz Innovation Campus, which opened in the Arts District in 2016

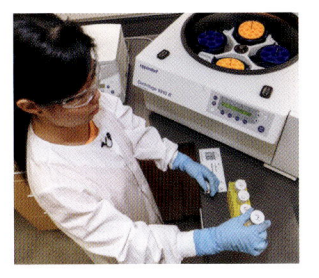

RAISING CLEAN AND GREEN

The Los Angeles Cleantech Incubator gives a leg up to environmentally friendly startups.

By Joe Bargmann

Diana Kim, LACI's Lab Coordinator, handles a centrifuge in the Advanced Prototyping Center's chemistry lab.

Omar Laldin (left) and Andrew Fortus operate a waterjet at the Prototyping Center.

A bike rack sits at LACI's entrance.

One of the biggest contributors to DTLA's deserved reputation as a hotbed of innovation is the Arts District's Los Angeles Cleantech Incubator (LACI). A nonprofit funded through L.A.'s Community Redevelopment Authority and the Department of Water and Power in 2011, LACI identifies and develops emergent companies and technologies that contribute to the city's green economy.

With 60,000 square feet of office and event space, as well as a lavishly equipped product prototyping center, LACI provides inventors and entrepreneurs with the hardware and the mentorship they need to launch purpose-driven businesses. It's led by president and CEO Matt Petersen, previously chief sustainability officer of the city of L.A.

"There is an emphasis on community, both inside and outside the building," says Ben Stapleton, LACI's senior vice president of operations and finance. "Most incubators are profit-focused, but our staff and our members have a collective belief in making the city a better place to live."

And if a business succeeds—and the founders get rich while also improving the environment—that's fine, too. Stapleton points to LACI-incubated company Repurpose, which has developed biodegradable, compostable cups, plates and utensils that are cheaper than similar products on the market. "Repurpose is going to be one of our biggest financial successes," Stapleton says, adding that the products will be sold by retail giants Walmart and Kroger.

A rendering of Ampaire's TailWind, a six-passenger electric aircraft due to launch next year

To become part of the incubator's portfolio, companies must apply and go through a rigorous selection process. If chosen, they agree to let LACI have a warrant for equity. According to LACI's website, costs are $500 a month for membership, plus $500 a month for each employee's desk.

Other LACI companies are developing clean transportation technologies such as electric airplanes and buses. Their goals are in line with L.A.'s Zero-Emissions 2028 Roadmap, which seeks to reduce smog in the city by 25 percent by the time the Olympic Games arrive here in 2028.

"The 2028 Roadmap is an incentive for everyone at LACI," Stapleton says. "We want all of our businesses to tie into the bigger picture." Here's a closer look at three such companies currently at LACI.

READY FOR TAKEOFF

Electric-airplane builder **Ampaire** *prepares for its first flight—soon.*

For the founders of Ampaire, LACI has been not just an incubator, but also an accelerator. They started their electric-aircraft company in 2016, joined LACI a year later and plan to put a fully electric six-passenger plane in the air in early 2019.

LACI BY THE NUMBERS

6
years of building an inclusive green economy for greater L.A.

72
companies in its portfolio

$159M
in funding raised

$220M
revenue generated by companies

1,700
jobs created by companies

60,000
square feet of office, event and workshop space

3.2
acre campus

175
kilowatt solar energy system

"We got started in Temecula, about an hour and a half south of L.A.—that's where Cory and I grew up," says Ryan Bilton, Ampaire's chief financial officer. He's referring to chief technology officer Cory Combs, whom Bilton describes as the company's "mad scientist." CEO Kevin Noertker completes the original team. Starting out in Temecula, recalls Bilton, "we had free office space, lived at home and took low salaries, and had a good network of friends, family and initial investors."

But after making their first hire, an engineer from L.A., the move to LACI became inevitable. "We reached the point where it wasn't just three guys in an office," Bilton says. "There was a lot of equipment and machinery we knew we'd eventually have to buy. We had a lot of hardware needs."

LACI fulfills those needs. "We use the welding lab, waterjet, CNC mills—we take advantage of the whole prototyping center," he says. Build-out of the aircraft components takes place in rented warehouse space across the street from the incubator, as well as in a hangar at Camarillo Airport in Ventura County.

But the incubator provides much more. CEO Noertker meets weekly with an Executive in Residence (EIR), who has started and run a successful company and now provides mentorship to LACI's fledgling enterprises. The EIR also counsels other Ampaire employees, helping them through the ups and downs and intricacies of starting a business.

"We sit next to a company that's building electric buses," Bilton says. "You get to learn about other areas where cleantech is gathering momentum."

As Ampaire prepares for its first test flight, Bilton reflects on the advantages of being at LACI. "It's not a magic pill," he says. "We still do all the grunt work. But the simple fact is, we could have had the idea for an electric plane before joining LACI—but we wouldn't have been able to build it."

SHINING STARS

*The founders of **Hive Lighting** are brightening movie and TV sets with reduced energy input.*

While enrolled at Brown University, Jonathan Miller and Robert Rutherford (class of 2005) worked together on the annual Ivy Film Festival, the world's largest student-run movie fest. Six years after they graduated, Miller was a cinematographer and Rutherford (after a stint in movie financing) worked as an energy-efficiency lighting consultant. They now run Hive Lighting, an LACI portfolio company whose products have illuminated the sets of photo shoots, movies, commercials and TV shows such as *The Mentalist* and *Veep.*

In 2011, Miller and Rutherford were "two guys in a garage," recalls the latter, creating one-offs of their innovative plasma lights. Then, Rutherford discovered LACI while researching co-working spaces.

"The idea of a hardware-centered prototyping facility seemed perfect for us," Rutherford says. "And as an energy-efficient lighting company with a uniquely L.A. focus—cleantech meets Hollywood—we were one of the very first companies to apply and start working at LACI. It was the perfect stepping stone from concept to company."

Like many breakthrough ideas, Hive's lighting begs the question "Why didn't someone think of that sooner?"

"Our lights use up to 90 percent less energy, last 100 times longer, generate virtually no heat and are made from recyclable aluminum," Rutherford says. "They are greener and cleaner in all categories compared to legacy technologies, like tungsten lighting."

Hive Lighting managing technician Eddie Pineda assembles a Wasp 100-C LED light in the prototyping center.

Hive Lighting's Wasp 250 Plasma

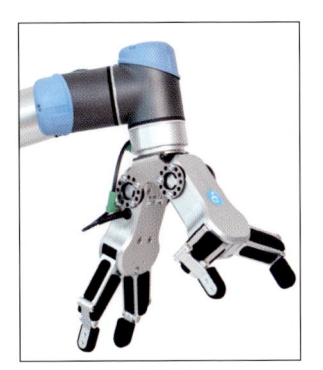

OnRobot's Dual Gripper end-of-arm tool

Key to Hive's success was LACI's Advanced Prototyping Center, where they created their first LED light, the Wasp 100-C. "This was the first product to be fully designed, prototyped and manufactured at the prototyping center," Rutherford says. "It was designed using computers and software in the CAD lab. Models were 3D-printed in the 3D printers. Aluminum parts were milled in the milling machines."

The Wasp 100-C anchored a Kickstarter campaign for Hive that generated $500,000 in pre-orders and millions more in follow-up business. Still growing, Hive now employs 15 people—and its future looks bright.

ROBOTS WITH FEELING

***OnRobot** is giving robots a sense of touch, designing hand-like grippers with tactile sensors.*

Imagine a robotic hand so sensitive that it can pick and pack greenhouse-grown herbs without bruising the plants' delicate leaves and stems. Sounds futuristic, right? But it is just one invention—already in use by Denmark's largest purveyor of fresh herbs—from the pioneering company OnRobot.

Launched out of LACI in 2013, OnRobot, which specializes in designing "grippers" that give robots a sense of touch, has grown to become an international powerhouse in the industry, with more than 100 employees. Co-founder and managing director Nick Wettels was employed by NASA's Jet Propulsion Laboratory when he began developing OnRobot's early prototypes. "I was working nights and weekends on the company. I wanted to join because of the supportive environment the incubator offers," he says.

He cites LACI's mentorship, through its Executive in Residence program, and access to high-tech equipment as primary factors in getting OnRobot off the ground and helping it continue to grow and innovate. "Being able to use the water jet, CNC mill and wet lab allowed us to accelerate our product development and R&D greatly, as there is no way we could have afforded that kind of equipment as such an early stage."

GOOD TIMES

Inside an enormous DTLA warehouse, high-tech "micro-amusement park" Two Bit Circus is bringing folks together with its unique brand of interactive fun: "We're making entertainment more personal."

By Joe Bargmann

Two Bit Circus founders Brent Bushnel (left) and Eric Gradman

"We are a bunch of clowns, make no mistake, but what we do is a serious undertaking." That's Eric Gradman speaking. He's the cofounder of Two Bit Circus, and he carries the title Chief Technology Officer and Mad Inventor. He and his longtime friend and business partner, Brent Bushnell, run a business unlike any other in Los Angeles—or in the world, for that matter.

With a tongue-in-cheek nod to an old-school carnival, Two Bit Circus, which calls itself a "micro-amusement park," is a thoroughly modern mashup of theatrical, interactive and high-tech entertainment, a playground for children and adults alike. You want a cocktail as well? The robot bartender will make it for you, with a little banter thrown in for good measure.

"You've got infinite opportunities during the day to hold your cellphone in front of your face and not interact with anybody, and you can go on the internet and argue politics all you want," Gradman says. "But what the world needs now is people going out, making new friends, hanging out in public, laughing together, grabbing a drink and having a good time."

Entering the 38,000-square-foot Two Bit Circus warehouse is like being sucked through a portal into a trippy futuristic party. There are video games created and built by Two Bit's team of engineers, a section devoted to VR-headset gaming, a carnival midway with a steampunk aesthetic, escape rooms, food offerings, roaming actors engaging with visitors, as well as Club01, a 100-seat theater—Bushnell prefers to call it an "interactive social club"—for everything from game shows and trivia to more traditional dramatic productions.

Well, somewhat traditional, anyway. "Our stage shows are interactive," Gradman says. "They're as much about the standup comedy on the stage as they are about using the touchscreens at your table to become part of the show."

Gradman says DTLA makes for the perfect home for Two Bit Circus. "It's at the crossroads of two important freeways," he notes. "You go down the 10 freeway, you wind up in Silicon Beach—high-tech companies doing high-tech things. You go up the 5 freeway, you wind up in Burbank, the center of the film and entertainment industries. We're right at the intersection of that. We draw from a very deep pool of talent in L.A."

The talent, working both behind the scenes and on the floor, now encompasses more than 100 employees. You see, it's still possible to run away and join the circus. Or just to visit it. Rest assured, an excursion to Two Bit Circus won't be your average night on the town.

"The people who come here are the same people you'd see out at a bar," says Gradman. "But they're able to have a better time because of the range of experiences they can engage in. We're able to create interactions with a very special quality to them because we apply technology. We can use projections, sensors to know how you're moving, computers to schedule a theatrical experience for you. Using technology, we're making entertainment more personal."

Patrons play against each other on Last Ball Standing.

TWO BIT CIRCUS
634 Mateo St., Arts District // 213-599-3188 // twobitcircus.com

WATCH THE FUN!
PEEK INSIDE TWO BIT CIRCUS

Scan this code with your standard iPhone camera or Android QR Code reader app, and play the video!

NOW PLAYING

TWO BIT CIRCUS

OUR FAVES – EAT –

FOR THE VIEW

The Rooftop at The Standard

BROKEN SHAKER
416 W. 8th St. // 213-395-9532
freehandhotels.com

For **ultimate vacation vibes**, order a playful cocktail—like B*tch Better Have My Money—and a tuna tostada or fried chicken at this kitschy and colorful rooftop bar, a James Beard Award finalist.

THE NOMAD ROOFTOP
649 S. Olive St. // 213-358-0000
thenomadhotel.com/los-angeles

Not much inhibits the sweeping views at this grand hotel's open-air rooftop. Designed by Jacques Garcia, the look is awash in **breezy sky blues and blush hues**, backed by the DTLA skyline. Play hooky with prawn rolls and piña coladas—frozen drinks are a specialty. At night, light bites abound.

OUE SKYSPACE LA BAR
633 W. 5th St. // 213-894-9000 // oue-skyspace.com

The best way to top off views from the ocean to the mountains, **the tallest open-air observation deck in California** and a slide that makes you float above the city is with a serious cocktail. The bar on the 69th floor has it all, including snacks should all that altitude make you hungry. (See page 9 for a cocktail shot.)

PERCH
448 S. Hill St. // 213-802-1770
perchla.com

Live band, festive flair. There is no better way to approach midnight than seated beside a fire pit on the 16th-floor rooftop lounge of this French bistro. Stellar sip: the signature Spicy Concombre, a mix of gin, St. Germain, cucumber, lime and jalapeño.

THE ROOFTOP AT THE STANDARD
550 S. Flower St. // 213-892-8080
standardhotels.com

You can nibble on pretzels, wieners, strudel and beer from the Biergarten. Or **settle into a waterbed pod with cocktails and sliders**. A DJ spins every night.

SORA
900 Wilshire Blvd., 69th Fl.
213-688-7777
dtla.intercontinental.com

Never has **conveyor-belt sushi** looked as good as it does at this 69th-floor eatery, where the most coveted stools are the ones along the expansive wall of windows.

SPIRE 73
900 Wilshire Blvd., 69th Fl.
213-688-7777
dtla.intercontinental.com

This open-air spot is perched atop **the tallest building west of Chicago**, with true bird's-eye views that seem to make everything you imbibe and eat taste that much better. $25 after 8 p.m.

TAKAMI
811 Wilshire Blvd. // 213-236-9600 //
takamisushi.com

Japanese robata-grilled favorites and sushi aren't the only things on offer at this 21st-floor rooftop restaurant. **Gorgeous panoramic views** take the experience to the next level, literally.

UPSTAIRS AT ACE HOTEL
929 Broadway // 213-623-3233 // acehotel.com

Described as "bunker-like," this isn't the most verdant rooftop in L.A. But it might be the hippest. Bring a crowd and enjoy a **pitcher of sangria or Pimm's cup**. Chips and the like are available when munchies set in.

WESTIN BONAVENTURE BONAVISTA LOUNGE
404 S. Figueroa St. // 213-624-1000
thebonaventure.com

The revolving bar on the 34th floor of an iconic L.A. hotel makes a **360-degree rotation in just under an hour**. It's the most efficient and *Mad Men*-chic way there is to see the city.

WP24
900 W. Olympic Blvd. // 213-743-8824
ritzcarlton.com

Wolfgang Puck's restaurant is on the 24th floor of The Ritz-Carlton, serving up a **panoramic view and modern Chinese dishes** like dan dan dumplings and lobster fried rice.

TO NEW HEIGHTS

71 vs. 71

A top-of-the-world war is waging in Downtown. The stakes? The title of L.A.'s loftiest, most awe-inspiring perch. DTLA's tallest skyscrapers pit their staggeringly high fine-dining restaurants—each on the 71st story—against each other.

71ABOVE
633 W. 5th St. // 213-712-2683 // 71above.com

At 950 feet, this gorgeously designed high-flier in the US Bank Tower is the ultimate date-night spot, with 360-degree panoramas and artfully composed dishes and tasting menus by chef Vartan Abgaryan. All tables are turned toward the view; there isn't a bad seat in the house. And the cocktails are worth the elevator ride alone.

LA BOUCHERIE
900 Wilshire Blvd. // 213-688-7777 // dtla.intercontinental.com

High up in the InterContinental hotel, the tallest building west of the Mississippi, this glassed-in dining room has jaw-dropping views, plus fanciful French-inspired steakhouse standards, an excellent wine list, and tons of charcuterie and cheese. VIP booths and privacy screens make for the perfect starlit private dinner.

TERI HATCHER
Actress, DTLA resident, founder of YouTube channel Hatching Change

BEST THING ABOUT DTLA *I love being able to walk to museums, coffee, music, breweries, bookstores, parks. I ride my bike around, too!*

FOOD SHOPPING *Urban Radish is the best curated spot for the finest edible offerings ever. They serve wonderful prepared foods—I've never had a lamb chop that wasn't perfectly medium-rare—and their wines offer obscure and delicious choices. Plus, there's great music on Wednesday nights!*

QUICK BITES *Back when Guerrilla Tacos was a food truck, I befriended the brilliant and sadly late Jonathan Gold as we waited in line for the duck hearts and persimmon special (which to this day is one of my favorites). I will never forget him and our conversations about food and life, and it all started over what have to be the best tacos in town.*

RESTAURANTS *ROW DTLA is the perfect place to find some special purchases. Have lunch at the Paramount Coffee Project; I love their tea, salads and toast. Or eat dinner at Rappahannock Oyster Bar, where every bite is a party in your mouth. There are plenty of places to just hang, read, check your computer, have a coffee and just breathe. Imagine that ... Downtown.*
—JOHN GRIFFITHS

GOURMET MEXICAN

GO FOR: *Throwback dishes*
Favorites get fancy at **Broken Spanish** (1050 S. Flower St. // 213-749-1460 brokenspanish.com), Ray Garcia's colorful modern-meets-classic cantina.

GO FOR: *Chorizo and papas tacos*
B.S. Taqueria (514 7th St. // 213-622-3744 // bstaqueria.com), Broken Spanish's little bro, excels at street eats like spicy ceviche and these beloved tacos.

GO FOR: *Tex-Mex*
Bar Amá (118 W. 4th St. // 213-687-8002 // bar-ama.com) skews toward the Texas-inflected—think queso with chorizo, Frito pie and enchiladas.

GO FOR: *Grilled Gulf shrimp tacos*
Border Grill (445 S. Figueroa St. // 213-486-5171 // bordergrill.com) has long set the standard for elevated modern takes on Mexican food.

GO FOR: *Grilled coastal cuisine*
Taking inspiration from the Yucatán, Baja and Oaxaca, **Pez Cantina** (401 S. Grand Ave. // 213-258-2280 // pezcantina.com) plays on vibrant Mexican dishes.

GO FOR: *Build-your-own nachos*
At **Corner Cantina** (630 W. 6th St. // 213-614-1900 // cornercantinala.com), make a mountain with everything from vegan queso to crispy pork belly and habanero salsa.

AMERICAN

BEST GIRL
927 S. Broadway // 213-235-9660
bestgirldtla.com

This all-day eatery inside the Ace Hotel is your chance to drool over impeccable crudo, oysters, pastas and even a **game-changing pork chop** by one of L.A.'s most beloved chefs, Michael Cimarusti (Providence).

BLACKSMITHS
117 Winston St. // 213-628-3847
blacksmithsla.com

"Elevated American" is the way this elegant Old Bank District gem is described, and the Southern-inflected menu—with items like buttermilk fried chicken, bacon truffle mac and cheese, and rye whiskey with smoked hickory honey—doesn't disappoint.

FAITH & FLOWER
705 W. 9th St. // 213-239-0642
faithandflowerla.com

You'll want to **dress up to dine** at this classy establishment, where the atmosphere and shared plates get A's for attractiveness. Order an English Milk Punch, then go to town on a panoply of proteins, veggies and pizzas.

MANUELA
907 E. 3rd St. // 323-849-0480 // manuela-la.com

It's not dinner, it's supper at this hip indoor-outdoor eatery and garden (with chickens!), where bites of cream biscuits and country ham, barbecued oysters, and beignets—with innovative cocktails, to boot—**transport diners to the South**.

OTIUM
222 S. Hope St. // 213-935-8500 // otiumla.com

This chic indoor-outdoor resto by The Broad embodies its name as a place where time is spent on leisure. There's no need to rush through creative cocktails and **fantastic New American plates**.

SIMONE
449 S. Hewitt St. // 424-433-3000
simoneartsdistrict.com

A stunning Art Deco dining room is the perfect setting for **James Beard Award-winner Jessica Largey's modern American cuisine** like abalone toast, grilled cabbage and ricotta dumplings. Leave time for impressive cocktails inspired by Arts District history in the Duello bar.

VERANDA
939 S. Figueroa St., Ste. 500 // 213-660-3032
verandadtla.com

The indoor/outdoor restaurant at the fantastically renovated Hotel Figueroa is **the perfect place for light bites during the day**, and dinner with a DJ backdrop (from the bar across the pool) at night. Flatbreads, salads, steaks and plancha-cooked branzino have a touch of seasonality.

WATER GRILL
544 S. Grand Ave. // 213-891-0900
watergrill.com

A **sustainable seafood–serving stalwart** since 1989, this refined restaurant excels at everything from chilled shellfish and bivalves to cioppino. A stiff martini pairs perfectly, as do the to-die-for sourdough rolls.

FRENCH

CHURCH & STATE
1850 Industrial St. // 213-405-1434
churchandstatebistro.com

The former 1925 Nabisco bakery is **a Francophile paradise** under chef Tony Esnault (page 36), who serves up steak frites and bouillabaisse in a charming bistro atmosphere. The cocktails are on point, too.

L.A. PRIME
The Westin Bonaventure Hotel and Suites, 404 S. Figueroa St., 35th Fl. // 213-612-4743
thebonaventure.com

Go for the prime beef, stay for the panoramic city view and **encyclopedic wine list** featuring hundreds of award-winning vinos. Seafood is also on the sophisticated menu, making surf and turf the right call.

LE PETIT PARIS
418 S. Spring St. // 213-217-4445
lepetitparisla.com

Husband-and-wife restaurateurs David and Fanny Rolland opened this **elegant two-story brasserie** back in 2015. While it's great for date night, it's also a beloved brunch spot, when classic French dishes are served up and mimosas flow freely.

ORIEL CHINATOWN
1135 N. Alameda St. // 213-253-9419
orielchinatown.com

This **photogenic little wine bar** is hidden under the Gold Line in Chinatown, but the classic French bites (like bavette steak and salad niçoise) and rare French wines make tracking it down worthwhile.

OUR FAVES - EAT -

ITALIAN

Rossoblu

BESTIA
2121 E. 7th Pl. // 213-514-5724 // bestiala.com

A shining star of the DTLA dining scene, Bestia serves up **creative multiregional Italian dishes** (pastas, pizzas, cured meats among them) in a hyper-masculine, loud, industrial space. (Note the meathook chandeliers.) Just be sure to make your reservations far in advance.

BOTTEGA LOUIE
700 S. Grand Ave. // 213-802-1470
bottegalouie.com

There's more to Bottega Louie than prized Technicolor macarons (still, don't miss them!). Italian staples including **particularly pretty pizzas** sit alongside Cali-influenced bites like portobello fries and avocado and chorizo toast.

CENTO PASTA BAR
128 E. 6th St. // 213-489-0131 // centopasta.com

This lunch-only pop-up—open indefinitely, thankfully—in wine bar Mignon is a **carb-lover's dream**. It's the most affordable handmade pasta in L.A., and maybe the most delish.

COLORI KITCHEN
429 W. 8th St. // 213-622-5950
colorikitchen.com

Italian countryside cuisine wows in the big city. Family-run and laid-back, it's all about rustic, authentic dishes that are easily customizable. Order the fettuccine Alfredo and BYOB.

DRAGO CENTRO
525 S. Flower St., Ste. 120 // 213-228-8998
dragocentro.com

Old World flavors undergo modern transformations with the help of **super-fresh ingredients** and contemporary techniques. Colorful creations and hand-cranked pastas shine in this large, marble-clad space.

FACTORY KITCHEN
1300 Factory Pl., Ste. 101 // 213-996-6000
thefactorykitchen.com

A reclaimed factory in the Arts District got a second—decidedly more delicious—life as a North Italian trattoria, churning out **mouthwatering traditional fare** that's rich in flavor.

GIULIA
701 W. 7th St. // 213-279-5025 // giuliadtla.com

When cravings hit for chic, modern Italian—think beautiful zucchini blossom and burrata pizzas, drool-worthy salumi—Giulia is the answer. Bonus: Most plates are **served until 2 a.m.**

MACCHERONI REPUBLIC
332 S. Broadway // 213-346-9725
maccheronirepublic.com

The name of this South Broadway staple should give a hint to its specialty: pasta. **Homey organic pastas** are handmade fresh daily in fanciful shapes and rival any Italian grandma's.

MIRO
888 Wilshire Blvd., Financial District
213-988-8880 // mirorestaurant.com

Charcuterie boards and big steaks, **wood-fired pizzas** and hand-made pastas are hallmarks to this bustling restaurant. Don't miss the extensive whiskey selection and "vault" in the basement lounge.

OFFICINE BRERA
1331 E. 6th St. // 213-553-8006 // officinebrera.com

This sleek and sophisticated spot is straight out of Northern Italy, serving up hearty meat dishes, homemade pastas and a few seafood standouts. **Ask about the off-menu farinata**, a chickpea pancake that draws raves from diners.

OLIVE BISTRO & CATERING
619 S. Olive St. // 213-327-1186
olivebistrocatering.com

Order in or go out, one thing is assured: It will hit the spot. This affordable, casual hideaway executes generous portions of all the standards flawlessly in a **warm, friendly atmosphere**.

ORSA & WINSTON
122 W. 4th St. // 213-687-0300 // orsaandwinston.com

Known for tasting menus of artfully plated dishes that span flavors from Italian to Asian, this restaurant with only 33 seats warrants a reservation.

PASTA E PASTA BY ALLEGRO
432 E. 2nd St. // 213-265-7003

Talk about turning Japanese. The new addition to Honda Plaza, hailing from Japan, turns out **heaping plates of squid ink pasta**, carbonara and uni spaghetti, best washed down with a draft Asahi or Italian vino.

ROSSOBLU
1124 San Julian St. // 213-749-1099 // rossoblula.com

Chef Steve Samson focuses on Bologna, beautifully represented in the pure expressions of **grandmotherly cooking**—like soul-warming tortellini en brodo—served family style (page 32).

TERRONI
802 S. Spring St. // 213-221-7234 // terroni.com

A 1924 bank-turned-restaurant, Terroni is as eye-catching as its food is authentic. **Passed-down Italian family recipes**—pizzas, pastas and addictive apristomaco—are unmodified, and stand the test of time. Also an excellent destination for oenophiles, the restaurant features an extensive list of Old World wines available in the adjoining grocery shop, Dopolavoro.

TESTA
1111 S. Hope St. // 213-973-5013 // testadtla.com

This South Park spot brings **romantic lighting and Italian inspiration** to the neighborhood alongside dishes that could pass as vibrant Californian. Craft cocktails like Hope Passion (bourbon and apple brandy) up the ante.

TOMGEORGE
707 S. Grand Ave. // 424-362-6263
tomgeorgela.com

Who says Italian food has to be made by Italians? This **Hungarian export** mixes covetable-cool design with modern, seasonal creations that reference the boot-shaped country as well as the Mediterranean and California.

GLOBAL

Plum Tree Inn's Sweet and Pungent Shrimp, Garlic Sauce with Vegetables, Vegetable Spring Rolls and Mai Tai

SZECHUAN STOP

The Classic Choice

For decades, **Plum Tree Inn** has been Chinatown's go-to culinary outpost for authentic—and addictive—Chinese favorites and Szechuan specialties, made with love and high-quality ingredients. Succulent and savory dishes aren't the only reasons to visit the spacious, elegant spot; their famous mai tais are hands-down the city's best.

PLUM TREE INN
913 N. Broadway // 213-613-1819 // plumtreeinn.com

BADMAASH
108 W. 2nd St. // 213-221-7466 // badmaashla.com

The menu at this beloved Indian spot (the name is Hindu for "badass") reflects its owners' Indian heritage and Canadian upbringing. Customers fall in love with the **fused flavors** of dishes like the Chicken Tikka Poutine, while a Bollywood-meets-Warhol design beckons a young, hip clientele.

BARCITO
403 W. 12th St. // 213-415-1821 // barcitola.com

Inspired by Buenos Aires' breezy corner cafés, this is a casual place for **inventive empanadas** (think jam and cheese), salads and sandwiches by day, and octopus grilled on the plancha and a Chegroni by night.

BAVEL
500 Mateo St. // 213-232-4966 // baveldtla.com

As busy as its sibling Bestia, this bustling haven with plants hanging from the rafters is jam-packed with Ori Menashe fans angling for his **inventive take on traditional Middle Eastern fare**. Must-gets include duck 'nduja hummus, foie gras halva and lamb neck shawarma, plus amazing desserts such as rose clove chocolate donuts.

BLOSSOM RESTAURANT
426 S. Main St. // 213-623-1973
blossomrestaurant.com

Sit inside or on the sidewalk of this popular Vietnamese spot to enjoy pho and other regional dishes. The restaurant itself is sleek and modern, a nice juxtaposition with its traditional take on **healthy, Saigon-style food**. Blossom's sophisticated wine list is a bonus.

BREVA
939 S. Figueroa St., Ste. 300 // 213-660-3006
brevadtla.com

This stunning Basque-inspired bistro at the renovated Figueroa Hotel is **where Southern California meets the Mediterranean**. Casey Lane's menu adds to the ambience with **everything from flatbreads to fish** (try the Vermouth-braised halibut). Spanish-style gin and tonics are a specialty.

DAMA
612 E. 11th St. // 213-741-0612
damafashiondistrict.com

In the same Fashion District pocket as Rossoblu, this **pan-Latin spot** is all about snacking and sipping with wild abandon. Set in a former banana warehouse, expect tastes (like clams and chorizo) from hideaways like Cuba, Colombia and beyond. Cocktails take a turn toward the tropics.

THE EXCHANGE RESTAURANT
416 W. 8th St. // 213-395-9531
freehandhotels.com/los-angeles/the-exchange

Vibrant colors and multicultural dishes pop inside this all-day restaurant clad in honey-hued wood. Though representative of urban L.A., the offerings **celebrate Israeli flavors** down to the drinks, like the yogurt-infused Kefir & Honey.

FOGO DE CHÃO
800 S. Figueroa St. // 213-228-4300 // fogo.com

One of the newest locations from the international churrascaria chain, this Brazilian steakhouse is a meat-lover's haven, where **servers slice from slabs of meat** (filet mignon, ancho ribeye, pork loin) tableside.

LASA
727 N. Broadway, #120 // 213-443-6163 // lasa-la.com

Run by two brothers, this **Filipino-American restaurant celebrates familial ties** and Southern California cooking. Hidden in the Far East Plaza in Chinatown, this casual gem is worth seeking out for lunch or dinner. Try the pancit noodles tossed with butter, calamansi lime and egg yolks cured with fish sauce.

LITTLE SISTER
523 W. 7th St. // 213-628-3146 // littlesisterla.com

In a city filled with pho restaurants, Little Sister offers a break from the norm with **contemporary Vietnamese cuisine**. While Little Sister bills itself as "East-meets-West-inspired dishes," *L.A. Times* food writer Jonathan Gold dubbed chef Tin Vuong's style "anti-fusion cooking." Expect modern dishes with traditional flavors.

MAJORDŌMO
1725 Naud St. // 323-545-4880 // majordomo.la

Only a celebrity chef like David Chang of New York's Momofuku could anchor a restaurant of this caliber in a previously no-man's-land neighborhood on the far edge of Chinatown. It's big and bustling, neither fully Korean nor American, and **great for groups to share giant smoked short ribs**, noodles, whole steamed fish and more.

PEKING TAVERN
806 S. Spring St. // 213-988-8308
pekingtavern.com

This underground gastropub is known for its '90s Beijing vibe and for serving up **street-style dishes** like delectable Sichuan fish dumplings (the red oil garlic sauce produces a numbing sensation) and hand-pulled noodles (made in the glass-walled kitchen). Also, it's the only place for Chinese baijiu cocktails.

DTLA BOOK 2019 117

WOLFGANG PUCK
Chef/owner, WP24

BEST THING ABOUT DTLA *I love the young, contemporary vibe of Downtown L.A. It has an energy that separates itself from the rest of the city.*

RESTAURANTS *Some of my favorite places to go in Downtown include—in addition to WP24—The Factory Kitchen, majordōmo and Otium.* —J.G.

GLOBAL Continued

PREUX & PROPER
840 S. Spring St. // 213-896-0090
preuxandproper.com

For **New Orleans delicacies** (po' boys, jambalaya, étouffée), head to this open-air patio with daiquiris downstairs. Whether you're seeking the hedonism of Bourbon Street or the refined beauty of the Garden District, you'll find it here.

RICEBAR
419 W. 7th St. // 213-807-5341 // ricebarla.com

One of **DTLA's first Filipino restaurants**, it serves up modern takes on comfort dishes. Seating is extremely limited at this fast-casual spot, where you'll craft a rice bowl from traditional Filipino flavors.

UNCLE JOHN'S
834 S. Grand Ave. // 213-623-3555
unclejohnsdtla.com

A Chinese-American diner may sound one-note, but actually the decades-old Downtown staple serves hangover-busting breakfasts and favorites like honey shrimp over noodles, and shifts to an **authentically Cajun seafood boil** at night.

WOODSPOON
107 W. 9th St. // 213-629-1765 // woodspoonla.com

You've likely never had **Brazilian food** like this, inspired by the country's African, European and Indian influences, served in an intimate shabby-chic environment. Not a steakhouse, it serves traditional street food, like its signature chicken pot pie with hearts of palm.

WURSTKÜCHE
800 E. 3rd St. // 213-687-4444 // wurstkuche.com

Open 'til 1:30 a.m. every night, Wurstküche is Downtown's **go-to spot for sausages** (served on fresh rolls with a variety of toppings and mustards) and Belgian fries. If you're feeling adventurous, the exotic sausages are what you've been lookng for.

QUICK BITES

PIZZA

Choose-Your-Own Toppings
Make the ultimate personal pizza at **800 Degrees Neapolitan Pizzeria** (800 Wilshire Blvd. // 213-542-3790 // 800degreespizza.com); it cooks in minutes.

Sweet Mary
Some call it extreme pizza, but strawberries, chicken and smoked bacon taste surprisingly good at **Baldoria** (243 S. San Pedro St. // 213-947-3329 baldoriadtla.com) in Little Tokyo.

Big Kahuna
While you can BYOP—build your own pizza—at **Firenza Pizza** (300 S. Grand Ave. // 213-687-8999 // firenzapizza.com), they're on to something with their ham, bacon and pineapple pie.

Mac 'n' Cheese Pizza
The carbo-loading extravaganza made famous at **Pizzanista!** (2019 E. 7th St. // 213-627-1430 // pizzanista.com) is only available on Sundays.

Salami Honey
Get a slice or whole pie of spicy salami with buckwheat honey at the hidden-gem **Superfine Pizza** (1101 San Pedro St., Unit F // 323-698-5677 superfinepizza.com).

The Ode
In a pizza rut? Try **Lupetti Pizzeria**'s (710 E. 4th Pl. // 213-415-1938 // lupettipizzeria.com) Brooklyn-style pie featuring pantaleo (a unique aged goat's milk cheese), almonds and rosemary.

The Sicilian
Topped with mozzarella, creamy ricotta, pesto and tomatoes, the square pie (or slice!) is a dream at Little Tokyo's new **Prime Pizza** (141 S. Central Ave. // 213-256-0011 // primepizza.la).

Margherita
Run and owned by Italians who use real Italian ingredients, the **Sixth + Mill Pizzeria and Bar** (1335 E. 6th St. // 213-629-3000 // sixthandmill.com) specialty might be the most authentic.

The Veggie
Like the WeHo original, this classic NYC-style, thin-crust pizza full of veggies is the ultimate in unpretentiousness at **Vito's** (124 W. 4th St., Harlem Alley // 213-816-1700 // vitosdtla.com).

A pie at Vito's

TACOS

CASA LA DOÑA
800 S. Main St. // 213-627-7441

When you're craving **flavorful Mexican**, head to this casa for tacos on homemade corn tortillas and an extensive salsa selection. On Tuesdays they'll only set you back $1 (tortillas are premade).

CHICA'S TACOS
728 S. Olive St. // 213-896-0373 // chicastacos.com

It may be tiny, but their tacos are **big on flavor**. Choose steak, chicken, pork, fish or veggie and enjoy your (quite hefty) meal at a communal picnic table out back.

GUERRILLA TACOS
2000 E. 7th St. // 213-375-3300
guerrillatacos.com

The **brick-and-mortar spot of Wes Avila's popular truck** has even more tacos, plus margaritas, murals and more in the Arts District.

GUISADOS
541 S. Spring St. // 213-627-7656 // guisados.com

This local chain is considered the gold standard by Angelenos. It's **great for simple tacos** on corn tortillas with fillings from chicharrón to veggie. Can't decide? Try the mini-taco sampler.

SONORATOWN
208 E. 8th St. // 213-290-5184 // sonoratownla.com

Pop into this 12-seater cooking **Sonora-style dishes** for carne asada tacos on fresh flour tortillas and fantastic agua frescas. (See page 37.)

FRIED CHICKEN

BIRDIES
314 W. Olympic Blvd. // 213-536-5720
birdiesla.com

If you're seeking something sweet to accompany that **fried bird craving**, look no further. Order a chicken sandwich or classic breast and wing, but leave room for a homemade doughnut.

COMFORT L.A.
1110 E. 7th St. // 213-537-0844
comfortla.net

At the **go-to spot for soul food** Downtown, you can't go wrong with the dinner special, consisting of five fried chicken wings, a piece of cornbread and two sides, from which you can choose collard greens, mac 'n' cheese and more. Heaven.

HOWLIN' RAY'S
727 N. Broadway, #128 // 213-935-8399
howlinrays.com

Anthony Bourdain famously threw shade at this Nashville-bred fad, which has seen **waits of up to two hours**. But the arrestingly spicy fried stuff the chef hates, many others adore.

LUCKY BIRD
317 S. Broadway // luckybirdla.com

This new Grand Central Market stall is all about gorgeously golden-fried bird. Lemon and herbs are what make the **extra-crispy coating** taste so good, and sides like pickled vegetables, macaroni salad, potato salad and biscuits are perfect accompaniments.

POKE BOWL

OHANA POKE CO.
735 S. Figueroa St., Mezzanine Level 1
ohanapokeco.com

Specializing in **true Hawaiian grindz**, chef Eric Park's poke bowls (and fried chicken!) are full of flavor, heirloom sushi rice and quality fish.

OKIPOKI
507 S. Spring St. // 213-628-3378 // okipokila.com

L.A.'s **Hawaiian poke obsession** gets the fusion treatment with cheekily named bowls (Straight Outta Tofu) and sushi burritos.

SWEETFIN POKE
735 W. 7th St. // 213-599-8050
sweetfinpoke.com

A modern space is the perfect place for **bright, fresh flavors to pop**. Build your poke bowl atop rice, kelp noodles or kale.

OTHERS

DUNE
199 W. Olympic Blvd. // 213-628-3586 // dune.kitchen

It's hard to choose between the **organic green falafel** with shoestring potatoes, lamb with turmeric yogurt, and fried eggplant with hummus and an eight-minute egg, but all come on housemade flatbread and tons of flavor and color.

KTCHN DTLA
428 S. Hewitt St. // 323-316-5311 // ktchndtla.com

Serving eggs all day, sandwiches and tasty sides, this spot **inside an Airstream trailer at Resident DTLA** is perfect for a lunch on the patio or a bite in between Resident's live music sets.

PHILIPPE THE ORIGINAL
1001 Alameda St. // 213-628-3781
philippes.com

This 1908 Chinatown institution serves nothing but old-school deli faves like **French Dip** at slightly nostalgic prices.

SPREAD MEDITERRANEAN KITCHEN
334 S. Main St. // 213-537-0284
spreadkitchen.com

Part of **L.A.'s Mediterranean moment** is this flavorful, vegan-friendly eatery with mix-and-match options (za'atar fried chicken) and Greek fro-yo.

URTH CAFFÉ
451 S. Hewitt St. // 213-797-4534
urthcaffe.com

Though "fast casual" technically describes this **ultra-relaxed café**, it's where many people take it slow, loitering over organic coffee, fresh-baked treats, artisan salads and sandwiches.

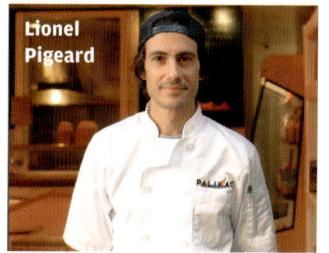

HEALTHY BITES

Art in a Bowl

Parisian restaurateur Lionel Pigeard opened his dream concept in DTLA's historic core, a charming Middle Eastern–influenced cafe featuring healthy build-your-own bowls. The name **Palikao** pays homage to his grandmother's hometown in Algeria, as well as to the cuisine he grew up eating, everything from pita wraps to tabbouleh, hummus, shakshuka and more. When you want to DIY your lunch, pick a base of either couscous or quinoa, then add proteins like merguez sausage, Moroccan-spiced chicken tagine or grilled keftas, plus fresh seasonal vegetables and sauces. It's like an artistic endeavor in bowl form.

PALIKAO
130 E. 6th St. // 213-265-7006 // pali-kao.com // Instagram: @palikaocouscous

OUR FAVES - EAT -

RAMEN

Rakkan Pearl salt ramen

RAMEN REPORT

Japanese Import

At the first U.S. location of **Rakkan**, a popular Tokyo ramen chain, the soup is as authentic as it gets. Unlike the ubiquitous and heavy bone-based broths, theirs are umami-packed and light. Shoyu, salt and miso soups are vegetable-and olive oil–based, and imported straight from the source. Minimalist décor allows flavors from Tokyo-style ramen, karaage (fried chicken) and miso eggplant to shine bright.

The newest Rakkan menu

RAKKAN RAMEN
359 E. 1st St. // 213-680-4166 // rakkaninc.com

A Ramen Broth Guide

LIGHT SALT / SHOYU / FISH / VEG BROTH

Hailing from Yokohama and Tokyo, the soy sauce–based shoyu broth is almost always clear, featuring chicken, vegetables or fish for the base.

For great vegan options: **DTLA RAMEN**
952 S. Broadway // 213-265-7641 // dtlaramen.com

For vegetable-based umami broth: **RAKKAN RAMEN**
359 E. 1st St. // 213-680-4166 // rakkaninc.com

HEAVY TONKOTSU BROTH

This style of broth was conceived in Hakata City, northwest of Kyushu. It can vary, but is usually a thick white soup made from pork bones. It's sometimes called tonkotsu (pork bone) ramen.

For filling soup with a wait: **DAIKOKUYA**
327 E. 1st St. // 213-626-1680 // dkramen.com

For free extra noodles: **HAKATA IKKOUSHA**
368 E. 2nd St. // 213-221-7920 // hakataikkoushausa.com

To select your own toppings: **SHIN SEN GUMI HAKATA RAMEN**
132 S. Central Ave. // 213-687-7108 // shinsengumigroup.com

Japanese Specialties

For karaage: **KARAYAMA**
136 S. Central Ave. // 213-265-7358

For kappo: **SHIBUMI**
815 Hill St. // 213-265-7923 // shibumidtla.com

For robata: **INKO NITO**
225 S. Garey St. // 310-999-0476 // inkonitorestaurant.com

For shabu shabu: **KAGAYA**
418 E. 2nd St. // 213-617-1016 // kagaya.dla.menuclub.com

For udon noodles: **MARUGAME MONZO**
329 E. 1st St. // 213-346-9762 // marugamemonzola.com

For yakitori: **HATCH YAKITORI & BAR**
700 W. 7th St., Ste. G600 // 213-282-9070 // hatchyakitori.com

Learn more words on the opposite page in the Go Little Tokyo section.

Kazunori

SUSHI & SASHIMI

HAMA SUSHI
347 E. 2nd St. // 213-680-3454 // hamasushila.com

Sushi connoisseurs know Hama is all about purity. There are no noodles or tempura bites here, and no flash. The intimate Little Tokyo favorite doles out **melt-in-your-mouth sashimi** that attracts lines.

KAZUNORI
421 S. Main St. // 213-493-6956
kazunorisushi.com

Calling itself "the original hand roll bar," KazuNori takes pride in being a first-of-its-kind sushi spot, serving only **made-to-order hand rolls** of crispy nori, warm rice and the freshest of seafood. An offshoot of Sugarfish, it has the same attention to detail with a more casual vibe.

KOMASA SUSHI
351 E. 2nd St. // 213-680-1792 // komasasushi.com

Locals line up at this Little Tokyo sushi den—**a staple for 20 years** with its 10-seater sushi bar and half a dozen tables—especially during peak hours. And it's for good reason, as it's hard to find fresher, better quality nigiri, sashimi and rolls than at this intimate spot.

Q SUSHI
521 W. 7th St. // 213-225-6285 // qsushila.com

With just 26 sought-after seats within its exposed brick walls, Q delivers **painstakingly perfect Edomae** (Tokyo style) cuisine. Chef Hiroyuki Naruke adheres to tradition when preparing his rice and imported seasonal fish, worth every pretty penny.

SUGARFISH BY SUSHI NOZAWA
600 W. 7th St. // 213-627-3000 // sugarfishsushi.com

Sushi surprises abound at this **renowned nigiri mecca**. Doing things the old-fashioned way is an option, but trust us, order Trust Me: seven enlightening courses of warm rice, creamy fish, hand rolls and edamame.

SUSHI ENYA
343 E. 1st St. // sushienya.com

There's usually a line to get into this **sweet little gem**, but it's worth the wait for the delicacies created at the hand of chef Kimiyasu Enya. Omakase is only available by reservation (ask for a seat at the bar), but a la carte orders will feature high-quality fish and excellent presentation.

SUSHI GEN
422 E. 2nd St. // 213-617-0552 // sushigen-dtla.com

Located in Honda Plaza, **sushi-lovers flock here for the sashimi deluxe plate**, which arrives at your table loaded with the day's freshest fish. It's a popular spot for an inexpensive lunch, too, even among some of the city's most renowned local chefs.

SUSHI ZO
334 S. Main St. // 424-201-5576 // sushizo.us

For special occasions there is no sushi sampler as storied as this stark white spot's **$160-per-person omakase** feast. Expect to experience perfect harmony between the neta (seafood) and shari (rice).

DELICIOUS LITTLE TOKYO

Meet and Eat All the Dishes!

CURRY · ONIGIRI · MATCHA · TEMPURA · GYOZA · RAMEN · MOCHI · YAKITORI · IMAGAWAYAKI · SUSHI

As one of Los Angeles' most vibrant cultural hubs, Little Tokyo is a historic and extremely walkable neighborhood full of unique destinations and landmarks, from incredible foodie finds to family-owned businesses that have made this corner of Downtown L.A. special for generations. Let **Go Little Tokyo** help you uncover all that there is to taste and see!

CURRY: Curry House, 123 Astronaut Ellison S. Onizuka St., #204
GYOZA: Daikokuya, 327 E. 1st St.
IMAGAWAYAKI: Mitsuru Café, 117 Japanese Village Plaza Mall
MATCHA: Tea Master, 450 E. 2nd St.
MOCHI: Fugestu-do, 315 E. 1st St.
ONIGIRI: Nijiya Market, 124 Japanese Village Plaza Mall
RAMEN: Kouraku, 314 E. 2nd St.
SUSHI: Sushi Gen, 422 E. 2nd St.
TEMPURA: Suehiro, 337 E. 1st St.
YAKITORI: Torigoya, 123 Astronaut Ellison S. Onizuka St., #203

GO LITTLE TOKYO

A Little Tokyo Community Council (LTCC) project developed and produced by Community Arts Resources (CARS) and made possible with support from Metro.
golittletokyo.com // Instagram: @golittletokyo

Learn more about Go Little Tokyo

OUR FAVES – EAT –

Inko Nito

IZAKAYA / ROBATA

INKO NITO
225 S. Garey St. // 310-999-0476
inkonitorestaurant.com

This beautifully designed robata restaurant seats 124 diners. **Charcoal cooking is king here**, with choices from crab tartare to pork ribs in a whiskey glaze.

IZAKAYA GAZEN
362 E. 1st St. // 213-613-1415
e-k-c.co.jp/gazen/la

Whether you're new to Japanese food altogether or a huge fan, this is a good place to start. Between **shabu shabu, the izakaya menu and sushi options**, you can't really go wrong. Be sure to get the tofu sampler, featuring tofu made in-house every morning.

IZAKAYA & BAR FU-GA
111 S. San Pedro St. // 213-625-1722
izakayafu-ga.com

It's not easy to find, but this sleek spot serves up **small plates, steaks and sushi in its underground lounge**. (You'll have to look for the tiny street-level sign.) Tradition is shrugged off for what is basically a Japanese take on delicious bar food and inventive fusion.

KINJIRO
424 E. 2nd St. // 213-229-8200 // kinjiro-la.com

Octopus ceviche, beef tongue and the bone-marrow dengaku are but three stars of the menu at this quiet Little Tokyo spot, **an artisanal izakaya** that serves both traditional and new-school small plates.

SAKE DOJO
333 E. 1st St. // 213-234-0957 // sakedojola.com

From the owners of neighborhood favorite Far Bar comes this **Tokyo-style, open-air izakaya**. The sake list is extensive with hard-to-find bottles and sake on tap, offered as flights to sample it all. Need help? Ask the sake sommelier.

GASTROPUB / TAPAS

BLUE COW KITCHEN
350 S. Grand Ave. // 213-621-2249
bluecowkitchen.com

Offering $6 cocktails, wines and sangria margaritas, happy hour here (4-6:30 p.m. on weekdays) is a guaranteed good time. Popular among those who work nearby, Blue Cow offers a ton of delicious small bites and a **casual patio area** in the middle of Downtown.

BRACK SHOP TAVERN
525 W. 7th St. // 213-232-8657
brackshoptavern.com

A love of sports isn't necessary to enjoy this comfy tavern, but games are always on as the kitchen churns out **comfort food like bacon-topped twice-baked potatoes** and bartenders shake up original cocktails.

THE EIGHT BAR
788 S. Grand Ave. // 213-873-4745
wholefoodsmarket.com

The location of this gastropub may surprise would-be patrons who find it inside Whole Foods. With a hip ambience, outdoor patio, **evening DJ and themed nights** (Taco Tuesday), The Eight Bar is more like a 10.

MIKKELLER DTLA
330 W. Olympic Blvd. // 213-596-9005
mikkellerbar.com

Expansive, high-ceilinged and glass-clad, this **craft beer heaven** hits a high note, pouring dozens of brews—not to mention kombucha and cold brew—and passing satisfyingly savory plates at all hours.

PATTERN BAR
100 W. 9th St. // 213-627-7774 // patternbar.com

This atmospheric bar takes its place in the Fashion District to heart, honoring iconic designers with **"haute" cocktails** named Lagerfeld and Chanel. Vibrant small plates and fashion-appropriate salads are the finishing touch.

PRANK
1100 S. Hope St. // 213-493-4786 // prankbar.com

An **open-air, walk-up bar** makes for perhaps DTLA's most pleasant place to drink. On-tap kombucha, cocktails made with experimental terpene (an anti-inflammatory oil from cannabis) and delectable bites don't hurt the cause.

PUBLIC SCHOOL 213
612 Flower St. // 213-622-4500
psontap.com

Throw it back to school days during Recess, aka happy hour, which, like lunch and dinner at this craft beer-slinging gastropub, features **grown-up, gourmet twists on lunchroom faves**: meatballs, PB&J and tots.

THE STOCKING FRAME
911 S. Hill St. // 213-488-0373
thestockingframe.com

It's a coffee shop during the day, but starting with happy hour (5-7 p.m. at the bar), it becomes a late-night spot with **cleverly concocted cocktails and sophisticated eats**. Plan to run into urban hipsters seeking craft beers and deep conversation.

YVETTE NICOLE BROWN
Actress (*Community*; Disney's remake of *Lady and the Tramp*)

RESTAURANT *At Simone, besides the amazing food courtesy of chef Jessica Largey, it's the décor! Every room tells its own story. Every area of Simone is crafted to be so welcoming, a delicious space for those who love good eats and ambience.*

MUSEUM *I love the GRAMMY Museum! Walking through those exhibits feels like home in the best way.*

TREATS *Birdies!!! Donuts, coffee and chicken! All complete perfection and they are open 24 hours a day from Friday to Sunday evening. They create donut art! GO!!!* —J.G.

THE MUST-ORDER

DTLA Specialty Burgers

100-DAY DRY-AGED BURGER, $23
It's all about the beef in **Belcampo Meat Co.**'s raclette- and caramelized onion-topped stunner.
Grand Central Market, 317 S. Broadway
213-625-0304 // belcampomeat.com

THE KIM PARK LEE, $9.75
Bulgogi, cheddar, kimchi and **Meatzilla**'s signature sauce are an undeniable combo.
646 S. Main St. // 213-623-3450
meatzilladtla.tumblr.com

THE SHACKBURGER, $5.69
Shake Shack has opened a new DTLA location, drawing crowds to taste the burger that made Danny Meyer a hit around the world.
801 Hill St. // shakeshack.com

SIMPLE BURGER, $10
The prime beef chuck and Tillamook cheddar burger at **Everson Royce Bar** sets the standard.
1936 E. 7th St. // 213-335-6166 // erbla.com

THE PATTY MELT, $12.79
The new **Cassell's Hamburgers** serves the diner classic: house-ground beef, oozy cheddar and grilled onions on toasted rye.
421 W. 8th St. // 213-372-5601
cassellshamburgers.com

THE BLACK SHEEP, $8
Topped with Gouda, arugula, caramelized onions and garlicky aioli, **The Black Sheep**'s eponymous burger is perfect with smothered tater tots.
126 E. 6th St. // 213-689-5022

THE IMPOSSIBLE TRUFFLEMAKER, $14
The impossibly good vegan patty comes topped with miso mustard, charred green chile salsa and truffle fondue at **Umami Burger**'s two outlets.
852 S. Broadway // 213-413-8626
738 E. 3rd St. // 323-263-8626
umamiburger.com

COURTESY MODERN TIMES

LATE NIGHT AND 24/7

24/7 RESTAURANT AT THE STANDARD
550 S. Flower St. // 213-439-3030 // standardhotels.com

Open 24 hours. Surprise, surprise—a big draw of this all-night diner is its consistent, no-brainer hours of operation. Comfort food is served all day to hotel guests and post-party revelers from either the mod counter or the party-ready patio.

BÄCO MERCAT
408 S. Main St. // 213-687-8808 // bacomercat.com

Open until midnight Friday and Saturday; 11 p.m. Monday through Thursday. Prolific chef Josef Centeno's trademarked bäco flatbread is joyously available until late at this hopping neighborhood spot. End-of-the-evening specials start at 10 p.m. during the week, 11 p.m. on weekends, and include Bäcobeer for $5.

BIRDIES
314 W. Olympic Blvd. // 213-536-5720 // birdiesla.com

Open 24 hours on Friday and Saturday. All kinds of late-night cravings are sated on weekends at this part-coffee, part-doughnut, part-fried chicken solution. The original chicken sandwich is crisp and juicy, while the made-on-the-hour artisanal pastries wow in a slew of inventive flavors.

COMFORT L.A.
1110 E. 7th St. // 213-537-0844 // comfortla.net

Open until 3 a.m. Thursday through Saturday; midnight Sunday through Wednesday (closed Monday). Soul food doesn't get more authentic in all of Downtown than at this go-to for the bar-hopping crowd. Fried chicken, collard greens and mac 'n' cheese are clearly made with love.

THE ORIGINAL PANTRY CAFE
877 S. Figueroa St. // 213-972-9279 // pantrycafe.com

Open 24 hours. This diner, open since 1924 and accepting only cash ever since, is rumored to not even have a lock on its door. The nostalgic stop is perfect for an old-school plate of steak and eggs or a late-night stack of buttermilk pancakes.

WURSTKÜCHE
800 E. 3rd St. // 213-687-4444 // wurstkuche.com

Open until 1:30 a.m. daily. When the sidewalk hot dog carts won't do the trick, there's Downtown's go-to for artisanal grilled sausages on fresh rolls, Belgian fries and craft brews. Exotics like rattlesnake and rabbit make for good late-night dares.

The Dankness Dojo by Modern Times

VEGETARIAN / VEGAN

BEELMAN'S
600 S. Spring St. // 213-622-1022 // beelmans.com

Like many an Angeleno, this former pub dropped the meat and went vegan. With an **Asian-Pacific bent**, its kitchen prepares plant-based fare—faux hot dogs, Impossible "meat" burgers—with tiki cocktails and craft beer.

CAFÉ GRATITUDE
300 S. Santa Fe Ave. // 213-929-5580
cafegratitude.com

This favorite spot among local veggies is a SoCal chain seeking to **promote consciousness and sustainability** by serving nothing but organic, plant-based food such as salads, sandwiches, wraps and warm entrées.

THE DANKNESS DOJO BY MODERN TIMES
832 S. Olive St. // 213-878-7008
moderntimesbeer.com

This brewery and restaurant serves over 30 tap beers and **a full menu of plant-based cuisine**. Think battered and fried seitan, onion rings, salads and meatless burgers.

P.Y.T.
400 S. Main St. // 213-687-7015 // pytlosangeles.com

Chef Josef Centeno's latest creation puts **veggies center stage**, featuring in-season produce from local farms in mouthwatering combos. But while veggies rule, you'll still find uni and ribeye on the menu, plus plenty of cheese and butter.

SHOJIN
333 S. Alameda St., Ste. 310 // 213-617-0305 // theshojin.com

This **upscale vegan and macrobiotic Japanese** spot holds its customers' health in the highest regard, which is why it replaces the fish you'd normally find in rolls and ramen with spicy tofu.

WILD LIVING FOODS
760 S. Main St. // 213-266-8254
wildlivingfoods.com

"Live Dirty, Eat Clean" is the slogan of this vibrant corner space in the Fashion District serving **raw food, smoothies and dairy-free gelato** alongside cold-pressed juices bottled in glass. The Gorilla Milk (cucumber, kale, almonds, dates, green apples and pink salt) is a fan favorite.

ZINC CAFE & MARKET
580 Mateo St. // 213-825-5381 // zinccafe.com

Serving up **vegetarian takes on American comfort food** (pizzas, burgers, sandwiches), this restaurant offers both a courtyard and a sleek dining room. Mixology lounge Bar Mateo sits out back.

OUR FAVES - EAT -

SWEET TOOTH

Little Damage's activated charcoal soft serve ice cream

Infinite Mint, Divine Dips' Vegan Ice Creme

SOFT SERVE SPOTLIGHT

The Big Chill

I scream, you scream, we all scream for…charcoal ice cream?! Step outside your comfort zone and into **Little Damage**, where rotating adventurous flavors—including one vegan option—are nothing short of innovative. The family-owned shop prepares their ice cream daily in small batches, using local ingredients supplied by organic dairy farmers. Don't forget to Instagram that freshly rolled signature black cone, naturally colored with activated charcoal.

LITTLE DAMAGE
700 S. Spring St. // 213-534-8363 // littledamage.com // Instagram: @little.damage

CREAMY + RICH

Vegan Goodness

This gleaming little shop on the edge of the Historic Core, **Divine Dips Vegan Ice Creme** is proof that vegan ice cream can be amazing. Owner Diane Jacobs uses all plant-based ingredients for unique flavors like turmeric-rich Bombay Gold, Black Sesame, NY Cheesecake and the beloved Infinite Mint. Try that last one in their signature classic brownie sundae (gluten-free as well)—divine indeed.

DIVINE DIPS VEGAN ICE CREME
601 S. Los Angeles St. // 213-265-7785 // divinedipsicecreme.com
Instagram: @divinedipsdtla

MORE ICE CREAM & GELATO

FOR ECO-MINDED CYCLISTS: PEDDLER'S CREAMERY
458 S. Main St. // 213-537-0257 // peddlerscreamery.com

FOR FLAVOR ADVENTURERS: SALT & STRAW
829 E. 3rd St. // 213-988-7070 // saltandstraw.com

FOR GELATO CONNOISSEURS: GELATERIA ULI
541 S. Spring St., Ste. 104 // 213-900-4717 // gelateriauli.com

FOR KOREAN CREATIONS: IHWAMUN ICE CREAM
333 Alameda St. // 213-537-0380 // ihwamun.com

FOR WAFFLE LOVERS: THE DOLLY LLAMA
611 S. Spring St. // thedollyllama.com

BIG MAN BAKES
413 S. Main St. // 213-617-9100 // bigmanbakes.com

This little Historic Core shop is a big magnet for those with a sweet tooth. Home of **incredibly moist, fluffy cupcakes**, the flavor rotation includes everything from red velvet to lemon and carrot. Best part: There are bite-size cakes for more mixing and matching.

BOTTEGA LOUIE
700 S. Grand Ave. // 213-802-1470
bottegalouie.com

Best known for their **French macarons and picturesque dessert cases**, the Downtown icon is part restaurant, grand market and patisserie, all under one gorgeous roof.

CAFÉ DULCE
134 Japanese Village Plaza // 213-346-9910; and ROW DTLA, 777 Alameda St., #150 // 213-536-9633
cafedulce.co

The **bacon doughnut made them famous**, but you'll find a full menu of breakfast and lunch items along with coffee, tea and matcha.

FUGETSU-DO
315 E. 1st St. // 213-625-8595 // fugetsu-do.com

A Little Tokyo staple since 1903, this tiny shop serves up a bit of history in each bite of **beautifully handmade mochi in various flavors** (green tea or strawberry are the most popular). Don't miss: seasonal red bean-filled rice cakes called manju.

THE PIE HOLE
714 Traction Ave. // 213-537-0115
thepieholela.com

This sleek local chain serves up **both sweet and savory from-scratch pies**—some by the slice, some personal hand pies—to Downtown denizens looking for a tasty treat. A slice is perfectly paired with The Pie Hole's medium-roast coffee, available as espresso, drip coffee or cold brew.

BENJAMIN MILLEPIED
Founder, L.A. Dance Project

QUICK BITE Guerrilla Tacos is a cool place. I love the food and atmosphere. It's a good place to take my staff out for margaritas after a big meeting.

CAFFEINE FIX Maru Coffee is close to the studios and our office. I love the sleek and simple design. Their matcha green tea latte with almond milk is the best.

RESTAURANT The Exchange has incredible food and incredible design.—J.G.

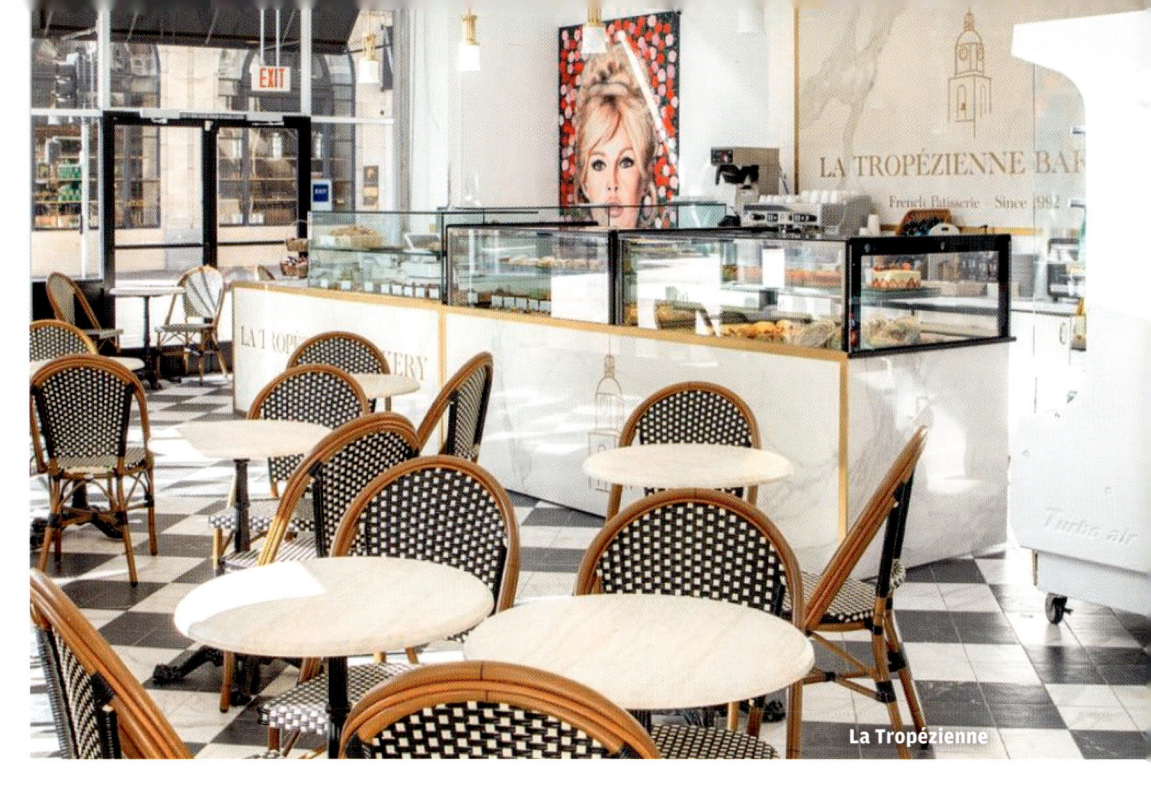

La Tropézienne

BREAKFAST / LUNCH

BLU JAM CAFE
541 S. Spring St., #110 // 213-266-8909
blujamcafe.com

The Spring Arcade is now home to an airy, expansive outpost of the **uber-popular brunch paradise**. Waits are almost guaranteed on weekends, but so is supreme satisfaction thanks to the magic made with eggs.

BRUNCH DTLA
718 S. Los Angeles St. // 213-944-8326

Inside a small food court is an extensive selection of **well-priced fusion dishes** (Thai and Korean among them). Local faves are the bibimbap breakfast burrito and creative waffles.

LATELY
970 N. Broadway #114 // 413-353-4276
eatlately.com

Proving good food can come from just about anywhere, this window-only (for now—a full restaurant is coming soon) spot serves **tasty bites like chicken-fried steak sandwiches** and rosemary Liège waffles to Chinatown crowds six days a week.

POPPY & ROSE
765 Wall St. // 213-995-7799 // poppyandrosela.com

Known for **American comfort food** (think chicken and waffles), this casual Flower District spot (open as early as 6 a.m. and serving breakfast, lunch and brunch 'til 3 p.m.) takes its inspiration from a Southern country kitchen.

STRADA EATERIA & COFFEE
119 E. 5th St. // 213-822-4558 // stradadtla.com

Expect global eats running from **sensational ceviche to sammies** and service with a giant smile at this eatery that stands out for its sworn-by Turkish coffee, sand-brewed for smoothness.

BAKERIES

BREAD LOUNGE
700 S. Santa Fe Ave. // 213-327-0782
breadlounge.com

From **house-made focaccia to Jerusalem bagels, plus quiche, soups and salads**, decisions aren't easy at this Arts District bakery and cafe.

LA TROPÉZIENNE
757-761 Main St. // 213-988-7282 // ltbakery.com

With a mural of Brigitte Bardot, this French cafe and bakery has everything from the **flakiest croissants to colorful macarons, quiche and more.**

PITCHOUN BAKERY & CAFÉ
545 S. Olive St. // 213-689-3240
pitchounbakery.com

The **artisan breads, gorgeous pastries and cakes are all made in-house,** along with salads, sandwiches and more at Pitchoun (an affectionate term meaning "kiddo" in French).

OUR FAVES - EAT -

JUICE & AÇAI BOWLS

AMAZEBOWLS
300 S. Santa Fe Ave. // 323-610-2099
amazebowls.com

The output at this Arts District açai go-to **couldn't be more Instagram-able**. Do your followers—and your belly—a favor with the Coconut Amazebowl, topped with fresh and dried fruit, granola and edible flowers.

PRESSED JUICERY
860 S. Los Angeles St. // 213-688-9700
pressedjuicery.com

Geared toward those seeking **cold-pressed juices for a cleanse** (and those seeking out the milkshake-like almond milk concoctions), Pressed Juicery sells a variety of fresh formulas perfect for a detox.

Three Hot Properties

1. Far Chinatown
No one quite knows what to call this little warehouse-heavy pocket, but Far Chinatown seems to be sticking. Chef David Chang was the first to anchor his debut L.A. restaurant, **majordōmo**, here, with New York's famed **Apotheke** cocktail bar opening right next door. Brooklyn-based music venue **Baby's All Right** is expected soon. With **Highland Park Brewery**'s tasting room, and the forthcoming **Angeleno Wine Company** throwing open their doors to the public, there's a food-and-drink crawl in the making along northern Spring Street. (See pages 7 and 14.)

2. Hewitt & 4th Place
There are still some Arts District corners to be discovered, like 4th Place near Hewitt Street, anchored by **Urth Caffe** and **Resident**, a hybrid bar, beer garden and music venue. Now there's also Jessica Largey's gorgeous Art Deco-inspired restaurant **Simone** and bar **Duello**. Along 4th Place, hidden newcomers **Lupetti Pizzeria** and **In Sheep's Clothing** (a hi-fi cocktail bar with heavy rotation of Japanese whiskies and jazz records) are helping make this one of the most dynamic new micro-neighborhoods.

3. City Market South
Building a neighborhood from one that didn't really exist before is no easy feat. However, when you get a couple of the city's top chefs involved, plus nightlife impresarios and coffee enthusiasts, a lot can happen. Chef Steve Samson and wife Dina were one of the first to put their stamp on this enclave of unused and historic warehouses in the Fashion District. **Rossoblu** is dedicated to creating food from Bologna with a SoCal twist. Now they also have **Superfine Pizza** for amazing pies next door. Across a courtyard, **Dama** has debuted a pan-Latin vibe with food from Antonia Lofaso and cocktails (yay, blended drinks!) from Steve Livigni and Pablo Moix. Coffee connoisseurs can pick up their expertly pulled espresso from **Cognescenti**. It's all just a short walk from quirky shopping area Santee Alley and the Bendix Building, a new haven for art galleries.

Juice Crafters' raw cold-pressed juice Greenest Plus #3.5

JUST THE JUICE

Nectar Nirvana

Live well and be well is the mantra at **Juice Crafters**, the rustic-chic Spring Street bar acclaimed for cold-pressed juices, wellness shots, powerhouse smoothies and açai bowls. Using only fruits and veggies handpicked by local farmers and delivered daily, these ultra-fresh raw organic ingredients deliver over-the-top flavor and nutrition. This is the place where healthy habits take hold.

JUICE CRAFTERS
702 S. Spring St. // 213-689-4555 // juicecrafters.com // Instagram: @juicecrafters

COFFEE / TEA

The light and airy interior of Don Francisco's Coffee Casa Cubana at the Spring Arcade building

CAFÉ CULTURE
Latin Flavor

Don Francisco's Coffee, the L.A.-born brand with more than 140 years of history, brings a new tropical oasis to DTLA's Spring Arcade. Patrons of the beautiful all-day café will experience Cuba not only in handcrafted coffee drinks, authentic house-made bites, and beer and wine, but also in affable charm that makes everyone family.

DON FRANCISCO'S COFFEE CASA CUBANA
541 S. Spring St., Ste. 124 // 213-537-0323 // dfcasacubana.com

---

BLUE BOTTLE COFFEE
582 Mateo St. // 300 S. Broadway
213-621-4194 // bluebottlecoffee.com

This newly trendy caffeine chain—selling beans and home brewing equipment along with its drinks and pastries—is beloved for its New Orleans-style iced coffee.

CAFE DEMITASSE
135 S. San Pedro St. // 323-844-3233
cafedemitasse.com

A spot for coffee obsessives, this café specializes in **Kyoto iced coffee** (which drips for over 14 hours in a weird alchemy contraption).

GIORGIPORGI
137 E. 3rd St. // 213-687-7753 // giorgiporgi.com

A **moss-laden tunnel** opens to a minimalist Italian-style espresso bar serving up quality coffee. (No Wi-Fi.)

GO GET 'EM TIGER
827 E. 3rd St. // gget.com

This hip growing local chain now has an Arts District spot for **perfectly pulled espressos and specialties like turmeric lattes**. An outpost at ROW DTLA is next.

IL CAFFE
855 S. Broadway // 213-612-0331 // ilcaffe.se

Find **Scando style**, Stumptown beans and house-made sammies at this Swedish coffee chain.

NO GHOST BEARS
305 E. 8th St., Ste. 103

Don't be intimidated by the punk rock attitude of this shop with sidewalk tables using **Japan's slow-roasting style**.

PHILZ COFFEE
801 S. Hope St. // 213-213-2616
philzcoffee.com

Specializing in its **own "secret blends,"** this Bay Area-based chain serves up custom blendeds, like the mint mojito iced coffee.

VERVE COFFEE ROASTERS
833 S. Spring St. // 213-455-5991 // vervecoffee.com

With its worldy roasts, **living plant wall** and home-brew kits, this Verve outpost with a relaxing patio is a magnet for creative types in the Fashion District.

Sharing your dessert tea is caring.

TEA TREATS
Dessert Goals

The "fluffy" tea trend is sweeping the country, and **Little Fluffy Head Cafe** was one of the first to bring the delicious sippable dessert to the West Coast. What's cheese tea exactly? The base is refreshing iced tea, like jasmine green or rose oolong tea, topped with a creamy, dreamy whipped cheese cloud. Flavor combos abound, like milk tea topped with coffee cream to matcha smothered in a crème brûlée cloud. Sweet and a little savory, it's the perfect treat.

LITTLE FLUFFY HEAD CAFE
203 W. 7th St. // 213-266-8495 // littlefluffyhead.com // Instagram: @littlefluffyhead

FOOD COURT / DINING DISTRICT

CORPORATION FOOD HALL

724 S. Spring St. // corporationfoodhall.com

The latest debut in L.A.'s food court scene is this seven-eatery collection, which comprises known restaurants, new concepts and now-stationary food trucks. **Buddha Belly** is an example of the latter, and, as the first brick-and-mortar by the Arroy food truck masterminds, doles out the same eclectic Southeast Asian fare. In fact, the selection at this food hall seems to circle the globe. **Funculo** serves a plethora of freestyle pastas, and **Soom Soom** (meaning "seed" in Hebrew) cooks up a 100-year-old falafel recipe and offers a salad bar of fresh Mediterranean flavors. At **South City Fried Chicken**, the crispy, golden free-range bird gets topped with crazy things like rojo red bean hummus on sandwiches. There are dumplings and more at the new **Gyoza Boyz**, while **Bardonna** keeps it simpler with easy salads, sandwiches and worth-the-trip coffee.

SPRING STREET ARCADE

541 S. Spring St. // springarcadebuilding.com

Built in 1924, this covered corridor in the historic Spring Arcade Building offers ways to sate every craving from breakfast (**Blu Jam Cafe**) to dessert (**Gelateria Uli**) to after-dinner drinks (**Clayton's Public House**). You'll also find amazing tacos at **Guisados**, wine and snacks at **Garçons de Café**, and modern takes on traditional Cantonese barbecue at **Ricebox**.

GRAND CENTRAL MARKET

317 S. Broadway // grandcentralmarket.com

L.A.'s original food court has been around for 100 years, yet still manages to attract crazy long lines for the likes of **Eggslut**, the wildly popular breakfast sandwich sanctuary. More than 30 food and beverage stalls make for a full experience—grab a falafel salad at **Kismet Falafel**, a smoothie at **Press Brothers Juicery**, then a scoop or two from the legendarily good **McConnell's Fine Ice Creams**. Addictive Asian food comes courtesy of **China Cafe**, **Sari Sari Store** and **Sticky Rice**, while **Wexler's Deli**'s new-traditional Jewish deli goods are just classic enough. **Belcampo Meat Co.** is among purveyors that sell both mouthwatering prepared foods and raw ingredients. And there's **Knead & Co. Pasta Bar + Market**, which hawks sustainably sourced staples and fresh pasta made like an Italian-by-way-of–New Jersey *nonna* would. Newcomers include modern takes on throwback sandwiches at **PBJ.LA**, and fried chicken madness at **Lucky Bird**.

SMORGASBURG LA

785 Bay St. // la.smorgasburg.com

The instantly legendary Brooklyn-born food market—a spinoff of Brooklyn Flea—has found a happy West Coast home at the five-acre ROW DTLA. Some 75 food and shopping vendors gather with their goodies every Sunday from 10 a.m. to 4 p.m. It's the place to discover up-and-coming businesses and cuisines. Standouts include **Hot Star**, selling giant pieces of Taiwanese-style fried chicken, and **Goa Taco**, a fusion spot featuring paratha, a flaky, buttery hybrid between tortilla and croissant. (Don't miss the crispy pork belly.) **Lobsterdamus**, for whole grilled lobster and lobster fries, and **Wanderlust Creamery**, for incredibly smooth scoops in cute colorful cones, are other hits.

L.A. LIVE

800 W. Olympic Blvd. // lalive.com/eat

When it comes to dining options, L.A. LIVE is an embarrassment of riches. You'll have plenty of restaurants to choose from depending on your vibe for the night, like **Yard House** with more than 160 beers on tap, **Triple 8 China Bar & Grill** for modern Chinese/Cantonese food, **Fleming's Prime Steakhouse & Wine Bar**, **Katsuya** for innovative sushi platters or **Rosa Mexicano** which prepares guacamole tableside—just to name a few. You can even hit the bowling lanes at **Lucky Strike**.

DINE X FIG

california pizza kitchen
coco fresh tea & juice
five guys
george's greek grill
gulp sushi alehouse
indus by saffron
the melt
mendocino farms
morton's the steakhouse
new moon café
ohana poké co.
oleego by parks bbq
pazzo gelato
pizza studio
salata
sprinkles cupcakes
starbucks
twist & grill

Hungry? We've Got 18 Restaurants & Eateries!

FIGAT7TH DOWNTOWN LA

THE INTERSECTION OF LIFE X STYLE

@FIGat7th FIGat7th.com

735 S. Figueroa St. · Downtown L.A. · Across from the 7th Street / Metro Center Station

OUR FAVES - DRINK -

HAPPY HOUR

BÄCO MERCAT
408 S. Main St. // 213-687-8808
bacomercat.com

From 5:30-7 p.m. Monday through Thursday, this **hopping neighborhood spot** offers great deals on fave food and drink items, like the bäco, a flatbread combining the best of pizza, tacos and gyros.

BLUE COW KITCHEN
350 S. Grand Ave. // 213-621-2249
bluecowkitchen.com

Offering $6 cocktails, wines and sangria margaritas, happy hour here (4:30-6:30 p.m. on weekdays) is a guaranteed good time. Popular among those working nearby, Blue Cow offers a ton of delicious small bites—think poke lettuce tacos and wings—and a casual patio area in the middle of Downtown.

COLE'S RED CAR BAR
118 E. 6th St. // 213-622-4090
colesfrenchdip.com

The restaurant is **renowned for its French Dip sandwiches**, but Red Car Bar is particularly popular among Downtown denizens for its happy hour, offering classic cocktails such as old-fashioneds and cheap eats from 3-7 p.m.

DISTRICT
711 S. Hope St. // 213-612-3185
districtdtla.com

From 2-7 p.m. daily, the bar and lounge areas offer incredibly great deals, including can't-miss Moscow Mules, wine and craft beer, $6 to $7 each. Small dishes of arugula hummus, tenderloin-and-kimchi tacos, tamari deviled eggs and shishito peppers are three for $22.

LAS PERLAS
107 E. 6th St. // 213-988-8355
213dthospitality.com

Five-dollar margaritas at this mezcal-bar favorite aren't super strong, but that just means you can have more. Palomas are also $5 from 5-8 p.m. on weekdays, and weekends from 1-8 p.m.

MEZCALERO
510 S. Broadway // 213-628-3337
mezcalerodtla.com

Every day from 3-7 p.m., this mezcal mecca serves specialty cocktails and beer, wine and **well drinks for a mere $3-$7**, but Tuesday 3 p.m.-midnight is the real get: $3 tacos and half off agave spirits (tequila and mezcal).

POUR HAUS WINE BAR
1820 Industrial St. // 213-327-0304
pourhauswinebar.com

Discover delectable bites—like papitas bravas and **flatbread white pizza—for just $5** at this daily 4-7 p.m. happy hour, which also boasts $5 vino (including sparkling!), sangria and beer.

SPRING STREET BAR
626-B S. Spring St. // 213-622-5859
springstbar.com

This laid-back bar and sandwich shop runs specials on its **tasty sammies and brews from 3-7 p.m., seven days a week.**

THE STOCKING FRAME
911 S. Hill St. // 213-488-0373
thestockingframe.com

It's a coffee shop during the day, but starting with **happy hour (weekdays 3-7 p.m. in the bar)**, it becomes a late-night spot with cleverly concocted cocktails and sophisticated eats. Plan to run into urban hipsters seeking craft beers and deep conversation.

Old Fashioned at Cole's Red Car Bar

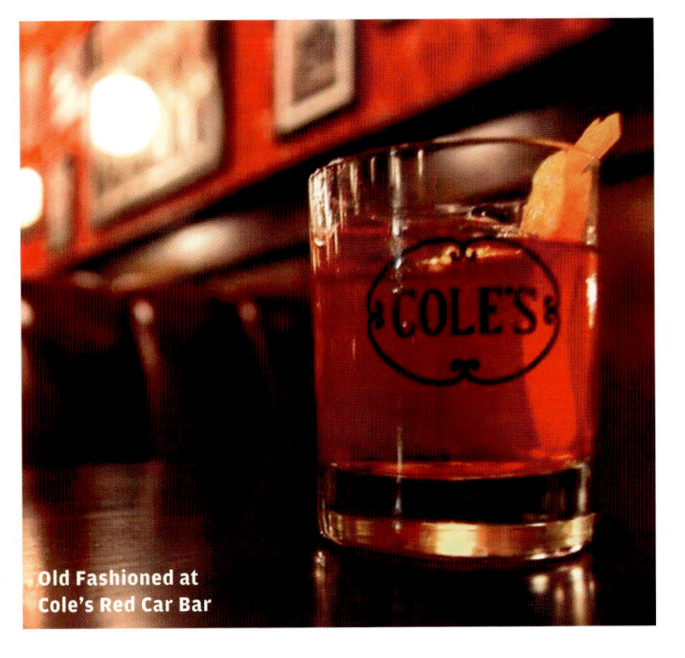

Apotheke LA

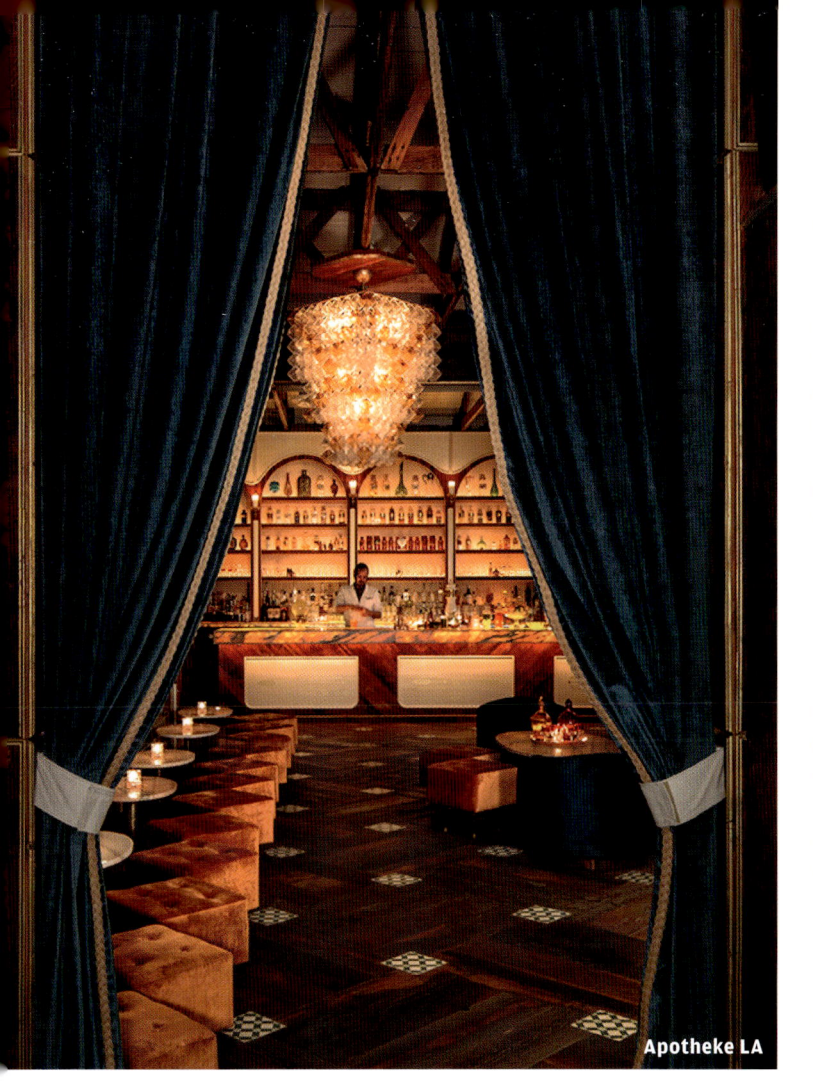

ONE OF A KIND

APOTHEKE LA
1746 N. Spring St. // 323-844-0717

The NYC bar best known for its **apothecary vibe and "prescription list" drink menu** has finally made its way to L.A. over by the L.A. River.

THE EDISON
108 W. 2nd St. // 213-613-0000
edisondowntown.com

Take in a live band—or a silent movie projected onto the walls—while enjoying inexpensive apps and reduced-price beer, wine and cocktails, every Wednesday through Friday (5-7 p.m.) at this **steampunk-meets-Art Nouveau spot**, formerly L.A.'s very first power plant.

EIGHTYTWO
707 E. 4th Pl. // 213-626-8200 // eightytwo.la

The "barcade" concept comes alive at this Arts District hot spot, where clever mixology mixes with **classic arcade games and pinball**. The cocktail menu features drinks with 8-bit-inspired names, plus caffeinated options (made with local roaster LAMILL coffee) to keep your mind sharp during long bouts of Ms. Pac-Man.

PACIFIC SEAS
648 S. Broadway // 213-627-1673
cliftonsla.com

Tucked inside Clifton's, through the Art Deco Map Room, is a **tiki-themed speakeasy** (with a dress code) that takes drinkers on a journey to the South Seas. Just the right amount of kitsch plus faves like a Navy Grog and Rum Barrel make it a sure bet.

RHYTHM ROOM LA
206 W. 6th St. // rhythmroomla.com

The rhythm is bound to get you in this **'20s-era underground jazz lounge**-turned-bar serving up infectious live music, billiards, shuffleboard and board games alongside craft cocktails and cold brew.

RUDOLPH'S BAR & TEA
416 W. 8th St. // 213-437-9496
freehandhotels.com

Tea time gets liquored up at this **vintage-feeling craft cocktail bar** inside the Freehand hotel lobby. Along with the traditional service are small plates (plus particularly yummy shoestring fries) and tea-infused concoctions such as Coquito con Matcha and the Russian Tea G&T.

SEVEN GRAND
515 W. 7th St. // 213-614-0736
sevengrandla.com

Built to resemble a **vintage hunting lodge** (think Don Draper's bar of choice), the emphasis here is on a well-curated whiskey selection so massive that it requires a bar-mounted ladder. While weekend evenings can get a bit raucous, happy hour offers a mellow spot to imbibe a Manhattan or an old-fashioned.

SPEAKEASIES

BAR JACKALOPE
515 W. 7th St., 2nd Fl. // 213-614-0736
barjackalope.com

There's an old-school vibe in this **hidden backroom bar inside Seven Grand** spotlighting U.S. and Japanese whiskeys.

BIRDS & BEES
207 S. Broadway // 213-537-0510

Find **mellow retro '50s vibes** at this secretive subterranean speakeasy, an industrial yet cozy lair for throwback classics and original recipes named after the likes of Lucille Ball and Ella Fitzgerald.

CAÑA RUM BAR
714 W. Olympic Blvd. // 213-745-7090
canarumbar.com

Featuring more than 250 varieties of the sugarcane spirit, this spot seeks to **elevate rum-based cocktails** you know and love. The bar's convivial crowd enjoys daiquiris, mojitos and Caña's popular rum punch.

EL DORADO
416 S. Spring St. // 213-621-7710 // eldo-stowaway.com

In the **historic El Dorado Hotel's basement** is a craft cocktail bar where you'll discover impeccable libations with zero attitude, plus DJs, occasional live jazz and 5-9 p.m. happy hour Wednesday through Sunday.

IN SHEEP'S CLOTHING
710 E. 4th Pl. // 213-415-1937
insheepsclothinghifi.com

Inside Lupetti Pizza, this hidden cafe and cocktail bar is inspired by Japan's kissaten, or hi-fi lounge, trend. The cozy space features coffee and **cool vinyl vibes** during the day and Japanese whiskies and jazz records at night.

THE SLIPPER CLUTCH
351 S. Broadway // 213-265-7477
theslipperclutch.com

Step back in time by stepping into the back room of Bar Clacson, where **vintage pinball machines and '80s arcade games** dot the funky, neon-lit space. Cocktails are $10 and include well-made classics like Jack Daniel's with housemade ginger syrup.

THE STREAMLINER
800 N. Alameda St. // thestreamlinerbar.com

This vintage-inspired cocktail lounge adjacent to the Imperial Western Beer Co. at Union Station is a **hidden gem for highballs and classic cocktails**. The midcentury vibe is alive and well with billboard ads from the 1940s and '50s.

THE VARNISH
118 E. 6th St. // 213-265-7089
thevarnishbar.com

Hidden behind iconic sandwich shop Cole's, this dark and moody spot serves up sophisticated old-school-era cocktails. **The 1920s serve as inspiration** here—for the bartenders, who are clad in suspenders; for the finely crafted daiquiris, Manhattans and gin fizzes; and for the clientele, who keep their drink-in-hand conversations hushed.

OUR FAVES - DRINK -

NEIGHBORHOOD BARS

Clayton's throwback vibe for the cocktail crowd

Clayton's signature cocktail, Modesta Avila

PUB LIFE

Classic Sips

A creative collage of forgotten time, **Clayton's Public House** is a lighthearted artistic rendering of what Victorian life would've been like if it included fish and chips and milk punch. It's fin de siècle in the Historic Core, with vintage photos and décor paying homage to the turn of the 20th century. There are 32 craft beers on tap, including many from local Southern California breweries, plus rare international beers and signature bygone-era craft cocktails. From the kitchen come elevated takes on classics for brunch, lunch and dinner.

CLAYTON'S PUBLIC HOUSE
541 S. Spring St. // 213-863-4327 // claytonspub.com // Instagram: @claytonsdtla

HISTORIC CORE

BAR CLACSON
351 S. Broadway // 213-265-7477 // barclacson.com

No pretense, only fun at this friendly bar with a comfortably lived-in aesthetic. Eighteen taps deliver brews, ciders and even cocktails; **bartenders work fast**, giving patrons plenty of time for foosball, pétanque and Pac-Man.

BAR FRANCA
438 S. Main St. // 213-935-8515 // barfranca.com

Tunnel vision isn't so bad when cocktails are involved. This **quirky little spot with floral décor**, long bar and high ceilings welcomes anyone with a curiosity for unique spirits and classically cool concoctions.

BERNADETTE'S
361 S. Broadway // 213-628-3354
bernadettesla.com

This throwback-themed drinking den does pretty much everything right, from allowing dogs inside to creating the perfect patio for sipping rotating frosé or IPA (check the palm-print board) while people-watching. It's decked in **primo midcentury décor**, with an enviable Garfield phone as the crowning touch.

BROADWAY BAR
830 S. Broadway // 213-614-9909
213hospitality.com

Part of the first wave of the Downtown renaissance, this **circular bar inside a Gothic Revival building** was one of the first to attract imbibers and history buffs alike. With cream and silk shades, lots of brass and smoking patios with views of historic theaters out front, it's a snazzy spot for a sip.

COLE'S RED CAR BAR
118 E. 6th St. // 213-622-4090 // colesfrenchdip.com

This famed French Dip restaurant has been a cherished landmark since 1908, and when you step up to Red Car's 40-foot bar, you'll feel like you've stepped back in time. Recalling the spot's own early years with penny-tiled floors and historic photos, the cocktails here—**classic but creative and changing with the seasons**—are timeless.

GOLDEN GOPHER
417 W. 8th St. // 213-614-8001
goldengopherbar.com

Formerly owned by President Teddy Roosevelt, this historic spot—a little retro and a lot glamorous—is now home to strong drinks and a liquor to-go booth where spirits and six-packs of beer are available for takeaway.

THE KING EDDY
131 E. 5th St. // kingeddyla.com

One of Downtown's favorite spots for cheap drinks, light bites and a round or two of darts, this spot has been **serving L.A.'s locals and visitors since 1933** (and bootlegging before that, according to the bar owners). Enjoy more than a dozen beers and a wide range of no-frills cocktails. Author John Fante used to hang out here. (Read about Fante on page 40.)

LOVE SONG BAR
450 S. Main St. // 213-284-5728

This place is groovy, literally. The reclaimed wood-clad craft cocktail lounge inside the revamped Regent theater not only boasts a vintage piano, but also a record player on which classic vinyl constantly spins. Top tunes are complemented by **cleverly named "rocktails"** like Black Flagg's Rise Above and Houses of the Holy.

SPRING STREET BAR
626-B S. Spring St. // 213-622-5859
springstbar.com

Happy hour isn't the only reason to visit this industrial-styled beer bar (a full selection of liquor is also on hand), but it's a darn good one. The centrally located brew hub **features 26 taps serving suds that pair particularly well with sandwiches**.

WENDELL
656 S. Main St. // 213-622-7200 // wendellbardtla.com

Named for Wendell Green, who opened some of the city's most legendary bars, the motto of this two-story space is "keep it simple." The beer selection ranges from **local drafts to cans of PBR (you won't find bottles here)**, which pairs nicely with a hot dog and the rock-filled old-school jukebox.

THE WOLVES
519 S. Spring St. // 213-265-7952
thewolvesdtla.com

It's like stepping into Paris during La Belle Époque, except this is the historic Alexandria Hotel in Downtown L.A. Only **incredibly fancy cocktails** (think: many ingredients, all made in-house, high-end spirits, etc.) could match this stunningly designed bar filled with antiques and vintage everything, and they don't disappoint. Even more discerning? Try the Le Néant omakase cocktail experience upstairs.

FASHION DISTRICT

CRANE'S BAR DOWNTOWN
810 S. Spring St. // 323-787-7966

Look for the neon "Cocktails" sign over the door of this mellow bar **inside an old bank vault**—perfectly positioned for a few bourbon cocktails before or after dinner at Terroni. Quirky décor, retro gaming consoles and a jukebox ramp up the fun.

DAMA
612 E. 11th St. // 213-741-0612
damafashiondistrict.com

Set up in the City Market South complex, in a former banana warehouse across from Rossoblu, cocktails here take a **turn toward the tropical**, including blended daiquiris and piña coladas.

PATTERN BAR
100 W. 9th St. // 213-627-7774
patternbar.com

Located in the Fashion District (hence the name), here's a bar that's as stylish as its patrons. The black-and-white décor is simple and sleek, with gigantic windows that make it a great place to drink and be seen. Keeping with the bar's fashionable theme, the **cocktails are named after fashion's finest**.

FINANCIAL DISTRICT

SHOO SHOO, BABY
717 W. 7th St. // 213-688-7755
shoobabyla.com

Take a trip back in time to the '40s inside the vintage-themed bar named for a WWII-era song by The Andrews Sisters about loving an enlisted man. Great vibes blend beautifully with cocktails like the perfect Moscow Mule and cheekily named Piss 'n Vinegar.

SOUTH PARK

FIRST DRAFT KITCHEN & TAPROOM
1230 S. Olive St. // 213-536-5267
firstdraftdtla.com

This Denver import lets you **pour your own draft beer** from more than 70 taps—with the appropriate prepaid wristband, that is. Also on tap are wine, cider cocktails and kombucha, plus snacks and bar food.

HANK'S BAR
840 S. Grand Ave. // 213-623-7718

Perfect for a **stiff drink with zero pretense** before heading to the nearby STAPLES Center, this hole-in-the-wall, attached to the lobby of the Stillwell Hotel, is the definition of a dive bar. It's the most packed when there's a game on TV, but you likely won't have a hard time finding a spot at the bar.

PRANK
1100 S. Hope St. // 213-493-4786
prankbar.com

An **open-air, walk-up bar** in South Park known for its inventive pairings, imperfect mischief and bitchin' music is a bar we can get on board with. At the helm is Dave Whitton, the guy behind Villains Tavern. Between that and the vegan nachos, things are off to a promising start for Prank.

LITTLE TOKYO

BALDORIA
243 S. San Pedro St. // 213-947-3329
baldoriadtla.com

Fantastic $8 pizzas during happy hour (4:30-7 p.m.) attract patrons to this chic, **welcoming** eatery/bar with a plethora of mouthwatering bites and sips.

FAR BAR
347 E. 1st St. // 213-617-9990 // farbarla.com

A favorite among beer aficionados, this spot has more than 30 selections on tap and hundreds of whiskeys.

THE MERMAID
428 E. 2nd St. // themermaidla.com

Like an underwater oasis, the tropical theme is strong at this cozy little bar. Aqua blues and seafaring lanterns set the stage for **tiki-leaning concoctions** like the Mermaiden Voyage, made with two rums and hibiscus, and boozy snow cones.

MISHEL PRADA
Actress, star of the Starz series *Vida*

HANGOUT *I have a huge soft spot for the nostalgic kitsch left over from L.A.'s history, and Clifton's Republic is an icon unlike any other place in L.A. It pulls you into a whimsical forest complete with a giant redwood tree, fossilized dinosaur eggs, a waterfall and so many other bizarre things. Go upstairs and drink in the tiki bar that's every bit the campy classic you wish you could be..*

NEIGHBORHOOD *Little Tokyo. I love to grab a bowl of ramen at Daikokuya and then head over to Nijiya Market supermarket. I get lost browsing and buying all the Japanese treats like melon cream soda, bento boxes and honestly the best produce.*

QUICK BITES *When I'm in serious need of comfort food, I find it at Guisados. This is not a typical street taco; this is food you find in a Mexican home. Which isn't surprising because Guisados is a family-run business and these are the de la Torre family recipes. They put so much love into their food. I order the quesadilla con chorizo. It's a giant slab of grilled panela cheese tucked into one of their thick, warm, handmade tortillas alongside crumbled chorizo.* —J.G.

ILLUSTRATION BY BRIAN BUSCH

NEIGHBORHOOD BARS Continued

Genbei San No Onikoroshi (aka The Demon Slayer) at Sake Dojo

SAKE DOJO
333 E. 1st St. // 213-234-0957 // sakedojola.com

From the owners of Far Bar comes this Tokyo-inspired restaurant and bar. Along with sushi and Japanese izakaya-style dishes, the **sake list is extensive** with hard-to-find bottles and sake on tap. Need help? Ask the sake sommelier.

WOLF & CRANE BAR
366 E. 2nd St. // 213-935-8249
wolfandcranebar.com

Japanese whiskey, small-batch American spirits and local craft beer are the specialties here. Whiskey connoisseurs are smart to splurge on a flight.

ARTS DISTRICT

EVERSON ROYCE BAR
1936 E. 7th St. // 213-335-6166 // erbla.com

Head through E.R.B.'s orange door for a welcoming night of cocktails, great eats and casual conversation. Its Arts District location guarantees a hip crowd, and the cocktail program—**best enjoyed on the spacious back patio** with the bar's comfort food options—is truly inspired.

GUERRILLA TACOS
2000 E. 7th St. // 213-375-3300
guerrillatacos.com

There's a full bar and wide array of tequila and mezcal cocktails to go along with the sweet potato taco and hamachi tostadas. Don't miss the **umami-rich micheladas**.

TONY'S SALOON
2017 E. 7th St. // 213-622-5523
tonyssaloon.com

Check the chalkboards inside for an extensive list of mezcal and other spirits on hand at this **dark dive bar, formerly a hangout of hipster hero Hunter S. Thompson**. Shoot pool, enjoy the jukebox, throw some darts or play ping-pong between drinks, and when you get hungry, you can order a slice from Pizzanista next door.

CHINATOWN

GENERAL LEE'S
475 Gin Ling Way // 213-625-7500
generallees.com

This **craft cocktail–slinging dance spot** is where the legendary Frank Sinatra once drank and bartenders can school patrons in artisanal gin and pour a vodka Red Bull.

MELODY LOUNGE
939 N. Hill St. // 213-625-2823

At this little hole-in-the-wall, a simple exterior gives way to a **gorgeous interior of vaulted ceilings and Chinese lanterns.** Creative cocktails and beer on tap fuel fun-seekers through long nights.

WITH LIVE MUSIC

DOWN & OUT
501 S. Spring St. // 213-221-7595
downandoutbar.com

Open 365 days a year, Down & Out offers everything from **video games and ping-pong during "game night" to karaoke backed by a live band.** DJs spin on weekends, with local and touring bands on deck weekdays.

THE ESCONDITE
410 Boyd St. // 213-626-1800 // theescondite.com

The name means "the hideout," and for good reason. Don't tell them we blew their cover, but this Little Tokyo dive bar is a **hidden gem and local favorite**. They offer an extensive burger menu, outdoor patio and live music from local bands.

FIVE STAR BAR
267 S. Main St. // 323-428-4492
fivestarbardtla.com

On the quest for **the ultimate dive bar**, add Five Star to your list. It offers more than 50 domestic and craft beers. The space is outfitted with billiards, art on the walls and a small stage for live bands to play while you rock out.

HAM & EGGS TAVERN
433 W. 8th St. // 213-891-6939
hamandeggstavern.com

Since 2012, this intimate hole-in-the-wall (**part beer-and-wine bar, part live-music setup**) has been treating patrons to small-scale rock concerts by local and indie bands. Drawing a crowd of regulars, it has achieved the impossible: respectable wines with a house-party vibe, perfect for the aging hipster.

LA CITA
336 Hill St. // 213-687-7111 // lacitabar.com

Don't come to La Cita unless you're ready to party. With a vast beer selection, its reputation as a Latin bar belies its **diverse clientele, from punks and hipsters to locals on the hunt for no-frills daytime drinks**. The divey spot dedicates different nights to different dance parties, so you'll want to check the calendar for what's in store, as rockabilly, punk, reggae and Latin cumbia beats are all on the roster.

THE LEXINGTON BAR
129 E. 3rd St. // 213-291-5723
thelexingtonbar.com

Live entertainment is the name of the game here. The Lexington is **best known for open mic nights** that range from comedy to music to variety show performances. You'll cozy up to a small stage and awesome graffiti décor. Stop in for happy hour Monday through Friday and score $2 PBRs.

THE MOROCCAN LOUNGE
901 E. 1st St. // 213-395-0610 // themoroccan.com

A **venue from the founders of the Teragram Ballroom** in Westlake, the Moroccan Lounge opened in the fall of 2017 in a Moorish-accented historic building in the Arts District. The front room is a restaurant serving falafel bites and tzatziki lamb burgers, while behind it lies an intimate venue where acts such as Grizzly Bear and Børns have performed.

REDWOOD BAR & GRILL
316 W. 2nd St. // 213-680-2600 // theredwoodbar.com

Every now and then, you just get a craving for **stiff drinks in a sunken pirate ship**. Full of nautical ropes, dark wooden planks and other aquatic ephemera, The Redwood offers live music every night of the week (plus a Sunday matinee performance) and pub grub that is itself worthy of stepping inside.

RESIDENT
428 S. Hewitt St. // 213-628-7503 // residentdtla.com

A classy, casual place in the Arts District, this space with a live music setup (DJs and indie rock, mostly) is **meant to recall the spirit of an Austin, Texas, neighborhood bar**. An outdoor beer garden uses a refurbished trailer to serve food.

LIVE JAZZ

Bop and Gin Date Night: BAR THIRTEEN
448 S. Hill St., 13th Fl. // 213-802-1770

Thirteen floors up, just below Perch, is this dressy gin and jazz den that offers not only swinging entertainment, but also epic vistas. Cocktails aren't cheap, but there's no cover charge, and the elegant digs and entertainment are more than worth it.

Jazzed About Jamming: BLUE WHALE BAR
Weller Court, 123 Astronaut E. S. Onizuka St. // 213-620-0908
bluewhalemusic.com

This intimate jazz club and art gallery is well loved by local L.A. music aficionados for the amazing acoustics inside. Step up to the bar for small-batch bourbons, modern artisanal cocktails and rotating craft beers on tap, or grab a table and a bite while enjoying jam sessions courtesy of its emerging talent.

Speakeasy-Style Music and Sips: THE BOARDROOM
135 N. Grand Ave. // 213-972-8556 // patinagroup.com/the-boardroom

Savory French food, creative cocktails named for iconic authors and excellent jazz are available to those who find this speakeasy under the Dorothy Chandler Pavilion, open Thursday through Saturday. The unpretentious atmosphere makes it even cooler.

New Wine Destination: Chinatown

Oriel Chinatown

Rosé With Classic French Bites: ORIEL CHINATOWN
1135 N. Alameda St. // 213-253-9419 // orielchinatown.com // more on page 105

Hidden under the Gold Line, this photogenic little wine bar is worth tracking down for classic French bites (bavette steak, oozy onion soup) and rare French wines.

California in a Glass: LA WINE
900 N. Broadway // lawineforever.com

Taste Central Coast wines without ever leaving DTLA at this cozy, sleek spot inside Blossom Plaza. Find something you loved? Take a bottle home for $10 less than the menu price.

Made in L.A.: ANGELENO WINE CO.
1638 N. Spring St. // angelenowine.com

This area was once filled with vineyards producing grapes for wine. Now, this urban winery is crushing and blending reds, whites and rosé.

MORE WINE BARS

Drink & Shop:
GARÇONS DE CAFÉ
541 S. Spring St. // 213-278-0737 // garcons-de-cafe.com

Easy on Your Wallet:
POUR HAUS WINE BAR
1820 Industrial St. // 213-327-0304 // pourhauswinebar.com

Rustic & Romantic:
MIGNON
128 E. 6th St. // 213-489-0131 // mignonla.com

Wines on Tap:
PALI WINE CO.
811 Traction Ave. // 213-372-5026 // paliwineco.com

DTLA BOOK 2019 135

OUR FAVES - DRINK -

BREWERIES

Friendlier, the American lager at Highland Park Brewery

ANGEL CITY BREWERY
216 Alameda St. // 213-622-1261
angelcitybrewery.com

This tap room and pub is also **a hub for gatherings,** including trivia nights and yoga. Enjoy popular brews and limited runs. Feel free to bring in outside food.

ARTS DISTRICT BREWING COMPANY
828 Traction Ave. // 213-817-5321
artsdistrictbrewing.com

Enjoy a couple of brews between games of ping-pong, darts and vintage Skeeball in a spot that produces **3,300 barrels of craft beer annually**. Bar snacks pair perfectly with stouts and IPAs.

BOOMTOWN BREWERY
700 Jackson St. // 213-617-8497
boomtownbrew.com

Boomtown seeks to create a community space through **gallery showings, block parties and live music**. Every beer label is designed by an L.A. artist, and the tap room is outfitted with foosball, darts and a pool table.

THE DANKNESS DOJO BY MODERN TIMES
832 S. Olive St. // 213-878-7008
moderntimesbeer.com

This San Diego-based brewery offers more than **two dozen taps and a plant-based menu**.

HIGHLAND PARK BREWERY
1220 N. Spring St. // 213-878-9017 // hpb.la

On the outskirts of Chinatown, this tasting room has a menu that features low-ABV brews and big sippers alike, and the **patio is both kid- and pet-friendly**.

IRON TRIANGLE BREWING CO.
1581 Industrial St. // 310-424-1370
irontrianglebrewing.com

At 40,000 square feet, Iron Triangle is **the largest of L.A.'s local breweries**. The tap room—offering 10 brews—has a sophisticated throwback vibe, echoing the 1920s with its long bar and fresh flowers.

MIKKELLER DTLA
330 W. Olympic Blvd. // 213-596-9005
mikkellerbar.com

This 100-year-old former auto repair shop was transformed into a high-ceilinged, industrial-chic nirvana for beer geeks featuring **50-plus taps**. Savory Scandinavian-inflected bites sidle up to brews including Mikkeller's own Waves IPA.

MUMFORD BREWING CO.
416 Boyd St. // mumfordbrewing.com

Mumford offers up a dozen beers on tap, including IPAs, porters and pale ales. The only food available are freshly baked pretzels, so BYOF, and **when you find your fave brew, have some canned to take home**.

DISTILLERY TOUR AND TASTINGS

GREENBAR DISTILLERY
2459 E. 8th St. // 213-375-3668 // greenbar.biz

This company, offering perhaps the **best-known distillery tour in the area**, has the world's largest organic, handcrafted spirits portfolio. You'll only be able to catch a tour on Saturdays ($12 per person) here, but they have plenty going on during the rest of the week, like cocktail classes and tastings for you to choose from.

LOST SPIRITS DISTILLERY
1235 E. 6th St. // 831-235-9400 // lostspirits.net

Disney meets distilling at this magical destination where science, innovation and art come together to create standout peated malt whiskeys and rum. The legendary laboratory is open only to those with online reservations for two-hour tastings, which comprise a tour, presentation and pours of truly one-of-a-kind spirits.

OUR/LOS ANGELES
915 S. Santa Fe Ave. // ourvodka.com/losangeles

Our/Vodka is a global brand that's all about local flavors. With micro-distilleries in nine cities worldwide, **each city's vodka has its own unique flavor and is sourced from local ingredients**. For $10, take a tour of their modern facility in the Arts District and taste their L.A. blend at the source.

THE SPIRIT GUILD
586 Mateo St. // 213-613-1498 // thespiritguild.com

This Arts District collaboration doesn't mess around when it comes to the art of distillation. Started by a sixth-generation California farmer and Scottish-Canadian distiller, it sets itself apart by producing **farm-to-glass gin and vodka completely in-house**. It's also gluten-free. Tickets are just $10 for a 45-minute tasting and tour to ooh and aah at their fab facility.

Lost Spirits Distillery

CLUBS

THE CONTINENTAL CLUB
116 W. 4th St. // 866-687-4449 // circa93.com

Don't expect to spend the entire night on Instagram or Tinder at this subterranean club with **zero cell reception. The hidden speakeasy is down an alley in Gallery Row**, and prospective clubbers without a reservation are subject to the whims of the bouncer. Expect Penicillins and draft Moscow Mules, DJs and a dressed-up, laid-back crowd.

ELEVATE LOUNGE
811 Wilshire Blvd., Ste. 2100 // 213-623-7100
elevatelounge.com

Like the name says, this club is on a different level—21 floors above Wilshire, to be exact. The **massive space offers panoramas** that reach the Hollywood Hills, but all the action is inside. Bottle service is the best bet for EDM fans who have something to celebrate, Vegas-style.

EXCHANGE L.A.
618 S. Spring St. // 213-627-8070
exchangela.com

Located in the **former L.A. Stock Exchange building**, this expansive, four-level nightclub is one of Downtown's most popular venues, inviting international DJs of the highest caliber to treat its patrons to a pulsing dance floor. You'll want to dress upscale for entry.

HONEYCUT
819 S. Flower St. // 213-688-0888
honeycutla.com

Known for its **multicolored light-up dance floor**, this slick spot with an old-school disco vibe invites you to get your groove on, but also to indulge in its expansive craft cocktail program of more than 50 drinks. Split into two rooms—one for drinking, one for dancing; you can choose your own adventure.

THE MAYAN
1038 S. Hill St. // 213-746-4674
clubmayan.com

It's not every day you come across a club with Mayan décor, but this former movie palace, opened in 1927, is one of the city's most popular venues for concerts and club nights. The Mayan offers **multiple levels of fun, usually with differing music** from Latin pop to hip-hop to Top 40.

THE RESERVE
650 S. Spring St. // 213-327-0057
thelareserve.com

Like most of DTLA's sophisticated nightlife hot spots, this place has history: It serves up its **handcrafted cocktails in the basement of a 1920s Beaux-Arts bank** (hence the name) and welcomes night owls with its talented DJs and three bars' worth of friendly staff.

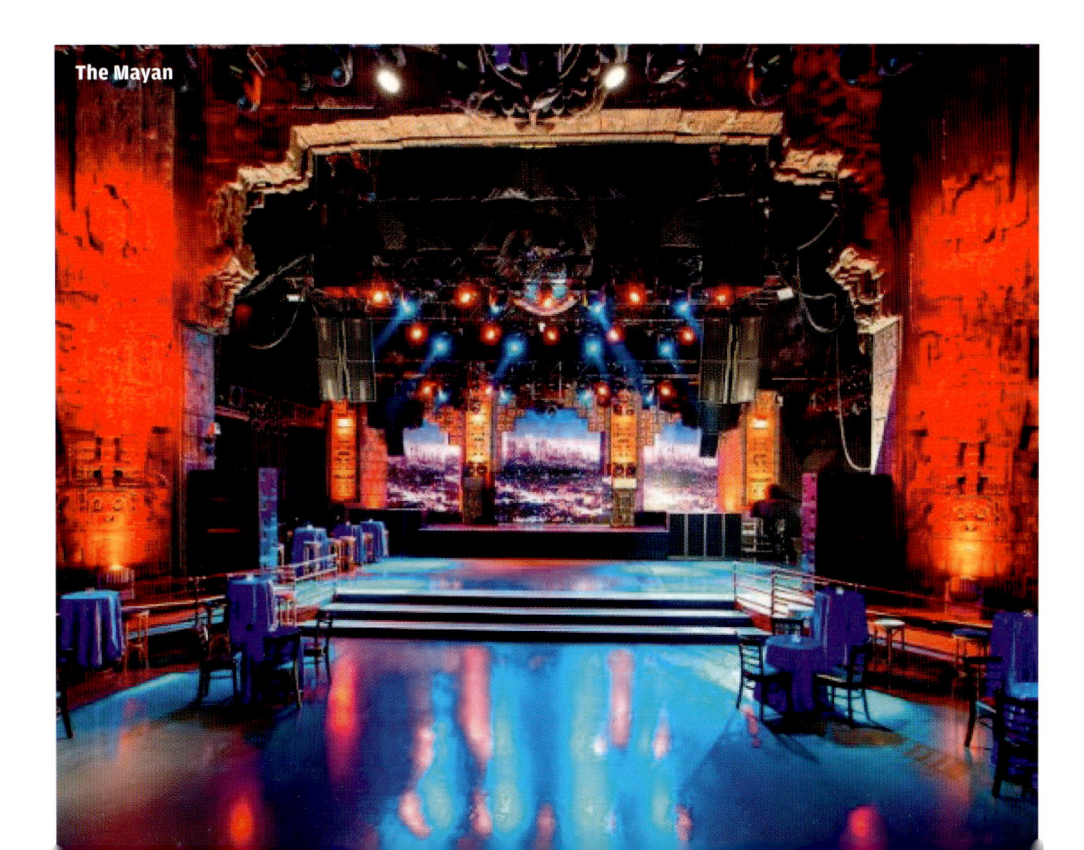

The Mayan

Drag show at New Jalisco

LGBTQA

NEW JALISCO
245 S. Main St. // 213-613-1802

The oldest of Downtown's batch of gay bars, the New Jalisco caters to a Latin crowd with **Spanish-language drag performances and Latino go-go boys**, though a mix of people call this neighborhood bar home. Step into this cash-only spot for a night of cumbia, reggaeton and pop music.

PRECINCT
357 S. Broadway // 213-628-3112 // precinctdtla.com

Located in a former police precinct, this multiroom nightclub has become Downtown's go-to spot for queer lovers of **drag, dancing and rock 'n' roll debauchery**. The second-floor spot's wrap-around patio acts as a refuge for smokers, while the main room's stage serves as a beloved home to talented local performers, comedians and musicians.

REDLINE
131 E. 6th St. // 213-935-8391 // redlinedtla.com

A sleek and modern gay bar located in the Historic Core, Redline draws boys and girls (mostly boys) with its **hunky bar staff, roster of rotating DJs and regular performances** by some of the city's most popular drag queens. Drinks are stiff and reasonably priced, and the patrons are a friendly bunch.

HISTORY LESSON
Riot, Sweet Riot

West Hollywood might be considered the prevalent LGBTQ area in L.A. today, but in the '50s and '60s, a stretch of DTLA's Main Street was the gay hangout. And what is considered the first gay uprising in America took place here, 10 years before NYC's Stonewall Rebellion. Known as the Cooper's Donut Riot, it happened in May 1959, when a group of drag queens and hustlers, tired of being harassed by the police, bombarded the LAPD with donuts, coffee and paper plates and caused Main Street to be closed down for a whole day.

OUR FAVES - WELLNESS -

YOGA

OUE Skyspace

YOGA WITH AN UNBEATABLE VIEW

High-Up Downward Dog

At **OUE Skyspace LA**, yoga classes take place on the observation space's 1,000-foot perch, making for blissed-out moments. Their Mind, Body & Soul program's balanced approach to fitness includes an empowering body workout led by SoHo Yoga and a spiritual Reiki healing with Celia Gellert (during spring/summer). Admission also includes a ride down the Skyslide as a fast-moving finale to your workout. Switching out seasonally from sunrise (spring and summer) to sunset (fall and winter) sessions, **OUE Skyspace LA** is the place to elevate your sun salutations game.

OUE SKYSPACE LA
633 W. 5th St., Financial District // 213-537-0323 // oue-skyspace.com

GET YOUR TICKET
Sunrise Yoga: $30
Sunset Yoga: $25

Scan this code with your standard iPhone camera or Android QR Code reader app to play the video or get your ticket!

YOGA

Good for Aerial Yoga: **THE BRIDGE MIND BODY MOVEMENT**
1820 Industrial St., #102B // 213-537-0159 // thebridgembm.com
Spins, beautiful poses and fun combos from an aerial hammock.

Good for Beginners: **EVOKE YOGA**
731 S. Spring St., #600 // 213-375-5528 // evokeyoga.com
Energetic playlists and uplifting instructors.

Good for Flow: **YOGA CIRCLE DOWNTOWN**
400 S. Main St. // 213-620-1040 // yogacircledowntown.com
Classes range from Solar Flow to Ayurvedic and Hatha.

Good for Hot Yoga: **BIKRAM YOGA L.A.**
700 W. 1st St. // 213-334-3949 // bikramyogala.com
Twenty-six specific postures are taught in a 105-degree room.

Good for Personal Posturing: **LOS ANGELES YOGA CLUB**
1206 Maple Ave., Ste. #846 // 323-977-4777 // losangelesyogaclub.org
One-on-one instruction at your pace.

Pilates+DTLA

PILATES

It's no surprise that Pilates, a fitness practice renowned for its unique ability to strengthen, lengthen and tone with low impact, has taken off in this body-obsessed city. Specializing in the classical method, **Kerri Baker Pilates** (408 S. Spring St. // 213-590-3703 kerribakerpilates.net) is an intimate go-to for newbies trying out the therapeutic modality, and experienced practitioners looking to be challenged one-on-one. At **Club Pilates Downtown Los Angeles** (1119 S. Hope St. // 213-204-6900 // clubpilates.com), the pure method is taught to groups on state-of-the-art equipment (also, your first intro class is free). Tradition is turned on its head at **Pilates+DTLA** (110 E. 9th St., AL-025 // 213-863-4834 // ppdtla.com), a Lagree Fitness studio where intense, sweaty classes test strength and muscular endurance for quick results.

FITNESS CLASSES

BAR EXPRESS
When you have limited time, but want the same results, hit this 45-minute class.
THE BAR METHOD
724 S. Spring St., #203 // 213-221-1237 // barmethod.com

THE BESPOKE RIDE
Get intense 45-minute workouts with cool choreography and upper-body moves.
BESPOKE CYCLING STUDIO
735 S. Figueroa St., #105 // 213-228-2828 // bespokecyclingstudio.com

BUDDY TRAINING
Grab a friend and get a discount for semi-private and personalized sessions.
FITPROSLA 123 S. Figueroa St., #140B // 818-319-3117 // fitprosla.com

BOXING
Learn how to box like a pro without having to get in a ring with this cardio-blasting workout.
THE JYIM 830 Traction Ave., #2B // 323-204-7604 // thejyim.com

HIIT IT
Check out these high-intensity interval trainings available at different gyms.
EQUINOX
444 Flower St. // 213-330-3999 // equinox.com
SANCTUARY FITNESS
718 Jackson St. // 213-266-8311 // sanctuaryfitnessla.com
SPEEDPLAY
1113½ S. Hope St. // 213-894-9944 // speedplayla.com

KRAV MAGA
Combine self-defense tactics and fitness in one dripping workout.
KRAV MAGA UNYTED
334 S. Main St., #1106A // 213-223-6233 // kravmagaunyted.com

THE MAIN BODY
The signature class blends dance, Pilates and yoga all in one.
The Main Barre
560 S. Main St., #4W // 213-623-1213 // themainbarre.com

WELLNESS / BEAUTY

BASE COAT
704 Mateo St. // 213-935-8330
basecoatnailsalon.com

This **nontoxic nail salon**'s expansive, airy Arts District space is as Instagram-able as the manicure you'll leave with. Fig & Yarrow custom-blends their plant-based products, and there's kombucha and cold brew on tap.

BENJAMIN
300 S. Santa Fe Ave. // 424-249-3296
benjaminsalon.com

Hairstyling guru Benjamin Mohapi's **art-filled cut-and-color salon** in the Arts District is not only exceptionally cool, but so are the looks coming out of it.

DRIP DOCTORS
1119½ S. Hope St. // 213-749-3747 // dripdoctors.com

This celeb-loved destination doles out **IV drips and vitamin infusions** that promise to boost immunity and energy, jump-start muscle recovery and reduce stress. Botox, fillers and weight loss programs are also available.

FRAIS SPA
819 S. Flower St. // 213-784-8194 // fraisspa.com

Everyone could likely use the Tech Neck Massage at this intimate spa with offerings such as **full-body rubdowns, facials and acupuncture** that end with chocolate and green tea.

HOTBOX INFRARED SAUNA STUDIO
835 S. Hill St. // 213-628-3221
hotboxsaunastudio.com

Netflix and chill—or heat—at this **infrared sauna destination**, where sessions to reduce chronic pain, alleviate stress and detoxify the body can be game-changing. Clean, private rooms allow guests to personalize lighting and entertainment and rinse off in a vitamin C-infused shower.

SOOTHE
866-473-6358 // Soothe.com

Like UberEats for massage, this on-demand service **delivers experienced masseuses to your doorstep**, whether it's an apartment, office or hotel room.

NAILBOX
300 S. Santa Fe Ave. // 213-229-8832 // nailboxla.com

Adorable décor and competitive pricing attract gel addicts for **manicures from basic to blinged out**, with chrome, holographic, jewels and nail art designs. Pedicures happen at cool copper basins.

NEIHULE
607 S. Olive St. // 213-623-4383 // neihule.com

This **relaxing full-service salon** across from Pershing Square offers skincare, massages, hair services, waxing and nail care.

THE RITZ-CARLTON SPA, LOS ANGELES
900 W. Olympic Blvd. // 213-763-4400 //
ritzcarlton.com

Feel like a king or queen for a day at this **opulent, expansive spa, where Champagne kicks off pampering** via luxe personalized treatments using ingredients from the rooftop garden.

OUR FAVES - WELLNESS -

CANNABIS WELLNESS

NOT FOR STONERS

CBD (cannabidiol) belongs to a class of ingredients called cannabinoids and is one of over 113 active compounds found in the cannabis plant. Instead of giving you a high, it helps curb anxiety, relieve pain and even reduce inflammation without any of that funny business. You can now stylishly calm yourself down with a CBD vape pen like **Beboe Calming Blend** (Right, $75). Visit beboeshop.com for store locations.

CANNABIS REPORT

Open Season

Once California Proposition 64 was enacted, it was only a matter of time before recreational marijuana use would impact businesses Downtown. The legalization of adult-use (over 21) weed ushered in a new era for where to get canna-goods. Oddly enough, the pre-Prop 64 use of cannabinoids (CBDs) in cocktails is now illegal, so those fun, calming, non-psychoactive sips are not available. The gist: Californians 18 and older with a cannabis recommendation ID card can still purchase medical marijuana, while anyone in the state—temporarily or permanently—21 and over can legally purchase and possess up to one ounce. There are a number of dispensaries to check out, from the clean and friendly **Buddha Company** (2038 Sacramento St. // 213-628-3144), where treats can be found alongside eye candy in the form of an intricate mural by artist Peter Greco, to slick **MedMen** (735 S. Broadway // 213-908 2244 // medmen.com) and the **Downtown Patient Group** (1320 Mateo St. // 213-747-3386 // dtpgla.com), which touts a large selection of edibles, topicals and even medicated pet treats. Many dispensaries now deliver as well.

NEW MONEY

Cannabiz Everywhere

There's a creative canna-business boom in Downtown. The Mystic Rebel offers **Stoned Yoga classes** (453 S. Spring St., Ste. 641 // 323-942-9484 // themysticrebel.com), which focus on awareness of the body with the enhancement of a little THC. No smoking is allowed, but you can vape or nosh an edible at will. ... **Supreme Organics** (supremeorganics.com) creates pop art–inspired edibles in its DTLA kitchen from gummies to peanut butter cups. ... You can also join, or host, a cannabis-laced dinner party with chefs from companies like **PopCultivate** (popsupperclub.com), **La Hoja** (lahoja.com) and Cannabis **Supper Club** (cannabissupperclub.com). ... And a cannabis-focused co-working space, anchored by branding company **Greet Street Agency**, will debut in a three-story Jewelry District building (718 S. Hill St.), offering workspace, retail and a restaurant.

TATTOO PARLORS

Ceora Ink
Private studio, by appointment only // ceoraink.com

Evol Arts Studio
S. Hill St. // edwinmarin.com

Heavy Gold Tattoo
814 S. Spring St. // 213-265-7627 // heavygoldtattoo.com

The Order DTLA Tattoo Parlour
122 E. 5th St. // 213-281-9353 // theorderdtla.com

Sketch Tattoo
453 S. Spring St. // 323-326-2534 // losangelestattooart.com

Tinta Rebelde Custom Tattoos
133 E. 3rd St. // 213-626-0051 // tintarebelde.com

SAMPLE SALES / VINTAGE & SPECIALTY STORES

OUR FAVES - SHOP -

ARTS DISTRICT CO-OP
453 Colyton St. // 213-223-6717 // adcoopla.com

Head here for **great flea market finds in block-party style**, with food trucks and live music. Shoppers are able to scope out handmade local goods, furniture, art, jewelry and clothing, too, all inside a funky brick building. Open every day but Monday.

BLUE MOON FABRICS
305 E. 9th St., Ste. 110 // 213-892-0401
bluemoonfabrics.com

This store sticks out in its 'hood for having the most organized, wide-ranging and **high-quality fabric selection** around, plus the friendliest, most knowledgeable staff to help navigate all the alluring options.

CALIFORNIA MARKET CENTER
110 E. 9th St. // 213-630-3600
californiamarketcenter.com

The showroom is almost always off-limits to the public for trade shows, but on **the last Friday of every month, they host a sample sale.** You'll know it by the line stretched around the block.

CALIFORNIA MILLINERY SUPPLY CO.
721 S. Spring St. // 213-622-8746
californiamillinery.net

A true one of a kind in the city, it's **the place to buy hat-making supplies.** The shop owned by a former stage and costume designer addresses every imaginable need—vintage ribbons, lace, bows, trims and fascinator bases.

MICHAEL LEVINE
920 S. Maple Ave. // 213-622-6259 // mlfabric.com

At the **"Disneyland of fabric stores,"** newbies and novices alike will enjoy weaving up and down the aisles of colorful fabrics to find just what they need. Prices are affordable, and the staff is happy to help.

MOSKATELS / MICHAEL'S
733 S. San Julian St. // 213-689-4830

It's **like Costco for crafters and party planners**, complete with a warehouse of ribbon, frames, art supplies and everything you need for a DIY wedding. The theme changes periodically according to the season, which means you'll rarely see the same store twice.

RAGGEDY THREADS
330 E. 2nd St. // 213-620-1188
raggedythreads.com

It's hard not to get nostalgic—and maybe even patriotic—in this **classic Americana vintage store**. From the décor to the treasure trove of shirts, shoes, overalls and dresses, you'll yearn for a simpler time, or at least want to look the part.

SANTEE ALLEY
Olympic Boulevard to 12th between Maple and Santee Streets // thesanteealley.com

With more than 150 vendors, you'll leave with your hands full after a day of shopping here. It's open daily, but weekends draw the biggest crowds. Bring cash, **be prepared to bargain** and pace yourself.

UNIQUE L.A.
110 E. 9th St., CMC Penthouse // uniquemarkets.com

If you've been hoping to shop at all your favorite Etsy stores in one place, this is it. The seasonal market has created a movement supporting **small American businesses and independent designers**, and it's just $10 cash to get in.

SHOPPING CENTERS

The Bloc 700 S. Flower St. // theblocla.com
After a pricey makeover, the former Macy's Plaza is now a sophisticated, open-air spot, complete with shops (luxe brands, jewelry, toys), restaurants (a steakhouse, pizza, juice bar) and soon an Alamo Drafthouse cinema.

FIGat7th 735 S. Figueroa St. // figat7th.com
Get all your shopping done in a dash at this one-stop retail haven—a lifestyle center complete with fashion, food, fitness and special events. It's home to Nordstrom Rack and Target, as well as H&M and Zara flagship stores, plus Gold's Gym and 18 restaurants and eateries.

ROW DTLA 777 S. Alameda St. // 213-943-4677 // rowdtla.com
With capacity for 100 retail outlets and 15 eateries and 1.4 million square feet of creative office space, this mecca for shoppers and aesthetes alike is major. Tightly edited womenswear at LCD, menswear at Banks Journal and sneakers at Bodega are just a few of countless reasons to go.

The Yards 300 S. Santa Fe Ave. // osfla.com
This 80,000-square-foot shopping center is anything but ordinary, and we wouldn't expect less in the Arts District. Part of the residential complex One Santa Fe, it hosts select shops like Wittmore, Malin+Goetz and The Voyager.

OUR FAVES - SHOP -

CLOTHING

Gucci at Dover Street Market

ACNE STUDIOS
855 S. Broadway // 213-243-0960 // acnestudios.com

The opening of this sleek Swedish brand's flagship in 2013 signified a new era in DTLA. Located in the Eastern Columbia Building, its 5,000 square feet of **world-famous denim, leather jackets and minimalist must-haves** await you.

ALCHEMY WORKS
826 E. 3rd St. // 323-487-1497
alchemyworks.us

A mix of retail and gallery space, **this carefully curated boutique is hip to the max** and includes men's and women's fashion, gifts, home goods, magazines and a Warby Parker showroom.

A.P.C.
125 W. 9th St. // 424-252-2762 // apc.fr

In good company at 9th Street and Broadway, this popular **ready-to-wear French brand** brought a whole lot of buzz with it when it opened. Both the collections and the space itself are minimalist with *très* chic flair.

APOLIS
826 E. 3rd St. // 855-894-1559 // apolisglobal.com

In a city where socially conscious equals sexy, this **minimalist menswear boutique** features shirts, swimwear, bags and shoes, all ethically sourced.

BLENDS LA
725 S. Los Angeles St. // 213-626-6607
blendsus.com

City-dwelling sneakerheads get their fix at the Downtown outpost of the **beloved shop that puts kicks front and center**. Everything from Vans to rare Nikes and Air Jordans draws hip-hop fans and skateboarders. (More on page 56.)

BNKR
901 S. Broadway // 213-327-0442
us.fashionbunker.com

This Australian retailer's cult following spans oceans. Luckily for us, the 6,800-square-foot flagship store is the only U.S. location. You'll find **women's fashion and accessories from Aussie brands** like C/MEO Collective and Jaggar Footwear.

COS
313 W. 8th St. // 213-271-2716 // cosstores.com

Clean and modern mark the men's and women's clothing and **Scandinavian-inflected design** of this London-based brand, a sibling company of H&M. Don't expect fast fashion—the everyday basics and minimalist ready-to-wear are quality and meant to last.

DOVER STREET MARKET
608 Imperial St. // 310-427-7610
losangeles.doverstreetmarket.com

Rei Kawakubo and Adrian Joffe have brought the **famed fashion haunt** to a massive warehouse in the Arts District. It has everything from Comme des Garçons and Gucci to lesser-known labels of T-shirts, shoes, jewelry and even a green Sqirl jam created just for DSM. There are shops-in-shops, art installations and its staple Rose Bakery serving light bites. The whole place feels bright, expansive and exploratory, whether you have the money to drop there or not.

EAST/WEST SHOP
727 N. Broadway, #115 // 213-440-2229
east-west-shop.com

This hub of sustainable fashion hidden in the Far East Plaza in Chinatown sells everything from gender-neutral ponchos to Hello Kitty denim masterpieces and limited-edition retro high tops, **all made from repurposed, reworked and vintage products**.

GENTLE MONSTER
816 S. Broadway // 213-935-8114
gentlemonster.com

Make any excuse to visit this massive, museum-like space with evocative kinetic sculptures and large-scale installations by famed film director Floria Sigismondi. Stimulating surroundings make the experience of shopping for **the Korean eyewear brand's cool creations** totally memorable.

HARPER
204 W. 6th St. // 213-489-1891

This jewel box of a shop packs a punch in a small amount of space, stocking **well-priced separates and dresses that speak to current trends**. The friendly salespeople are known to offer styling advice with purchases, too.

THE HOUSE OF WOO
209 S. Garey St. // 213-687-4800 // ilovewoo.com

Nestled in the Arts District, designer Staci Woo's flagship store **brings a bit of the beach to Downtown—upscale but comfortable**. You'll find clothing and accessories for men, women and children, and, of course, beach towels.

JUICE
801 Mateo St. // juicestore.com

This is the **first U.S. outpost of the Chinese streetwear retailer**, co-founded by Hong Kong-Canadian hip-hop performer Kevin Chen. The shop sells bomber jackets, shirts, kicks and bags from labels, including its own collection, CLOT.

LE BOX BLANC
1100 S. Hope St., C1 // 213-519-3400
leboxblanc.com

From head to toe, Le Box Blanc's store—an **airy brick-and-mortar shop opened by the DTLA-**

142 DTLA BOOK 2019

COURTESY DOVER STREET MARKET

THE INTERSECTION OF

LIFE X STYLE

SHOP X FIG

bath & body works · bespoke cycling studio · downtown hi-tech · gold's gym · h&m · lenscrafters · l'occitane
mac cosmetics · nordstrom rack · pink by victoria's secret · sunglass hut · target · t-mobile · victoria's secret · zara

DINE X FIG

california pizza kitchen · coco fresh tea & juice · five guys · george's greek grill · gulp sushi alehouse
indus by saffron · the melt · mendocino farms · morton's the steakhouse · new moon café · ohana poké co.
oleego by parks bbq · pazzo gelato · pizza studio · salata · sprinkles cupcakes · starbucks · twist & grill

FIGAT7TH

@FIGat7th   FIGat7th.com
735 S. Figueroa St. · Downtown L.A. · Across from the 7th Street / Metro Center Station

OUR FAVES — SHOP

CLOTHING

Continued from page 142

based e-commerce retailer in 2016—has you covered. Local designers like Janessa Leoné hang alongside faves from Equipment and IRO.

MYKITA
847 S. Broadway // 213-335-5815 // mykita.com

This German brand is known for **custom-fit prescription eyewear** (all done in-house), with designs that straddle the line between edgy and classic.

POCKET SQUARE CLOTHING
205 W. 7th St. // 213-375-5111
pocketsquareclothing.com

Since 2011, this stylish shop has been the go-to place for dapper gentlemen looking for **made-to-measure custom suits and accessories**. With a focus on superior craftsmanship, their entire in-house collection is carefully handcrafted right here in L.A., favored by creatives, musicians and stylists.

RAISED IN LOS ANGELES
548 S. Sprint St., R110 // 213-265-7488
raisedinlosangeles.bigcartel.com

Repping L.A.'s transplants and natives alike, this **urban/skate brand** carries hoodies, tees and accessories. Their collection also features one-of-a-kind "hand canned" pieces from local artists with spray-painted designs.

THE ROGUE COLLECTIVE
305 S. Hewitt St. // 213-436-1160
theroguecollective.com

See what the Arts District used to be while you shop their premium lifestyle goods. The space **pays homage to the iconic Al's Bar that once was here**, and you'll even find the original stage and authentic band posters.

ROUND 2 LA
605 S. Los Angeles St., Ste. D
213-884-6409 // round2la.bigcartel.com

A fun place to play dress-up in both modern and vintage finds—from punk rock to disco—this store has a vibrant, playful vibe. They offer men's and women's clothing, accessories and **mind-blowing platforms**.

RSVP GALLERY
905 S. Hill St. // rsvpgallery.com

This Chicago-based conceptual streetwear store—a brainchild of Virgil Abloh, Kanye West's style advisor—blurs the lines between **luxury clothing boutique and art gallery**. Kaws, Channel and Bape are on display.

SKINGRAFT
758 S. Spring St. // 213-626-2662
skingraftdesigns.com

Play with your edge as you sift the racks of this L.A.-based brand ruled by sleek designs, dark colors and fine craftsmanship. You'll **feel more badass** wearing their men's and women's clothing, leather goods and accessories. (See pages 5-10 for their collection.)

SUB_URBAN RIOT
111 W. 7th St. // 213-689-3271
suburbanriot.com

You've likely gotten a chuckle from someone wearing their signature KALE shirt, and you can expect more clever designs here. It's a **lighthearted U.S-made brand**, and it's all about that comfy and casual life.

URBAN OUTFITTERS
Rialto Theatre, 810 S. Broadway
213-627-7469 // urbanoutfitters.com

Inside the architecturally significant Rialto Theatre building, this hipster juggernaut's DTLA store is epic in size and content. With almost 10,000 square feet, there's **almost nothing you can't find here,** from clothing to cosmetics and vinyl to décor.

VIRGO
216 E. 9th St. // 213-988-8899
virgodowntown.com

Snag all the best vintage finds without all the digging. From denim to dresses to accessories, the owners have you covered. Not your size? **Have their in-house tailor alter your find** to fit you like a glove.

VISVIM
304 S. Broadway // visvim.tv

This East-meets-West brand with a huge celebrity following—Drake, Pharrell Williams and John Mayer are all fans—has landed **in the historic Bradbury Building**. The shop features a rotating collection of products and goods, including Visvim's Indigo Camping Trailer offshoot.

LIFESTYLE / HOME / GIFT

3.1 PHILLIP LIM
734 E. 3rd St. // 213-246-2588 // 31philliplim.com

After closing in WeHo, Phillip Lim made DTLA its new home: 5,000 square feet of home, to be exact. Men's and women's clothes share the **minimalist concept space** with Patrick Parrish Gallery, M. Crow, Apparatus Books and Li, Inc. Studio.

AESOP
862 S. Broadway // 213-265-7487 // aesop.com

A pioneer of 9th Street and Broadway's transformation, the Aussie brand has a cult following for its **plant-based skin and hair products**.

CLEVELAND ART
451 Colyton St. // 213-626-1311 // clevelandart.com

Long a secret trove for designers looking for **industrial chic vintage furniture**, Cleveland Art's warehouse carries lighting, factory carts, cast-iron tables and selections from its own line.

THE GOOD LIVER
705 Mateo St. // 213-947-3141 // good-liver.com

This gift boutique is all about **home and personal items with history and craftsmanship**.

Need a brass pencil sharpener? Or a $153 hand-carved wooden bowl? You might after you walk in.

HAMMER AND SPEAR
255 S. Santa Fe Ave., Ste. 101
213-928-0997 // hammerandspear.com

L.A. interior designers rely on power couple Kristan Cunningham and Scott Jarrell for **amazing vintage and new home finds**. This showroom is a retail mecca and interior design firm.

HATCHET OUTDOOR SUPPLY
941 E. 2nd St., Ste. 101 // 213-935-8065
hatchetsupply.myshopify.com

With brick walls and a tight selection of designer and artisan gear, this Arts District store is **made for the stylish outdoorsman**, stocking gifts and everything for a camping trip.

PLEASE DO NOT ENTER
549 S. Olive St. // 213-263-0037
pleasedonotenter.com

Contrary to its name, this luxury retail/art exhibition space really does want you to visit. Design-loving men will especially love the **curated collection of art books, home décor and accessories**.

144 DTLA BOOK 2019

LITTLE TOKYO

THE BOWLS
311 E. 1st St. // 213-628-8866 // bowlsla.com

The Bowls has all the vibes of **an old-school men's general store, only more refined**. Shop here for all your manly goods like grooming products, men's clothing, hats and accessories.

DAISO
333 S. Alameda St., #114 // 213-265-7821 // daisojapan.com

Move over, Dollar Tree, because for $1.50 you'll find an assortment of household items, beauty supplies, gifts and more. You never know what you'll find each time you go, but **the overload of cuteness is guaranteed**.

JAPANGELES
335 E. 2nd St. // 310-920-2383 // japangeles.com

Shopping bags for this Little Tokyo shop read "dope things inside," and indeed the goods are covetable **for guys who love streetwear**. Just like the name would seem, this brand represents the intersection of Japanese and Los Angeles styles.

KINOKUNIYA BOOKSTORE
123 Astronaut E. S. Onizuka St.
213-687-4480 // usa.kinokuniya.com

This spot has long been a pillar in L.A.'s Japanese-American community. Find **eclectic Japanese fashion magazines**, manga and plenty of great reads in English as well.

MAKE ASOBI
130 Japanese Village Plaza // 213-620-0181

Long before Asian skincare products were all the rage, Angelenos were coming here for **affordable beauty supplies**. It's fully stocked with Asian brands, and impossible to leave this shop empty-handed.

POKETO
ROW DTLA, 777 S. Alameda St., #174 & 374 E. 2nd St.
213-537-0751 // poketo.com

Artsy but organized is the vibe here—with everything from **one-of-a-kind planters and books to wallets and backpacks with a colorful minimalist spin**.

POPKILLER
300 E. 2nd St. // 213-625-1372 // popkiller.us

You can't go to Little Tokyo and not stop at this shop, known for its **unique selection of cheeky T-shirts and funky accessories**. Everyone leaves this edgy boutique feeling a little more hip than they were before.

RAFU BUSSAN
414 E. 2nd St. // 213-614-1181 // rafubussaninc.com

If you're in need of a grown-up gift, look no further than the **largest gift shop in Little Tokyo**. The 7,000-square-foot space offers plenty of gorgeous tea sets, ceramics, Japanese dolls, lanterns and more to choose from.

Poketo Project Space at ROW DTLA

GILLIAN JACOBS
Actress, star of the Netflix series *Love* and the Disney film *Magic Camp*

SHOPPING *ROW DTLA has my favorite coffee shop, Go Get 'Em Tiger, and many great stores like Charlotte Stone and Myrtle, which sells my favorite independent female clothing designers like Rachel Antonoff and Samantha Pleet.*

MUSEUM *I love the Geffen Contemporary at MOCA in Little Tokyo. The museum is amazing and there are so many great shops and restaurants within walking distance.*

RESTAURANT *Simone is a beautiful restaurant with great food, and I love supporting female chefs. I've been waiting for Jessica Largey to open her own place and Simone does not disappoint.* —J.G.

TAILOR MADE

Custom Fit: GROOM STUDIO
833 S. Spring St., 4th Fl. // 213-265-7074
groomstudioweddings.com

Formal men's attire, dress shirts, dress shoes, ties and other accessories for **stylishly reasonable prices**. By appointment only.

Bespoke: JB CLOTHIERS
859 S. Spring St. // 213-785-8998 // jbclothiers.com

Starting with **34 measurements, this tailor painstakingly creates** your custom suit, tuxedo, sport jacket and dress shirt. By appointment only.

Feel-Good Goods

Imagine if you could help provide housing for women in Skid Row by walking into a café and enjoying an organic pastry, or by shopping for a vintage handbag or an upcycled teacup candle made with hand-poured soy wax (shown at right). You can in DTLA, thanks to MADE by DWC's Café and Gift Boutique and Resale Boutique, two innovative social enterprises created by the Downtown Women's Center.

Since 1978, the center has been serving women by providing supportive housing and a safe community. Its handmade products—also sold online—are created onsite by the center's women. The program helps the women develop new skills and restore self-esteem. "It allows them the space to work through barriers they've been facing living in poverty or homelessness," says Dena Younkin, product and merchandise senior manager. Proceeds support the DWC, which includes 119 housing units and a women's health clinic.

MADE BY DWC CAFÉ AND GIFT BOUTIQUE
438 S. San Pedro St. // 213-213-2881 // madebydwc.org

MADE BY DWC RESALE BOUTIQUE
325 S. Los Angeles St. // 213-225-8020

OUR FAVES
- SHOP -

SHOP 'TIL YOU DROP OFF...

If you enjoyed shopping in Downtown—and picked up more than can fit in your suitcase—**City Business Shipping** has got you covered. Residents and business owners of the Fashion District have long depended on this one-stop shop for all their logistics and packaging needs. Opened in 1995 on 9th Street, it now has multiple area locations. It makes shipping easy, whether you need to send something small back home or are looking for freight consolidation to restock inventory at your boutique in, say, Chicago. Just bring any item into a location near you and the company will pack and box it and recommend the most appropriate carrier for delivery (UPS, FedEx, DHL or USPS). The company even offers same-day service for urgent shipments. Services include packaging and building custom crates for paintings, statues and antiques of all sorts.

CITY BUSINESS SHIPPING INC. cbshipping.com
FASHION DISTRICT 225 E. 9th St. // 213-612-4949
LITTLE TOKYO 308 S. Los Angeles St. // 213-622-2426
GARMENT DISTRICT 967 E. 12th St. // 213-239-8877
MARKET SOUTH 1147 S. San Pedro St. // 323-831-2022

BOOKSTORES

A.G. GEIGER
502 Chung King Ct. // 213-505-6957

Part bookstore, part co-working space, this Chinatown shop named for a character in *The Big Sleep* carries **fine art books with a spotlight on California artists**.

HENNESSEY + INGALLS
300 S. Santa Fe, Ste. M // 213-437-2130
hennesseyingalls.com

This well-known bookstore moved from Santa Monica to the Arts District's One Santa Fe. The shelves are packed with **gorgeous books on art and design**.

THE LAST BOOKSTORE
453 S. Spring St. // 213-488-0599 // lastbookstorela.com

A true L.A. icon, this indie bookstore is **home to that infamous book tunnel** you've seen on Instagram. You'll find books old and new, and they even have a music section featuring vintage vinyl.

THE LIBRARY STORE
630 W. 5th St. // 213-228-7500 // shop.lfla.org

With **all sales supporting the L.A. Public Library**, it takes a lot of restraint not to go on a book shopping spree. This curated selection of literary gifts also includes toys, stationery, notebooks and more.

OOGA BOOGA
943 N. Broadway // 213-617-1105 // oogaboogastore.com

This **hip offbeat upstairs shop** in Chinatown not only offers books, jewerly, clothing and music, but also obscure zines and even mix cassette tapes—in the most earnest throwback '80s style.

PETS

JUST FOOD FOR DOGS
333 S. Spring St. // 213-709-2963
justfoodfordogs.com

Owners of picky or sickly pups flock to this specialty store, conveniently located beside a veterinarian's office. The brand's proprietary recipes address a number of dietary concerns and preferences using **high-quality ingredients and creative combinations**.

PET PROJECT LA
548 S. Spring St., Ste. 107 // 213-688-7752
petprojectla.com

Raw, organic food isn't only trending for people, thanks to the presence of one pet supply store that sells only top-of-the-line food for your favorite four-legged family members. Super-friendly staff treat all customers with care.

PUSSY & POOCH
564 S. Main St. // 213-438-0900 // pussyandpooch.com

Cats and dogs are more than family here—they're almost royalty. This location **features a "Pawbar" cafe** where your four-legged baby can choose from raw meats, stews or made-to-order options. That's luxe living.

POINTS OF VIEW

A historic icon and two modern towers offer three takes on the city's epic vista and beyond.

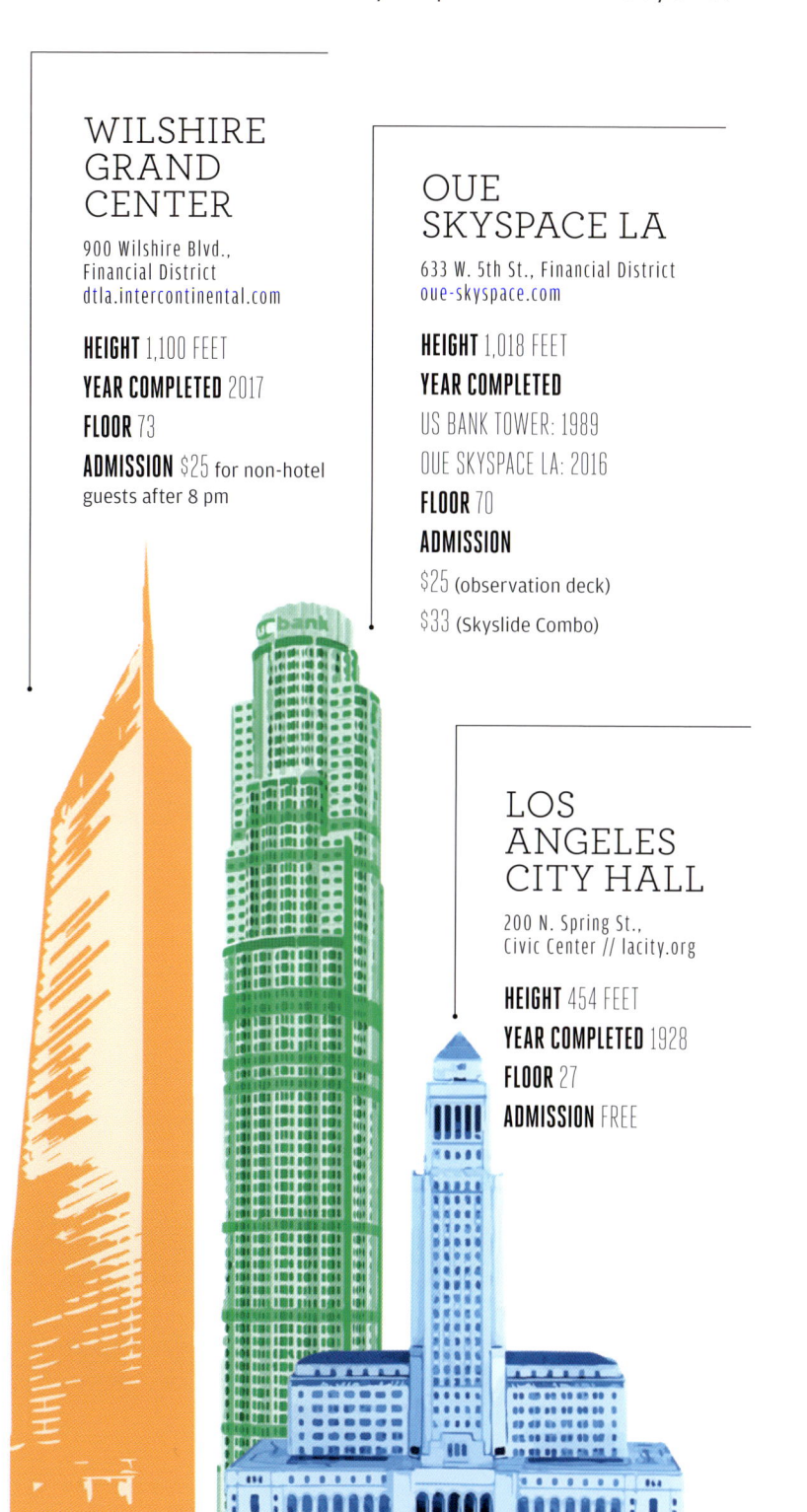

WILSHIRE GRAND CENTER

900 Wilshire Blvd., Financial District
dtla.intercontinental.com

HEIGHT 1,100 FEET
YEAR COMPLETED 2017
FLOOR 73
ADMISSION $25 for non-hotel guests after 8 pm

OUE SKYSPACE LA

633 W. 5th St., Financial District
oue-skyspace.com

HEIGHT 1,018 FEET
YEAR COMPLETED
US BANK TOWER: 1989
OUE SKYSPACE LA: 2016
FLOOR 70
ADMISSION
$25 (observation deck)
$33 (Skyslide Combo)

LOS ANGELES CITY HALL

200 N. Spring St.,
Civic Center // lacity.org

HEIGHT 454 FEET
YEAR COMPLETED 1928
FLOOR 27
ADMISSION FREE

ENHANCING DTLA'S VIBRANCY AND INCREASING INVESTMENT IN THE REGION.

CCA
CENTRAL CITY ASSOCIATION OF LOS ANGELES

Visit ccala.org for more information.

OUR FAVES - ART -

MUSEUMS

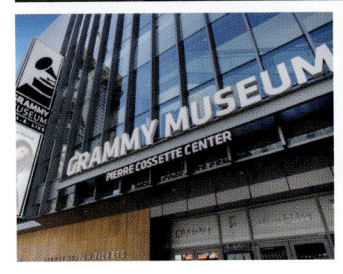

PERFECT PITCH

Music Has a Home

The GRAMMY Museum is one of L.A.'s best-kept secrets. Celebrate all forms of music throughout four floors of immersive and interactive exhibits, essential music education programs, and star-studded live performances in the Clive Davis Theater. The museum features everything from Michael Jackson's iconic "Thriller" jacket to Taylor Swift's handwritten lyrics, plus great moments and artists in rock, hip-hop, country, classical, Latin, R&B, jazz and more. See how the storied legacy of music is the thread that connects us all.

THE GRAMMY MUSEUM
800 W. Olympic Blvd., South Park // 213-765-6800 // grammymuseum.org // Instagram: @grammymuseum

---

A+D ARCHITECTURE AND DESIGN MUSEUM
900 E. 4th St. // 213-346-9734 // aplusd.org

Celebrating progressive design, A+D moved to DTLA in 2015. Shows have included architect retrospectives and a look at never-built L.A. projects.

THE AFRICAN AMERICAN FIREFIGHTER MUSEUM
1401 S. Central Ave. // 213-744-1730
aaffmuseum.org

L.A. has **the country's only African American firefighter museum,** housed in Fire Station 30 and established in 1913.

AMÉRICA TROPICAL INTERPRETIVE CENTER
125 Paseo de la Plaza // 213-485-6855
theamericatropical.org

This small museum, **dedicated to Mexican artist David Alfaro Siqueiros,** showcases his mural "América Tropical."

CHINESE AMERICAN MUSEUM
425 N. Los Angeles St. // 213-485-8567
camla.org

Located in El Pueblo's Garner Building, SoCal's oldest surviving Chinese building, the museum **spotlights the experience of Chinese Americans** in California.

EL PUEBLO DE LOS ANGELES HISTORICAL MONUMENT
125 Paseo de la Plaza // 213-485-6855
elpueblo.lacity.org

This monument includes **27 historic buildings,** four of them museums, and Olvera Street market. (Read more on page 76.)

FIDM MUSEUM AND GALLERIES/ ANNETTE GREEN FRAGRANCE ARCHIVE
919 S. Grand Ave., 2nd Fl. // 800-624-1200
fidmmuseum.org

The museum draws from its **collection of 15,000 costumes, accessories and textiles** with shows on midcentury women designers, antique corsets

---

MICHAEL STICKA
Executive director,
the GRAMMY Museum

PERFECT DTLA DAY *Morning stroll up Spring Street, lunch at L.A. LIVE, afternoon poking around in the Fashion District, and dinner at Bestia.*

PLACES TO HEAR LIVE MUSIC *Definitely Walt Disney Concert Hall and the GRAMMY Museum's Clive Davis Theater.*

CULINARY PICKS *For lunch, The Carving Board at District with roasted chicken and mac and cheese. For dinner, anything at Bestia. When I'm feeling gluttonous, a spicy shredded beef burrito from Cilantro.*

DRINK SPOTS *I drink a good cab or Macallan on the rocks. Favorite spots include Broken Shaker, Perch, and NoMad Rooftop Bar.* —J.G.

and more, while the Fragrance Archive is **the country's only perfume museum**.

THE GEFFEN CONTEMPORARY AT MOCA
152 N. Central Ave. // 213-625-4390 // moca.org

A **hipster favorite for its industrial setting**, this second MOCA location features a mix of exhibitions and events.

ICA LA
1717 E. 7th St. // 213-928-0833 // theicala.org

Formerly the Santa Monica Museum of Art, the ICA LA (Institute for Contemporary Art, Los Angeles) is now located in an industrial building in the Arts District and is led by talked-about curator Jamillah James.

ITALIAN AMERICAN MUSEUM OF LOS ANGELES
125 Paseo de la Plaza // 213-485-8432 italianhall.org

Opened in 2016, this institution **exploring the lives of Italian Americans** is in El Pueblo's historic Italian Hall, built in 1908.

JAPANESE AMERICAN NATIONAL MUSEUM
100 N. Central Ave. // 213-625-0414 // janm.org

The beating heart of Little Tokyo, it's the country's only museum **dedicated to the history of Japanese Americans**.

LA PLAZA DE CULTURA Y ARTES
501 N. Main St. // 213-542-6200 // lapca.org

Located near historic Olvera Street, this museum is the nation's premier **center of Mexican-American culture**.

LOS ANGELES UNITED METHODIST MUSEUM OF SOCIAL JUSTICE
115 Paseo de la Plaza // 213-613-1096 museumofsocialjustice.org

Housed in the historic La Plaza United Methodist Church, this small **social-justice museum** plans a show on economic inequality in 2019.

THE MAIN MUSEUM
114 W. 4th St. // 213-986-8500 themainmuseum.org

Still in beta phase—with exhibits in a temporary space—The Main, co-founded by developer Tom Gilmore, **will eventually inhabit three historic buildings** and include a café, rooftop garden and resident artist studios.

MOCA AT GRAND
250 S. Grand Ave. // 213-626-6222 // moca.org

With more than 5,000 pieces in its phenomenal collection, MOCA, which recently welcomed new director Klaus Biesenbach, is **a force in the global art scene**, staging acclaimed shows by the likes of Kerry James Marshall and Anna Maria Maiolino.

SCI-ARC GALLERIES
960 E. 3rd St. // 213-613-2200 // sciarc.edu

Since 2002, more than 50 **experimental projects by contemporary architects** have been staged at SCI-Arc architecture school's gallery.

The Broad

5 TIPS TO FULLY ENJOY **THE BROAD**

1. General admission is free at this sublime museum—designed by Diller Scofidio + Renfro and built by philanthropists Eli and Edythe Broad—but you still need a ticket, so reserve ahead of time at *ticketing.thebroad.org*. Tickets are released at noon on the first of every month for the following month.

2. If tickets are sold out online, do not fret. Do it the old-fashioned way and line up. But you'll want to go early to beat the crowd. Thursday morning is your best bet. The museum is closed on Mondays.

3. Download the app at *thebroad.org*. It's user-friendly and has a searchable, interactive map, and it even uses your location within the museum to queue up the right audio guide.

4. Reserve a time for Yayoi Kusama's stunning *Infinity Mirrored Room—The Souls of Millions of Light Years Away* by finding the tablet outside the work and signing up for a 45-second slot. You'll get a text 10 minutes before your entrance time.

5. Take a sneak peek through a glass window at The Vault, a 21,000-square-foot storage space. It's a glimpse behind the scenes of the workings of the museum.

THE BROAD 221 S. Grand Ave. // 213-232-6200 // thebroad.org

GALLERIES IN BOYLE HEIGHTS

This area across the L.A. River is a hub for art. But be warned: It's been roiled by activists fighting gentrification, including protests of galleries.

COREY HELFORD GALLERY
571 S. Anderson St. // coreyhelfordgallery.com
Its street-art roster includes D*Face and Ron English.

IBID
670 S. Anderson St. // ibidgallery.com
A London transplant whose lineup includes David Adamo.

LITTLE BIG MAN
1427 E. 4th St. S. // littlebigmangallery.com
Dedicated to showing photography.

MACCARONE GALLERY
300 S. Mission Rd. // maccarone.net
NYC gallerist Michele Maccarone's L.A. satellite.

MUSEUM AS RETAIL SPACE
649 S. Anderson St. // marsgallery.net
Despite its cheeky name, this is a commercial gallery.

NICODIM GALLERY
571 S. Anderson St. // nicodimgallery.com
Mihai Nicodim spotlights European art, including works from his native Romania.

PARRASCH HEIJNEN
1326 S. Boyle Ave. // parraschheijnen.com
Co-founded by NYC dealer Franklin Parrasch and repping seminal L.A. artist Billy Al Bengtson.

SELF HELP GRAPHICS & ART
1300 E. 1st St. // selfhelpgraphics.com
Since 1973, this nonprofit has supported the Latinx community with shows and workshops.

DTLA BOOK 2019 149

OUR FAVES – ART –

GALLERIES

BOBBY BERK
DTLA-based interior designer and *Queer Eye* cast member

CULINARY PICKS Otium, next to The Broad, is a great place pre- or post-"Broad-ing," as it's always a solid meal after you tour one of L.A.s most iconic museums. Otium's warm service and efforts for fresh food by supporting L.A. Urban Farming makes this an easy go-to with friends any day of the week. The fresh frojito certainly helps in good company.

SHOPPING Alchemy Works is a small artisan shop/gallery carefully curated with local goods and high-end accessories. Additionally, it's my go-to for gifts as know I can find something with an elevated feel that's local or supporting an artist.

GALLERY I love the intimacy of Hauser & Wirth, and every few months exhibits rotate. Whether you hang out at their beautiful courtyard or Manuela for a quick bite, this experience is worth a visit. —J.G.

ARTS DISTRICT

ART SHARE L.A. GALLERY
801 E. 4th Pl. // 213-687-4278 // artsharela.org

With 30 subsidized artist lofts, this complex is a **community-minded space** with two galleries.

THE BOX GALLERY
805 Traction Ave. // 213-625-1747 // theboxla.com

Founded by Mara McCarthy, daughter of Paul, it **reps crucial L.A. figures**, such as Barbara T. Smith, as well as younger international artists.

DENK GALLERY
749 E. Temple St. // 213-935-8331
denkgallery.com

Meaning "think" in Flemish and representing Tim Hawkinson, Denk was opened in 2017 by an endrocrinologist and her superyacht-captain husband.

GARIS & HAHN
1820 Industrial St. // 213-267-0229
garisandhahn.com

Showing L.A.-based painter Sarah Awad and performance and video artist Kalup Linzy, Garis & Hahn **relocated from NYC** in 2017.

HAUSER & WIRTH
901 E. 3rd St. // 213-943-1620
hauserwirthlosangeles.com

Opened in a former mill, Swiss-founded Hauser & Wirth is a **giant complex** that includes Manuela restaurant, Artbook bookshop and a public garden. It represents major L.A artists Paul McCarthy, Mark Bradford and Thomas Houseago.

JASON VASS
1452 E. 6th St. // 213-228-3334 // jasonvass.com

The son of painter Gene Vass and fashion designer Joan Vass, Jason Vass **moved his eponymous gallery here in 2016**.

MASH GALLERY
1325 Palmetto St. // 213-325-2759 // mashgallery.com

A new gallery, owned by Haleh Mashian, that **works with independent curators**.

OVER THE INFLUENCE
833 E. 3rd St. // 310-921-5933
overtheinfluence.com

A new gallery with a roster that includes tattooist Scott Campbell and Portugese muralist Vhils.

PDP GALLERY
806 Mateo St. // 213- 265-1765 // pdpgallery.com

This new gallery, **an outpost of the original in Paris**, is fronted by a striking mural by Morocco-born artist Mohammed L'Ghacham.

ROYALE PROJECTS
432 S. Alameda St. // 213-595-5182
royaleprojects.com

Paige Moss and Rick Royale's gallery **spotlights West Coast abstract** artists including Phillip K. Smith III and Ken Lum.

WILDING CRAN GALLERY
939 S. Santa Fe Ave. // 213-553-9190
wildingcran.com

Husband-and-wife dealers Naomi deLuce Wilding and Anthony Cran opened in 2014, showing work by Martin Bennett and Karon Davis.

FASHION DISTRICT

AVENUE DES ARTS
807 S. Los Angeles St. // 213-232-8676
avenuedesarts.org

The gallery, which has a location in Hong Kong, **spotlights street artists** like Hebru Brantley. (See page 67 for their muralists.)

THE HIVE GALLERY
729 S. Spring St. // 213-955-9051
hivegallery.com

Boasting 22 studio spaces, it spotlights affordable, **neo-pop illustration**.

MARIE BALDWIN GALLERY
814 S. Spring St., Ste. 2 // 310-600-4566
mariebaldwingallery.com

This new gallery represents *DTLA Book* **cover artists** such as Tommii Lim and Peter Greco. By appointment only.

MUGELLO GALLERY
818 S. Spring St. // 213-374-5959 // mugelloart.com

Opened in 2015, this space leans toward **colorful abstraction**.

REN GALLERY
743 S. Santee St., Unit B // 213-293-4877
rengallery.com

Ren exhibits **pop and urban** artists, including Futura.

THE SPACE BY ADVOCARTSY
924 S. San Pedro St. // 213-372-5096
advocartsy.com

A new-in-2018 gallery, by appointment only, highlighting **Iranian art**.

GALLERY ROW

DAC GALLERY
431 S. Broadway // 213-627-7374 // dacgallery.com

Active since 2009, this space focuses on large **group shows**.

Gallery Hopping at the Bendix

You can enjoy multiple gallery openings in one night under one roof–just like Chelsea gallery hopping in N.Y. The historic Bendix Building (read on page 78 & 86) has become home to six art galleries, plus numerous artist studios. Check the galleries' websites for opening nights and hop around from one floor to the other, a Tecate beer in hand (the opening-night drink offering of choice for some of the art spaces.) *Bendix Building 1206 Maple Ave.*

CHÂTEAU SHATTO Ste. 1030. // 213-973-5327 // chateaushatto.com
Showcasing work by young international artists

DURDEN & RAY Ste. 832. // DandRart@gmail.com // durdenandray.com
Artist-run nonprofit with 24 artist/curator members

JOAN Ste. 715 // 213-441-9009 // joanlosangeles.org
Nonprofit committed to showing emerging and under-represented artists

MONTE VISTA PROJECTS Ste. 523 // montevistaprojects.com
This artist-run space relocated from Highland Park

TIGER STRIKES ASTEROID Ste. 523 // 209-553-0462
tigerstrikesasteroid.com
Part of a national network of artist-run spaces

TRACK 16 Ste. 1005 // 310-815-8080 // track16.com
Showcasing genre bending exhibitions since 1994, when it co-founded Bergamot Station in Santa Monica

LOS ANGELES CENTER FOR DIGITAL ART
104 E. 4th St. // 323-646-9427 // lacda.com

Devoted to new media, LACDA also holds juried competitions.

THESE DAYS
118 Winston St., 2nd Fl. // thesedaysla.com

This **gallery and design shop** was opened by Stephen and Jodie Zeigler in 2014.

HISTORIC CORE

FOLD GALLERY
453 S. Spring St. // 213-221-4585 // folddtla.com

This gallery/store, above The Last Bookstore's main floor, focuses on **street art and pop surrealism**.

INDUSTRIAL DISTRICT

PRODUCE HAUS
1318 E. 7th St. // hello@produce.haus produce.haus

This appointment-only spot is operated by Zadik Zadikian, known for his **gold-covered art**.

SUPERCHIEF GALLERY
739 Kohler St. // superchiefgallery.com

An artist-run outpost of the NYC original, it **spotlights street art**.

LITTLE TOKYO

GEORGE J. DOIZAKI GALLERY
120 Judge John Aiso St. // 213-617-3274 laartcore.org

Located inside the Japanese American Cultural & Community Center, this gallery presents shows ranging **from Japanese** artifacts to contemporary Japanese-American art.

LA ARTCORE UNION CENTER FOR THE ARTS
120 Judge John Aiso St. // 213-617-3274 laartcore.org

Founded in 1979, this **nonprofit mounts shows in an old church building**, as well as in a second location at the Brewery Arts Colony.

NOH/WAVE
420 E. 3rd St. // info@nohwave.co // nohwave.co

Artist collective that also includes a retail shop and **runs artist workshops**.

SOUTH PARK

MAXWELL ALEXANDER GALLERY
406 W. Pico Blvd. // 213-275-1060 maxwellalexandergallery.com

Specialist in contemporary realism and **Western art**.

BELOW THE 10 FWY

BAERT GALLERY
2441 Hunter St. // 213-537-0737 // baertgallery.com

This **contemporary gallery** reps such artists as Ludovica Gioscia.

CIRRUS GALLERY
2011 S. Santa Fe Ave. // 213-680-3473 cirrusgallery.com

A **DTLA pioneer**, Cirrus moved from Hollywood in 1979. It's known for fine printmaking with such names as Lita Albuquerque.

GHEBALY GALLERY
2245 E. Washington Blvd. // 323-282-5187 ghebaly.com

Previously in Culver City, this **gallery with a conceptual art bent** moved to DTLA in 2014.

THE MISTAKE ROOM
1811 E. 20th St. // 213-749-1200 // tmr.la

This nonprofit space founded by Cesar Garcia **showcases international artists**.

MIXOGRAFIA
1419 E. Adams Blvd. // 323-232-1158 mixografia.com

Known for its **3-D paper printing technique**, Mixografia has produced editions with everyone from Ed Ruscha to Alex Israel.

NIGHT GALLERY
2276 S. 16th St. // 323-589-1135 // nightgallery.ca

Davida Nemeroff's space hosts **acclaimed shows**, performance art and even comedy nights.

PIO PICO
3311 E. Pico Blvd. // 323-645-5955 piopico.us

This gallery debuted in late 2017 with a show of **Vanessa Beecroft's ceramics**.

SIMARD BILODEAU
1923 S. Santa Fe Ave., Ste. 100 // 213-935-8253 simardbilodeau.com

Two French-Canadian dealers opened this **L.A. outpost of their Shanghai space**, showing young artists like Harmonia Rosales.

Chung King Road

Chinatown's Little Gem

Back in the late '90s, gallerists began taking unused spaces on Chung King Road, a 500-foot pedestrian alley. Since then, the art scene has spread throughout Chinatown, all from this intimate spot hung with red paper lanterns.

ACTUAL SIZE 741 New High St. // actualsizela.com
Curator collective located in a 250-square-foot former convenience store.

BEL AMI 709 N. Hill St. // belami.info
The brainchild of a writer, an artist and a co-founder of Human Resources.

CHARLIE JAMES GALLERY 969 Chung King Rd. // cjamesgallery.com
A strong L.A. player since 2009, repping Lars Jan and Sadie Barnette.

EASTERN PROJECTS 900 N. Broadway // easternprojectsgallery.com
New gallery committed to a culturally diverse program.

THE GOOD LUCK GALLERY 945 Chung King Rd. // thegoodluckgallery.com
A spotlight on self-taught (aka outsider) artists.

HUMAN RESOURCES 410 Cottage Home St. // humanresourcesla.com
Inclusive, artist-run nonprofit staging highly effective shows since 2010.

INSTITUTE FOR ART AND OLFACTION 932 Chung King Rd. // artandolfaction.com
Saskia Wilson-Brown's brainchild offers perfumery education, exhibitions and events dedicated to the intersection between the nose and art.

JOSEPH GROSS GALLERY 978 Chung King Rd. // josephgrossgallery.com
A New York transplant new to Chinatown.

LEIMIN SPACE 443 Lei Min Way // leiminspace.com
Draws a young crowd for artists like Vanessa Gingold and Laura Soto.

MAKE ROOM 1035 N. Broadway // makeroom.la
An installation-minded space with a sister gallery in Beijing.

O-O LA 818 N. Spring St., Ste. 202 // O-Ola.com
From the founders of Got It for Cheap, a traveling show of affordable art.

OUR FAVES — ART

PERFORMANCE THEATERS

Walt Disney Concert Hall

AHMANSON THEATRE
135 N. Grand Ave. // 213-628-2772
centertheatregroup.org

Dear Evan Hansen, Come From Away, Something Rotten!... there's a reason this 2,000-seat Center Theatre Group venue has the **largest theatrical subscription base** on this coast.

DOROTHY CHANDLER PAVILION
135 N. Grand Ave. // 213-628-2772 // laopera.org

This 1964 **hall with gigantic chandeliers** is home to LA Opera and Glorya Kaufman Presents Dance at The Music Center.

EAST WEST PLAYERS
120 Judge John Aiso St. // 213-625-7000
eastwestplayers.org

The **Asian-American theater company** collaborates on plays with such companies as Rogue Artists Ensemble.

FOUR LARKS
fourlarks.com

Known for its **immersive junkyard operas** around town (including at its hidden Basic Flowers space in the Historic Core), this company moved from Melbourne to L.A. in 2015.

LOS ANGELES THEATRE CENTER
514 S. Spring St. // 213-489-0994 // thelatc.org

Operated by the Latino Theater Company and **encompassing several stages**, it offers dance, theater and spoken word.

MARK TAPER FORUM
135 N. Grand Ave. // 213-628-2772
centertheatregroup.org

There's not a bad seat in the house at the Center Theatre Group's **adventurous stage at The Music Center**, thanks to its half-circle shape.

REDCAT
631 W. 2nd St. // 213-237-2800 // redcat.org

Inside Walt Disney Concert Hall, REDCAT offers **cutting-edge plays, dance and performance art** in a black-box theater, plus a lounge-bar and art gallery.

WALT DISNEY CONCERT HALL
111 S. Grand Ave. // 323-850-2000 // laphil.com and lamasterchorale.org

Home to the L.A. Philharmonic and Los Angeles Master Chorale, this **Frank Gehry-designed hall** also offers free tours of its architecture and gardens.

ZIPPER HALL
200 S. Grand Ave. // 213-621-1050
colburnschool.edu

This **classical-music hall** at the Colburn School is a main venue for the Los Angeles Chamber Orchestra.

LIVE CONCERTS

BELASCO
1050 S. Hill St. // 213-746-5670 // thebelasco.com

Enjoy live music at this historic theater, where the real star has been the **ornate, gilded dome ceiling** since 1926.

CICADA RESTAURANT AND CLUB
617 S. Olive St. // cicadarestaurant.com

The **1920s Art Deco** and 30-foot ceilings make for an elegant night out with live music.

CONGA ROOM
800 W. Olympic Blvd. // 213-745-0162
congaroom.com

Catch live musical acts from global artists at this **Latin dance club** and venue.

THE MAYAN
1038 S. Hill St. // 213-746-4674 // clubmayan.com

Bring the drama. Outside is a distinguished 1920s façade, while the inside boasts a 5,000-square-foot stage for the ultimate show.

MICROSOFT THEATER
777 Chick Hearn Ct. // 213-763-6020
microsofttheater.com

This **7,100-seat music venue at L.A. LIVE** sits in the middle between STAPLES Center and The Novo in terms of size.

THE NOVO BY MICROSOFT
800 W. Olympic Blvd., Ste. A335 // 213-765-7000
thenovodtla.com

Formerly Club Nokia, this music/event venue at L.A. LIVE has just over 2,000 seats and is known for **good acoustics**.

THE REGENT THEATER
448 S. Main St. // 323- 284-5727 // regenttheater.com

Thanks to the ingenious slanted floor, there are **no bad seats** in this theater.

SPORTS & CONCERT ARENAS

Dodger Stadium 1000 Vin Scully Ave. // 866-363-4377 // losangeles.dodgers.mlb.com
Go blue or go home. Dodger Stadium has been hosting Dodger fans since 1962 and has a capacity of 56,000 seats, making it a prime concert venue for big acts like Guns N' Roses and Beyoncé as well.

STAPLES Center 1111 S. Figueroa St., Ste. 3100 // 213-742-7100 // staplescenter.com
Welcome to the hub of DTLA. Between Lakers, Clippers, Sparks and Kings games and concerts, STAPLES Center sees about 4 million visitors a year.

Dodger Stadium

BROADWAY THEATERS

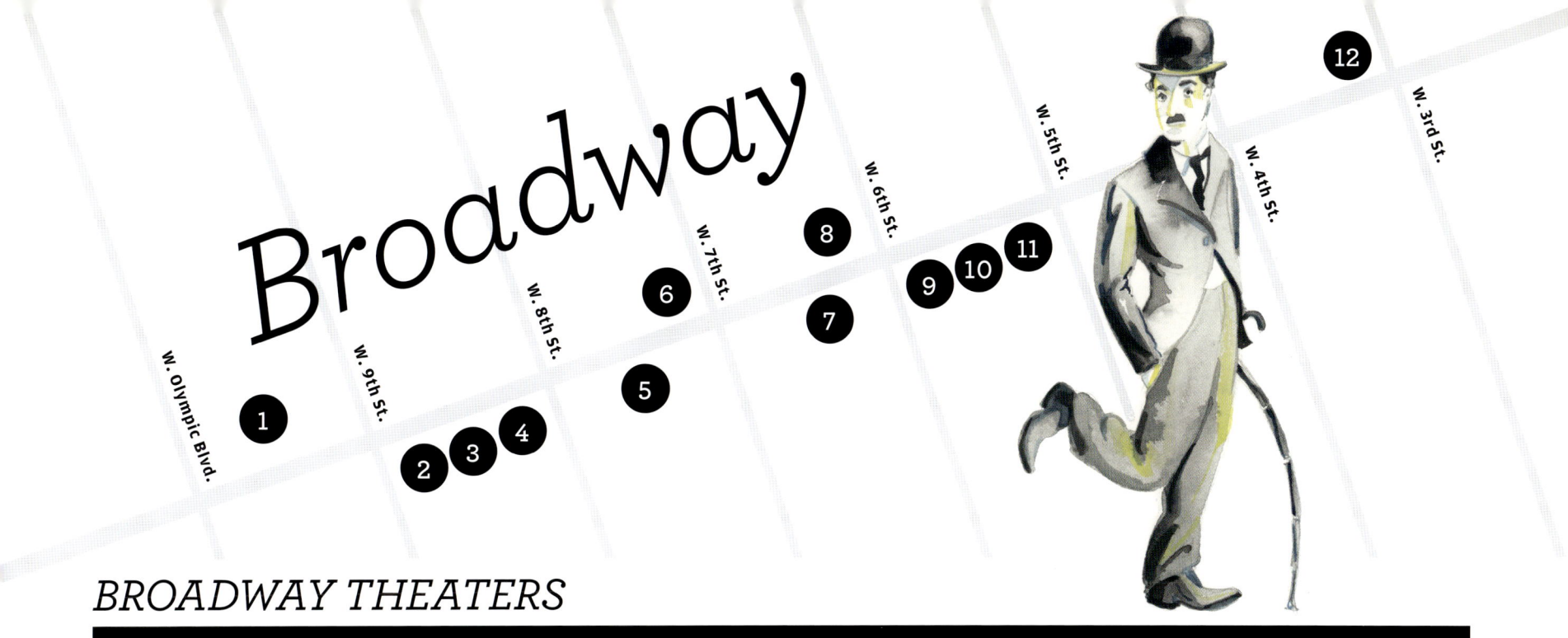

1. UNITED ARTISTS THEATRE
Opened in 1927 // 1,600 seats

LITTLE-KNOWN FACT This theater was built for United Artists, the company formed by Charlie Chaplin, Douglas Fairbanks, Mary Pickford and D. W. Griffith to gain independence from the big studios of the time.
THE LATEST Now The Theatre at Ace Hotel, it hosts concerts and events. UCLA's Center for the Art of Performance brings some of its programming here as well, including performances by The Gloaming and Carrie Mae Weems.

2. ORPHEUM THEATRE
Opened in 1926 // 2,000 seats

YOU'VE SEEN IT IN Broadcasts of *American Idol, America's Got Talent*, the seventh and eighth season finales of *RuPaul's Drag Race*.
THE LATEST The theater's $4 million makeover in 2003 has really paid off. The Orpheum is alive and thriving as a concert venue, film location and movie theater.

3. RIALTO THEATRE
Opened in 1917 // 800 seats

LITTLE-KNOWN FACT The Rialto opened with *The Garden of Allah* starring Broadway favorite Helen Ware.
THE LATEST Urban Outfitters restored the theater's marquee and opened a retail outlet in December 2013.

4. TOWER THEATRE
Opened in 1927 // 900 seats

LITTLE-KNOWN FACT This theater was the first one in Los Angeles to be wired for talking pictures.
THE LATEST: It's a future home of an Apple store, the first in DTLA.

5. GLOBE THEATRE
Opened in 1913 // 782 seating capacity

YOU'VE SEEN IT IN Jennifer Lopez's video "On the Floor" (2011) was filmed here.
THE LATEST Reopened in July 2015. Twice a month, the theater hosts *TEASE, if you please!*, a modern burlesque show.

6. LOEW'S STATE THEATRE
Opened in 1921 // 2,450 seats

LITTLE-KNOWN FACT A six-year-old Judy Garland debuted here as Francis Gumm, appearing as part of performance trio The Gumm Sisters in 1929.
THE LATEST Currently called the State Theatre and home to a Spanish-language church, the Catedral de la Fe.

7. PALACE THEATRE
Opened in 1911 // 1,956 seats originally; 1,068 seats currently

YOU'VE SEEN IT IN *Dreamgirls* (2006), *The Big Lebowski* (1988) as Maude's apartment and in Michael Jackson's "Thriller" music video (1983).
THE LATEST After years as a filming location, the theater was given a $1 million renovation in 2011, opening the doors to concerts, movie screenings and other events.

8. LOS ANGELES THEATRE
Opened in 1931 // 2,000 seats

LITTLE-KNOWN FACT Charlie Chaplin invested his own money to finish this lavish theater in time for the premiere of his movie *City Lights*. With a construction price tag of $1.5 million, it was the most expensive theater built up to that time on a per-seat basis.
THE LATEST The theater is now earning its money as a film location and event space.

9. ARCADE THEATRE
Opened in 1910 // 1,400 seats originally; 850 seats currently

YOU'VE SEEN IT IN If you made the unfortunate mistake of seeing *Daredevil* (2003), starring Ben Affleck and Jennifer Garner, you saw the theater's rooftop, with L.A.'s Broadway played off as New York City.
THE LATEST Retail space in the lobby.

10. CAMEO THEATRE
Opened in 1910 // 900 seats

LITTLE-KNOWN FACT Until it closed in 1991, the Cameo Theatre was the longest continuously operating movie theater in the United States.
THE LATEST Retail space in the lobby.

11. ROXIE THEATRE
Opened in 1932 // 1,600 seats

LITTLE-KNOWN FACT It was the very last historic theater built on Broadway, designed by famed architect John M. Cooper. Its claim to fame as the only Art Deco theater in the district makes it easy to spot.
THE LATEST Retail space in the lobby.

12. MILLION DOLLAR THEATRE
Opened in 1918 // 2,024 seats

LITTLE-KNOWN FACT Opened February 1, 1918, by impresario Sid Grauman (of Chinese Theatre fame) as one of the earliest and largest movie palaces in the country, the theater hosted big band stars such as Billie Holiday, Artie Shaw and Lionel Hampton in the '40s.
THE LATEST Located next door to a thriving Grand Central Market, it's enjoying new life as prime real estate for live events and movie screenings.

ILLUSTRATION: CHRIS SHARP

Mural by Retna, Risk, Revok and Abel seen along Cartwheel Art's new Graffiti + BBQ tour

OUR FAVES
- PLAY -

WALKING TOURS

Cartwheel Art 213-537-0687 // cartwheelart.com

Started in 2013 by Arts District local Cindy Schwarzstein, these immersive walking adventures ($25–$85) blend art, food and history. **Underground L.A.** unearths stories of everything from notorious Prohibition-era murders to famous speakeasies. Journalist Hadley Hall Meares brings famed criminals and victims to life on **L.A. Vice**. Or view street art and eat some fine 'cue with **Graffiti + BBQ**.

Downtown L.A. Walking Tours 213-399-3820 // dtlawalkingtours.com

Formed in 2009, this company has a variety of tours ($20). **Old & New Downtown L.A. Tour** focuses on the past and the present; **L.A.'s Beginnings** looks back at the history that shaped the city; and the **Filming Location Tour** shows the Hollywood history of DTLA.

L.A. Art Tours 670 Moulton Ave., #9A // 310-503-2365 // laarttours.com

For more modern-day enjoyment of all the fun things Downtown L.A. has to offer, there's artist-led L.A. Art Tours. They paired up with SoCal Brew Bus for their **Craft Beer and Urban Art Tour** ($65), covering three craft breweries, graffiti and murals in the Arts District. If beer flights aren't your thing, the **Downtown L.A. Graffiti/Mural Tour** ($12) takes you through the Arts District to discover galleries and street art.

Los Angeles Conservancy 523 W. 6th St., Ste. 826 // 213-623-2489 // laconservancy.org

This influential nonprofit has championed historical preservation for decades. As part of its work, there's a selection of walking tours ($15). The **Historic Downtown Walking Tour** starts at Pershing Square and showcases historic and cultural landmarks, including the Central Library and Grand Central Market. There's also the **Art Deco Tour**, spotlighting the fine architecture of buildings from the 1920s and '30s, with stops at the Eastern Columbia Building and the Title Guarantee & Trust Building. And for those who love vintage movie palaces, the **Broadway Historic Theatre and Commercial District Tour** focuses on Broadway's evolution. If you're lucky, you'll get to see a few theaters from the inside.

SPECIALTY TOURS

ARCHITECTURE

ARCHITECTURE TOURS L.A.
323-464-7868 // architecturetoursla.com

It's not every day that you get to take a **tour of L.A.'s oldest buildings with an actual architecture historian** like Laura Massino Smith. This tour gets you up close and personal. Cost: $75 per person/$80 single traveler. Duration: 2–3 hours.

BIKE

LA CYCLE TOURS
lacycletours.com // 323-550-8265

They say **biking is the best way to really experience L.A.** With this leisurely paced tour, you're sure to discover new pockets of the city you thought you knew. Cost: $55–$75.

BUS

ESOTOURIC
213-915-8687 // esotouric.com

If you're looking to mix it up, you've come to the right place. This is no cookie-cutter company. You can **choose from tours like true crime or literary (think Raymond Chandler)**. Cost: $58–$65.

FOOD

AVITAL TOURS
213-394-0901 // avitaltours.com

For $79, you'll experience four courses in three hours and get a chance to **go behind the scenes with local chefs** and restaurant owners. Group size is limited to 12 people to keep it cozy.

SIDEWALK FOOD TOURS OF LOS ANGELES
877-568-6877 // foodtoursoflosangeles.com

Looking for just the highlights? These **family-friendly tours will take you to six renowned stops** that are bustling with tourists and locals alike, including the can't-miss Grand Central Market. Tickets are $75; free for kiddos ages 1–3.

SIX TASTE
213-798-4749 // sixtaste.com

Experience this city's **culinary diversity on a walking tour** and get to know eclectic Downtown eateries in neighborhoods like Little Tokyo and the Arts District. For $65–$70, you'll eat well at five to seven spots and learn about the area's culture and history, all in about 3½ hours.

Grand Central Market

GAMES & RECREATION

HISTORIC LIBRARY

CENTRAL LIBRARY TOUR
630 W. 5th St. // 213-228-7168 // lapl.org

Marvel at this prized historic building, including the Tom Bradley Wing with its awe-inspiring chandeliers. They offer **free daily docent-led tours** for an in-depth experience, and free walk-in tours on certain days.

MURDER & MYSTERY

THE REAL LOS ANGELES TOURS
213-316-8687 // therealosangelestours.com

This company offers a dozen different options including a tour (2½ hours, $30) that looks at the **noir underbelly of the Historic Core** from days gone by.

NEON

NEON CRUISE
818-696-2149 // neonmona.org

The Museum of Neon Art's Saturday night Neon Cruise ($65) has been around for 17 years, highlighting the **best neon signs and movie marquees**.

BOWLING

LUCKY STRIKE
800 W. Olympic Blvd. // 213-542-4880
bowlluckystrike.com

Between DJs, mood lighting and 18 lanes, **bowling night is an elevated experience**. Enjoy drinks from expert mixologists and a gastropub menu.

XLANES FAMILY ENTERTAINMENT CENTER
333 S. Alameda St., Ste. 300 // 213-229-8910
xlanesla.com

XLanes has everything you'd ever need under one roof: **bowling, billiards, an arcade, even a karaoke room**.

ESCAPE GAME

ESCAPE ROOM
120 E. 8th St. // 213-689-3229
escaperoomla.com

Test your sleuth skills in their **themed mystery rooms**. Your team has 60 minutes to uncover clues and solve puzzles.

THE VIRUS
1500 S. Los Angeles St. // 310-922-4562
getthefoutroom.com

With **more than 22 puzzles to solve against the clock**, The Virus is an immerse adventure in VR.

KARAOKE

MAX KARAOKE STUDIO
333 S. Alameda St., Ste. 216
310-421-2550

This BYOB/food karaoke bar is where you can **rent a private room and sing your heart out** without the weirdos (except the ones you bring).

GAME HALL

TWO BIT CIRCUS
634 Mateo St. // 213-599-3188
twobitcircus.com

Don't go looking for elephant and tiger acts. More like rooms full of **vintage video games, carnival games, virtual reality** and more. (More on page 112.)

BARBARA BESTOR
Architect, author of *Bohemian Modern: Living in Silver Lake*

GALLERY *SCI-Arc has a fantastic gallery to see shows by emerging, idea-heavy designers.*

SELF-GUIDED TOUR *Walk from the Department of Water & Power Building (one of my favorites) past Walt Disney Concert Hall to the Central Library, the Biltmore, Ricardo Legorreta's Pershing Square and then the wonderful Bradbury Building. Eat at Grand Central Market or do brunch at Redbird in the former St. Vibiana's Cathedral.* —J.G.

ILLUSTRATION: BRIAN BUSCH; LUCHA VAVOOM: POUL LANGE

SPECIAL EVENTS

Chinatown Summer Nights chinatownsummernights.com
The **crowds flock to Chinatown for this seasonal block party**, which usually takes place on the first Saturday of the summer months. The festivities include cooking demos by Chinese chefs, cultural activities and music by KCRW.

Downtown Art Walk downtownartwalk.org
This free, self-guided walking tour has turned into a **full-grown street fair with food trucks and entertainment**. It attracts huge crowds every second Thursday of the month. For info and maps, start at the Art Walk Lounge, located at 634 S. Spring St.

Grand Performances 617 S. Olive St. // grandperformances.org
People wait all year for this **spectacular summer concert series at Grand Park**. Not only is it free and family-friendly, but you can bring your own food and drink and enjoy live performances under the open sky.

Lucha Vavoom The Mayan, 1038 S. Hill St. // luchavavoom.com
Part *lucha libre* (Mexican wrestling), part burlesque show, part comedy, this fun night out is an adrenaline-pumping experience you have to see for yourself.

Tuesday Night Café
Aratani Courtyard/Union Center for the Arts, 120 Judge John Aiso St.
tuesdaynightproject.org

On the first and third Tuesday of every month from April to September, this **free open mic night** features visual and performing artists of Asian American, Native Hawaiian and Pacific Islander descent. The shows emphasize art and community and are held in Little Tokyo.

Lucha Vavoom at The Mayan

DTLA BOOK 2019 155

CONTRIBUTORS

MOLLY CREEDEN, who profiles cover artist Leticia "Tiza" Maldonado, is a Venice resident and former *Vogue* editor who writes about culture, fashion and celebrity. Her work has appeared in publications including *The Wall Street Journal*, *T* magazine, *Condé Nast Traveler* and *Elle UK*. "Tiza sees elegant possibilities within the medium, and she is mesmerized by the fact that she can illustrate with fire. I was mesmerized, too."

See page 48

JOE BARGMANN, who writes about cleantech incubator LACI and the "micro-amusement park" Two Bit Circus—has either written for or held senior editorial positions at *Popular Mechanics*, *The New York Times*, *The Washington Post*, *Garden & Gun*, *Road & Track* and *Glamour*. He lives in Charlottesville, Virginia. "LACI takes the 'makerspace' model to the absolute top level. It's a place where dreamers can realize their ideas."

See pages 108, 112

L.A.-based **BRIAN BUSCH**—who illustrates the noir tales of DTLA and drew caricatures for the OUR FAVES section—has more than 20 years of experience as an illustrator. When he's not creating work for the film and advertising industries, he's usually found eating a pastrami reuben at Canter's Deli. "As a recent transplant from Chicago, working on this project gave me an opportunity to research and learn about my new city. The fact that I'm an avid fan of all things noir was a bonus."

See pages 72, 115-155

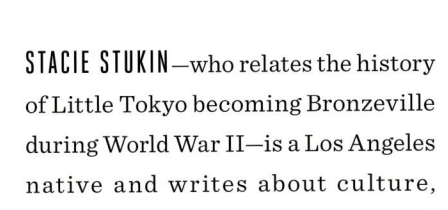

STACIE STUKIN—who relates the history of Little Tokyo becoming Bronzeville during World War II—is a Los Angeles native and writes about culture, design and food for publications like the *Los Angeles Times*, *W* magazine and *Robb Report*. "The repercussions of the internment of Japanese Americans and the improbable cultural opening for African Americans in Little Tokyo reveal a story of adaptation and creativity in the midst of oppression that holds relevance today."

See page 94

LIZ OHANESIAN, who writes about where to find nature in and around Downtown as well as recommends day trips to make via Metro—is an arts and culture journalist whose work has appeared in the *Los Angeles Times*, *Los Angeles* magazine and other publications. A Metro rider and avid walker, she loved strolling through Downtown's gardens.

See pages 12, 26, 102

Born in L.A., **JOSHUA SPENCER**—who photographed model Meng for the "5 Rules" feature—shoots portraits, fashion and video. "My favorite part of the day was shooting in the super-crowded Santee Alley. I was using a long lens and was kind of hidden, so it looked like Meng was dressed to the nines stomping through the crowd for no good reason. People didn't know what to make of her."

See page 4

JIRO SCHNEIDER—who photographed and created the video for the cover story on neon artist Leticia Maldonado—is known for his portraits of people in the music, fashion and entertainment industries. "What was mesmerizing was learning about the artisan skill set needed to execute Tiza's medium. The pure craftsmanship is astonishing."

See the cover and page 48

LESLEY MCKENZIE—who profiles DTLA's restaurateur couples as well as shines a spotlight on four need-to-know fashion labels—is the deputy editor of *C* magazine. She's a regular contributor to *The Hollywood Reporter* and the *Los Angeles Times*, covering style. Raised in the Middle East, she now calls L.A.'s East Side home. "I've been a longtime cheerleader for the city's fashion scene, including Raquel Allegra, whose signature dresses currently occupy a large portion of my closet. The Fashion District is still thriving."

See pages 18, 32

LESLEY BALLA—writer and editor of the OUR FAVES section—has written about food, wine and travel for *Los Angeles* magazine, *Angeleno* and *Zagat*. Covering the expansive L.A. dining scene, she admits DTLA is her favorite place to explore, even if it means driving from her Santa Monica home on the other side of the 405. "The best part about contributing to OUR FAVES is walking through the map of my mind, picking and choosing from my usual haunts, up-and-comers, hidden gems and great finds in every neighborhood."

See pages 114-155

With a background in filmmaking, **JORDAN RIEFE**—who writes about DTLA's fertile dance scene—became an entertainment reporter, covering for *The Wrap* and Reuters. He now serves as West Coast theater critic for *The Hollywood Reporter*, and writes on culture and cinema for *L.A. Weekly, OC Register* and Truthdig.com. He enjoyed "chatting with dancers and choreographers fueled by the love of their medium."

See page 84

DTLA BOOK

KAYOKO SUZUKI-LANGE
Co-Founder & Chief Creative Officer
kayoko@district8media.com

SHANA WONG SOLARES
Co-Founder & Publisher
shana@district8media.com

DEGEN PENER
Consulting Editorial Director

DEBRA DILGER
Business Development Director

LESLEY BALLA
OUR FAVES Editor

ROBIN OKMAN
Account Director

MELISSA BRANDZEL
Copy Editor

ABOUT OUR EDITORIAL DIRECTOR

For the 2019 edition, we asked **Degen Pener** to oversee our editorial vision. He's the former culture editor of *The Hollywood Reporter* and previously was editor in chief of *Angeleno* magazine. He has contributed stories on design, art, philanthropy and timepieces to such publications as *Los Angeles* magazine, *The New York Times, C* magazine and *Santa Barbara Magazine*. He wrote about DTLA's plethora of murals for this issue: see page 60.

SPECIAL THANKS TO:
Poul Lange, Richard Solares and our families for their unconditional support and contributions.

PUBLISHER'S NOTE:
While every effort was made to ensure accuracy at the time of publication, it is always best to call ahead and confirm that the information is up to date.

All rights reserved. No part of this book may be reproduced in any form or by any electronic or mechanical means, including information storage and retrieval systems, without permission in writing from the publisher. Scanning, uploading and electronic distribution of this book or the facilitation of such without the permission of the publisher is prohibited. Opinions in *DTLA BOOK* are solely those of the editors and writers and are not necessarily endorsed by our distribution partners.

Copyright © 2019 by District 8 Media, LLC.
3rd Edition // First published in the United States of America in 2017
Printed in Korea

DISTRICT 8 MEDIA, LLC
315 E. 8th St., Ste. 702
Los Angeles, CA 90014
info@district8media.com
district8media.com // Social: @DTLAbook

ADVERTISING
sales@district8media.com
808-386-0872